JOURNAL FOR THE STUDY OF THE OLD TESTAMENT
SUPPLEMENT SERIES
334

Sheffield Academic Press
A Continuum imprint

Queer Commentary and the Hebrew Bible

edited by
Ken Stone

Journal for the Study of the Old Testament
Supplement Series 334

Copyright © 2001 Sheffield Academic Press
A Continuum imprint

Published by Sheffield Academic Press Ltd
The Tower Building, 11 York Road, London SE1 7NX
71 Lexington Avenue, New York NY 10017-653

www.SheffieldAcademicPress.com
www.continuum-books.com

British Library Cataloguing-in-Publication Data

A catalogue record for this book is available from the British Library

Typeset by Sheffield Academic Press
Printed on acid-free paper in Great Britain by MPG Books Ltd, Bodmin, Cornwall

ISBN 1-84127-237-X

CONTENTS

Acknowledgments   7
Abbreviations   8
List of Contributors   9

KEN STONE
Queer Commentary and Biblical Interpretation:
An Introduction   11

Part I:
QUEER READINGS

THEODORE W. JENNINGS JR
YHWH as Erastes   36

ROLAND BOER
Yahweh as Top: A Lost Targum   75

LORI ROWLETT
Violent Femmes and S/M: Queering Samson and Delilah   106

KEN STONE
Lovers and Raisin Cakes: Food, Sex and Divine Insecurity in
Hosea   116

MONA WEST
The Gift of Voice, the Gift of Tears: A Queer Reading of
Lamentations in the Context of AIDS   140

MICHAEL CARDEN
Remembering Pelotit: A Queer Midrash on Calling Down Fire   152

TIMOTHY R. KOCH
Cruising as Methodology: Homoeroticism and the Scriptures   169

Part II:
RESPONSES

TAT-SIONG BENNY LIEW
(Cor)Responding: A Letter to the Editor   182

DANIEL T. SPENCER
A Gay Male Ethicist's Response to Queer Readings of the Bible   193

LAUREL C. SCHNEIDER
Yahwist Desires: Imagining Divinity Queerly   210

Bibliography   228
Index of References   245
Index of Authors   248

ACKNOWLEDGMENTS

I would like to thank a number of individuals whose collective support and assistance made this volume possible. Thanks to Philip R. Davies at Sheffield Academic Press for inviting a collection of essays on a rather unconventional topic in biblical studies; to Douglas A. Knight and Amy-Jill Levine for feedback in the early stages of the project; to Wil Brant for various types of assistance in the preparation of the manuscript; to Wil Brant and Theodore Jennings for feedback on the introduction and to Horace Griffin for support throughout the process.

While soliciting contributors to this volume I spoke with several scholars who were interested in the project but felt that, given the focus of the volume, institutional or ecclesial politics prevented their participation. Thus I want to thank my colleagues at Chicago Theological Seminary, including its president Susan Brooks Thistlethwaite, for creating an environment in which a potentially controversial project was always enthusiastically supported.

Above all, though, I must thank the contributors, each of whom has transformed my own view of the possibilities for biblical interpretation in general and queer readings of the Hebrew Bible in particular.

ABBREVIATIONS

AB	Anchor Bible
BibInt	*Biblical Interpretation: A Journal of Contemporary Approaches*
BTB	*Biblical Theology Bulletin*
HTR	*Harvard Theological Review*
Int	*Interpretation*
JFSR	*Journal of Feminist Studies in Religion*
JSOT	*Journal for the Study of the Old Testament*
JTS	*Journal of Theological Studies*
KJV	King James Version
NIV	New International Version
NRSV	New Revised Standard Version
OTL	Old Testament Library
RSV	Revised Standard Version
TheolSex	*Theology and Sexuality*
VTSup	*Vetus Testamentum*, Supplements

List of Contributors

ROLAND BOER
Centre for Studies in Religion and Theology, Monash University, Victoria, Australia

MICHAEL CARDEN
University of Queensland, Queensland, Australia

THEODORE W. JENNINGS JR
Chicago Theological Seminary, Chicago, IL, USA

TIMOTHY R. KOCH
Boston University, Boston, MA, USA

TAT-SIONG BENNY LIEW
Chicago Theological Seminary, Chicago, IL, USA

LORI ROWLETT
University of Wisconsin, Eau-Claire, WI, USA

LAUREL C. SCHNEIDER
Chicago Theological Seminary, Chicago, IL, USA

DANIEL T. SPENCER
Drake University, Des Moines, IA, USA

KEN STONE
Chicago Theological Seminary, Chicago, IL, USA

MONA WEST
Cathedral of Hope, Dallas, TX, USA

QUEER COMMENTARY AND BIBLICAL INTERPRETATION: AN INTRODUCTION

Ken Stone

I

'In different ways queer politics might…have implications for any area of social life.' So argues Michael Warner in his introduction to a collection of essays on queer politics and social theory (Warner 1993: vii). One of the motivating assumptions behind the present volume is the assumption that biblical interpretation is one of those 'area[s] of social life' for which 'queer politics might…have implications'. Such an assertion will surely seem dubious to some readers, including not only readers affiliated with biblical interpretation but also readers involved in queer politics. Nevertheless, the much-discussed interdisciplinary explosion of multiple approaches and methods within biblical scholarship, on the one hand, and the rapid growth in lesbian and gay studies and queer theory outside of biblical scholarship, on the other hand, combine to produce a situation in which the proliferation of queer readings of the Bible seems today like a real future possibility—if not, unfortunately, very much of a present reality.

Most observers of contemporary biblical studies are aware that the discipline has been undergoing a rapid transformation in the last few decades with the appearance of a range of new interpretative questions and types of reading, many of which are now often conveniently (if somewhat simplistically) grouped together by friend and foe alike under the rubric of 'postmodern' biblical interpretation (see Adam 1995; 2000; Bible and Culture Collective 1995). While there are biblical scholars who have tried to ignore the changing shape of biblical scholarship, and others who have expressed critical reservations about the changes in question (see, e.g., Barr 2000), it does increasingly seem to be the case today that, as two writers heavily involved in the development of the newer trends put it, 'there are no holds barred, and no automatically inappropriate angles of vision upon our texts' (Clines and Exum 1993: 13). Nevertheless, at least a few biblical scholars, aware of the varieties of intellectual discourse flourishing outside the domains of biblical, religious and theological studies, have also noted the striking absence of lesbian and gay studies and of queer theory from the expanded toolbox of biblical scholarship and have therefore called for the application of these particular 'angles of vision' within biblical interpretation (see, e.g., Stone 1997a; Moore 1998; Clines 1998; cf. Boer 1999: 13-32; Goss and West 2000). The essays in this volume seek, if only initially and still, perhaps, somewhat tentatively, to answer that call.

But the implications of queer politics and queer reading strategies for biblical interpretation are very far from being clear or (pun intended) 'straight'-forward. What might it mean to produce readings of the Bible that function as something like 'queer commentary'? The latter phrase, borrowed from an argument made by the literary critics Lauren Berlant and Michael Warner in a different context (Berlant and Warner 1995), has been appropriated here precisely because of the way in which the phrase's juxtaposition of two very different terms calls to mind both continuity and radical discontinuity with conventional practices of biblical interpretation.

'Commentary' is a term with a long and respected tradition of use in connection with the Bible. It often refers to a specific genre of written biblical interpretation, a genre that is well known even outside of academic biblical studies in spite of the fact that the genre itself has only occasionally been the object of critical reflection (cf. Sherwood 1996: 22-25). The production of individual 'commentaries' on the Bible is frequently assumed to be the result of sustained academic analysis of particular books of the Bible by knowledgeable, competent experts who are well socialized into the traditional practices and norms of biblical scholarship. These norms can include (explicitly or by implication) the cautionary stricture that careful, scholarly attention to the text will allow the text to speak for itself, in its own terms, within the expectations, linguistic and social conventions, and presuppositions of its own time and culture, and without excessive interference from the interests and assumptions of the commentator. Thus Bernhard Anderson, explaining why one must approach commentaries critically, suggests that the biblical text 'ought to be allowed to make its claims first' so that the reader will be able to recognize those unfortunate situations in which 'the commentator subtly or openly imposes his or her inter-pretative categories' on the object of analysis (Anderson 1982: 342-43).

Today, of course, observers from many different points of view would probably agree that the relationship between commentary and 'interpretative categories' is more complicated than any simplistic account (pro or con) of scholarly 'objectivity' allows. Anderson him-self rightly notes, for example, that the production of biblical com-mentary has often been linked to disputes over religious orthodoxy in which competing sides attempt to ground their own views in the inter-pretation of Scripture (Anderson 1982: 344). Stated concerns about the assistance that commentaries do or do not give Christian ministers in the production of sermons and in the theological appropriation of the Bible (see, e.g., Fretheim 1982) also testify to the multiple interpretative agendas that shape the writing and reception of commentaries. Indeed, as Burke Long's fascinating discussion of the circumstances which gave birth to the influential Anchor Bible commentary series reveals, even those modern commentaries that focus most insistently on 'scien-tific' textual criticism, philological analysis and historical-archaeologi-cal contextualization are often conceptualized and produced on the basis of a complex combination of political, religious and more tradi-tionally 'academic' motives (Long 1997: 59-68). Thus the 'imposition' of 'interpretative categories' in the creation of commentary, about which Anderson cautions, is widely recognized today to be a necessary constraint within which all interpreters of the Bible must work to some degree rather than a problem that could ever be completely avoided. In spite of such recognition, however, it seems fair to suggest that the term 'commentary' continues to carry with it, in biblical studies at least, connotations of a careful, judicious analysis which is dutifully submissive to the norms of the community of scholars that precedes and authorizes it (cf. Anderson 1982: 343), which attempts to explicate a text first of all in terms of its original, ancient context of production rather than its contemporary contexts of reception, and which aims to achieve in terms of reliability and widespread acceptance what it frequently sacrifices in terms of excitement.

'Queer', on the other hand, is a term that, in radical distinction from 'commentary', has only rarely appeared in the context of biblical interpretation. The conjunction of the two terms in the title of the present volume will surely be viewed with dismay by some readers precisely because the introduction of the word 'queer' seems to flaunt the imposition of a modern 'interpretative category'—and, perhaps more importantly, an interpretative category that remains somewhat suspect, especially in circles where biblical interpretation is encouraged—upon the hallowed tradition of commenting on biblical texts. Although the term 'queer', especially when used in such phrases as 'queer theory', is now common enough outside of biblical scholarship that introductory overviews of its possible significance and use are available (see, e.g., Jagose 1996), 'queer' continues to be a contested term even among those who use it, and it is likely to remain so for some time to come. My point in using the term here is neither to resolve the many disputes that have emerged around it nor even necessarily to take a position in all of those disputes (though some of the positions that I do inevitably take will no doubt become apparent in the discussion that follows). Rather, I wish to suggest that the productive questions, debates and energies generated around 'queer' projects outside of biblical studies might also be deployed in useful or interesting ways by scholars involved in biblical interpretation; and that the essays in the present volume begin to point toward this possibility. However, since 'queer' projects have been, up to now, almost nonexistent in biblical studies, it will be necessary in this introduction to consider briefly some of the ways in which 'queer' is or has been used in other fields of discourse and how those uses might be related both to trends in biblical interpretation and to the individual essays collected in this volume.

II

In order to explicate some of the possible connotations of 'queer', let me begin with what may appear to be, at first, a historical digression. The US historian George Chauncey has argued in a remarkable book (Chauncey 1994) that there existed in New York City, roughly between the late nineteenth century and the Second World War, a particular social milieu in which male same-sex sexual acts were surprisingly frequent. The self-understanding of most of the men who participated in these acts is not adequately grasped, however, if approached in terms of the binary distinction so common today between 'homosexual' and 'heterosexual'. Rather, the acts in question took place between so-called 'fairies'—men whose gestures, styles of dress and grooming, social interactions, speech patterns, etc. were thought to be effeminate and flamboyant, with the result that the men in question were considered something very close to female prostitutes—and 'normal men'—usually men from the working classes, often Italian, Irish, or African American, whose gender presentation was in most respects conventionally 'masculine' and who generally enjoyed sexual relations with women but were also willing, and sometimes even eager, to obtain sexual pleasures from 'fairies'. So long as their sexual partners submitted to the passive, conventionally 'feminine' sexual role in oral or anal sexual penetration, these 'normal men' seem to have understood their own same-sex sexual contacts not as evidence for a 'homosexual identity' but, rather, as sexual conquests that confirmed their own 'normal' masculinity in much the same way that liaisons with female prostitutes did.

Chauncey goes on to point out, however, that a third group of men who enjoyed or desired sexual contacts with other men increasingly found it difficult to fit themselves into this widely accepted opposition between 'fairies' and 'normal men'. This third group of men tended to eschew activities and modes of self-presentation that were associated with the flamboyant 'femininity' of the fairies. On the other hand, their near-exclusive sexual attraction to men rather than women, as well as their willingness to take both active and passive roles in sexual relations with other men, distinguished them also from the 'normal' male partners of the fairies. In addition, the 'normal' partners of the fairies were often characterized by a kind of tough, working-class masculinity that seemed as far from the self-presentation of this third group of men (many of whom came from middle-class backgrounds) as the actions and mannerisms of the fairies. Attempting to find a way to talk about the distinctive nature of their situation vis-à-vis the various, and sometimes competing, norms of gender, class and sexual practice prevalent in their time and place, this third group of men, according to Chauncey, often referred to themselves as 'queer'.

While the connotations of 'queer', as that term seems to have been used among the men discussed by Chauncey, are not entirely identical to the connotations of 'queer' in much recent academic writing, nevertheless this example from the history of the word's use does serve as a convenient illustration of one recurring context in which 'queer' is often deployed. The English word 'queer' has frequently been used, at least during the twentieth century, to refer to particular individuals who participate in or desire same-sex sexual contact, although as Chauncey's discussion shows not all such individuals are necessarily subsumed under the term in every context. Still today one can find the plural noun 'queers' used in a loose sense to refer to persons who participate in or desire same-sex sexual contact—for example, gay men, lesbians and bisexuals. While such a use of the word 'queer' served for a number of decades in the middle of the twentieth century primarily as a sort of insult uttered by persons who did not identify with it, today the earlier use of the term as a self-appellation has been reclaimed by many individuals who desire and/or participate in same-sex sexual contact and who identify with the label with pride or, in any case, without shame. This seems to be the sense attributed to 'queer' by the ethicist Daniel Spencer, for example, when, in his response to the queer readings of the Bible collected in this volume, he refers to himself as 'one of an increasing number of openly queer seminarians seeking ordination in the early 1980s' (p. 192).

Now in societies that privilege heterosexual relations and stigmatize sexual relations between persons of the same sex, such 'queers' are inevitably positioned in a distinctive fashion in relation to a wide range of social practices, norms, ideologies and institutions. Because of this distinctive positioning, one can build on this first use of 'queer' as a label for those who desire and/or participate in same-sex sexual contact to argue for an understanding of 'queer' as a kind of location in society, and then go on to explicate the notion of 'queer readings of the Bible' within the framework of conversations already taking place among biblical scholars about 'social location and biblical interpretation'. Developed in part under the influence of contemporary theories of reading and reception, these conversations stress the fact that different readers, shaped in diverse ways by the complex interaction of such variables as race, ethnicity, gender, class, national origin, religious tradition, political affiliation and a host of comparable social factors, often attribute multiple meanings to the 'same' biblical texts. Thus, if the role of the biblical scholar is to analyze and reflect critically upon meanings of biblical texts, then biblical scholarship should involve an analysis not only of the linguistic and literary structures of those texts (as important as such structures obviously are for textual meaning), and not only of the ancient contexts in which the biblical texts were produced (though, again, a thorough knowledge of such contexts of origin is clearly a valuable component of biblical interpretation), but also of the context—or, better, multiple contexts—in which those texts are read by a range of differentially positioned readers and of the many complex factors which together make up those contexts of reading (see Tolbert 1990; Felder 1991; Sugirtharajah 1991; 1998; Segovia and Tolbert 1995a; 1995b; G. West 1999).

Picking up on these conversations, one of the contributors to the present volume, Mona West, has pointed out elsewhere that '[w]hile sexual orientation is often mentioned as one of the factors that shapes who we are as readers and members of particular social communities', nevertheless discussions of social location and biblical interpretation almost never analyze in detail the impact of this particular type of shaping on the practice of reading the Bible. West therefore argues that it is important 'to add the voice of the gay/lesbian/bisexual and trans-gendered community (Queers) to those marginalized groups who are reading the Bible from particular social locations...' (M. West 1999: 30) and goes on to suggest that new light is shed on those texts when they are subjected to 'a Queer reading of the Bible' (36). For West, then, as for many others who use the word, 'queer' seems to be a sort of inclusive term for lesbians, gay men and bisexuals, as well as transgendered persons (though this latter addition introduces important nuances into our understanding of the term 'queer', to which I return below); and a 'queer reading' is a reading produced by a reader who is located socially within this collective.

Such a conception of 'queer reading' seems also to be at work in West's contribution to this volume. Here, though, West adds to her earlier picture of queer social location by calling attention to the devastating effects of AIDS among those who share that location. West suggests that the book of Lamentations can serve as a crucial resource for members of what she calls 'queer life and culture' who are working through the 'trauma' associated with AIDS. In making this suggestion West's essay taps into a resurgence of interest in the biblical lament tradition which considers that tradition not simply in terms of its ancient production or literary form but also, or even primarily, in terms of its reception and use (cf., e.g., Linafelt 2000).

One possible contribution of an approach to the biblical lament tradition such as that proposed by West, at least in my view, is the fact that it might move lesbians, gay men and bisexuals away from a ten-dency to restrict their questions about the Bible almost exclusively to the question, 'What does the Bible say about same-sex relations?' Although a growing body of work has been produced within biblical scholarship in recent years that deals in one way or another with the latter question (see, e.g., Fewell and Gunn 1993: 105-108, 148-51; Olyan 1994; Boyarin 1995; Stone 1995; Martin 1995; 1996; Brooten 1996; Nissinen 1998; Carden 1999; Bird 2000), the contemporary significance of the question is clearly overdetermined by political and ecclesial conflicts over the morality of homosexuality and by particular assumptions about the Bible's religious authority (cf. Martin 1996: 130). With such factors looming in the background, the heavy emphasis upon the question tends to push some lesbian, gay or bisexual readers into an unfortunate false alternative where one's only options appear to be a denial that the Bible condemns homoeroticism or a rejection of the value of biblical interpretation altogether. West, however, like most of the authors in this volume, helpfully shifts the focus away from the handful of texts that are endlessly analyzed in discussions of 'the Bible and homosexuality'. Here she considers instead another body of biblical literature which, when subjected to queer commentary, will in West's estimation produce helpful effects among a particular group of contemporary socially-located readers referred to by West as 'queers'.

One complaint that is occasionally (and more and more frequently) voiced within biblical studies about the recent interest in reading and social location is the complaint that one may learn a great deal from such studies about the interpreter but relatively little about the biblical text or ways of understanding it (see, e.g., Provan 1998: 206). Certainly it has to be admitted that one can leave particular 'queer readings' of the Bible, as one can leave examples of other types of reading of the Bible (whether they call attention to the social location of the reader or not), wondering whether the reading in question has allowed one not simply to learn more about the individual reader but also to see the text in a new light. Yet every biblical scholar knows that the high degree of ambiguity, obscurity and lack of descriptive detail in the biblical texts frequently makes the interpretation of those texts heavily dependent upon inference and a certain sort of choosing among alternative scenarios, all of which have varying degrees of relative plausibility. When such choices are made, even by scholars with no stated interest in the question of social location, the social location and personal experiences of the scholar who does the choosing can impact the selection among interpretative alternatives.

Thus, Theodore Jennings notes at one point in his contribution to this volume that the nature of the relationships one plausibly understands the biblical characters Saul, Jonathan and David to be having with other male characters depends to some degree upon 'the experience of the reader', and in particular upon the sexual experiences different readers have had with different types of partners under different types of socio-cultural circumstances (or at any rate upon the exposure readers have had to the existence of such experiences). Inasmuch as this argument is put forward by Jennings in the course of a very close reading of texts from the books of Samuel, it helpfully underscores, in relation to a specific question of textual analysis, the important role played in biblical interpretation by social locations and experiences that might be characterized as 'queer'.

Working with a somewhat similar emphasis on the social location of the reader, Timothy Koch asserts in his contribution to this volume that he necessarily reads and writes out of his own experiences as a gay man (just as, one would probably conclude from Koch's discussion, anyone else reads and writes out of his or her own experiences). Thus, far from worrying about the possibility that he as commentator will impose his own modern interpretative framework on the ancient text, Koch seizes upon a particular set of experiences shared by many gay men—experiences of 'cruising', in which one searches in numerous subtle and not-so-subtle ways for possible sexual partners with whom one can establish a range of different types of relationship—and uses that set of gay male experiences as a sort of tool for thinking about various ways in which a gay male reader might interpret, and position himself relative to, the biblical text. While Koch's comments about specific biblical texts are brief and await further explication, they nevertheless indicate some of the ways in which the experience of participation in a particular gay male social practice can impact the kinds of meaning one derives from, attributes to, or develops in interaction with the biblical texts.

To summarize this first major point, then: one possible understanding of a 'queer reading of the Bible' is a reading produced by a reader who is 'queer', where 'queer' is understood to communicate lesbian, gay, or bisexual identities, experiences, or social locations; and where those identities, experiences, or social locations are thought to impact both the questions that one puts to the biblical texts and the answers one can imagine giving to those questions.

III

A difficult problem arises, however, when one attempts to elaborate further upon the relations between reading and social location. 'Social location' can be construed in a fairly rigid sense, so that all readers associated with a particular social location are spoken about in a homogenizing and universalizing fashion that has come to be criticized, in much contemporary thought, as 'essentialist'. Attempts to grapple with this problem are far more widespread outside of biblical scholarship than within it, and many helpful discussions exist (see, e.g., Fuss 1989); but manifestations of concern appear in biblical scholarship as well, if less frequently. So for example Mary Ann Tolbert, writing in a collection of essays on social location and biblical interpretation, has suggested that until one recognizes that there is 'no one feminist perspective or feminist reading of a text...no one womanist perspective, no one Hispanic perspective, no one Asian perspective, no one lesbian perspective, and so on', the attempt to reflect on social location often 'replicates anew the oppressiveness and exclusivity of hegemonic culture' by insisting that individuals who identify with these various 'perspectives' ignore or suppress their differences from one another (Tolbert 1995: 273). Such warnings should not be misconstrued as attempts to deny the importance of social location for reading. Rather, they serve as calls to acknowledge the complexities involved in accounting for such phenomena as social location, identity and experience when reflecting on biblical interpretation.

I mention these calls here because similar concerns about the complexity of identity and experience have been prominent in one realm of contemporary academic discourse that contributes a great deal to the possible connotations of 'queer commentary' on the Bible: specifically, the development of 'queer theory' out of the intersection of lesbian and gay studies and so-called 'postmodern' thought. Some of the emphases of queer theory, and the possible relevance of these emphases for biblical interpretation in general (cf. Schneider 2000) and the essays in this volume in particular, therefore require a brief discussion.

The origins of 'queer theory' as a term of academic discourse are often associated with an influential essay by Teresa de Lauretis, written to introduce a collection of papers on lesbian and gay sexualities. Interestingly, one of the reasons that de Lauretis gives in that essay for the new terminology, 'queer theory', is her discomfort with a particular move that now often takes place in connection with the word 'queer' itself. While 'queer' is now often used, as we saw above, as a sort of inclusive, convenient shorthand for much longer terminological lists such as 'gay and lesbian' or 'lesbian, gay, bisexual and transgendered', de Lauretis's original stated motivations for using 'queer' rather than 'lesbian and gay' include a concern that the phrase 'lesbian and gay' has in practice come to be used in ways that obscure rather than clarify differences between lesbians and gay men (de Lauretis 1991: v-vi). Thus, while 'queer theory' would continue to recognize the need for political cooperation among those who participate in same-sex sexual activity in societies where such activity is stigmatized or becomes the basis for discrimination and persecution, it would also, according to de Lauretis, specify and analyze differences within that same population, turning a critical eye upon simplistic assumptions about gay or lesbian identity that obscure such differences. Indeed, the differences that concern de Lauretis are not restricted to gender differences between lesbians and gay men but also include, for example, 'difference between and within lesbians, and between and within gay men, in relation to race and its attendant differences of class or ethnic culture, generational, geographical, and socio-political differences' (viii). An important source of inspiration underlying de Lauretis's vision of 'queer theory' seems to be her own prior involvement, as a prominent feminist theorist, in discussions about the need for feminists simultaneously to cooperate politically around issues of women's oppression while taking into account the many differences that exist among actual women, women who therefore experience such oppression (as well as their own identities as women) in multiple particular ways (see especially de Lauretis 1986; 1990).

While de Lauretis herself has subsequently expressed discomfort about the ways in which 'queer theory' has come to be used by the academic publishing industry (de Lauretis 1994: 297), a significant portion of the work associated with 'queer theory' is in fact devoted to the critical analysis of simplistic accounts of lesbian and gay identity that de Lauretis seems to have hoped for. Some of this work is focused, for example, upon the issues of race and ethnicity highlighted by de Lauretis. Such projects ask about the interrelations that are constructed in various times and places between sexuality (including but not restricted to homosexuality) and racial/ethnic categorizations (see, e.g., Somerville 2000; cf. Phelan 1994; Seidman 1997). Although none of the contributions to the present volume takes this particular question as its point of departure (a fact that Tat-siong Benny Liew rightly and critically notes in his response to the essays gathered here), it is not difficult to imagine projects within biblical studies that might do so in the future. So, for example, the trend in contemporary biblical scholarship to analyze rather than accept uncritically biblical references to ethnic groups such as 'Israelites' and 'Canaanites' (see, e.g., Lemche 1991; 1998) may offer opportunities to reconsider the ways in which ethnic boundaries between various groups represented in the biblical texts have been constructed by both those texts and later readers in relation to assumptions (ancient and modern) about sexual practice (cf. Bailey 1995; Stone 1997b). Further exploration along such lines is a desideratum for the future development of 'queer commentary' on the Hebrew Bible.

Moreover, as part of its attempt to complicate notions of gay and lesbian identity and experience, queer theory has also interrogated a particular conceptual distinction that might be understood by some as foundational to the lesbian and gay movement which, in so many respects, gave birth to queer questions. Specifically, queer theorists have problematized the sharp distinction frequently made between 'homosexual' and 'heterosexual' as two categories of human type, or 'sexual orientation', defined by the preferred gender of one's sexual partners. Indeed, the historical work by Chauncey referred to above is only one study among many by historians, social scientists, philosophers, literary scholars and others which point out that the modern Western emphasis upon the binary opposition between 'heterosexual' and 'homosexual' persons and identities has occurred under quite specific historical and sociocultural circumstances (see, e.g., Foucault 1978; 1985; Weeks 1985; 1989; Halperin 1990; Seidman 1997). The fact that individuals living in the wake of those circumstances come to understand their 'sexual identity' or 'sexual orientation' so completely in terms of the 'homosexual/heterosexual' differentiation is in certain respects a contingent effect of history, social organization and modern discourses of sexuality. Rather than accepting without qualification the adequacy of contemporary construals of sexual identity or sexual orientation, queer theorists often attempt to problematize our culture-specific assumptions about the relations between sexual practices and desires, on the one hand, and ways of understanding individual and collective 'identity', on the other hand. Such an attempt at problematization is apparent, for example, when Eve Kosofsky Sedgwick, one of the more influential scholars associated with queer theory, refers critically to the following 'puzzle':

> It is a rather amazing fact that, of the very many dimensions along which the genital activity of one person can be differentiated from that of another (dimensions that include preference for certain acts, certain zones or sensations, certain physical types, a certain frequency, certain symbolic investments, certain relations of age or power, a certain species, a certain number of participants, etc. etc. etc.), precisely one, the gender of object choice, emerged from the turn of the century, and has remained, as *the* dimension denoted by the now ubiquitous category of 'sexual orientation' (Sedgwick 1990: 8, emphasis in original).

Clearly Sedgwick wishes to raise the possibility that, under different circumstances, alternative ways of thinking about and organizing 'sexual orientation' which do not place so much emphasis on 'the gender of object choice' might displace the central role so often granted to the binary distinction between 'heterosexual' and 'homosexual'.

This sort of suggestion is sometimes perceived as presenting a problem to lesbian and gay politics, at least to the extent that such politics try to appeal to 'homosexuality' as an ahistorical category of identity which can serve as the stable foundation for an identity-based political movement. By extension, it might also be thought to present a problem to any understanding of 'queer reading' of the Bible that presupposes a similar stable foundation. It should be stressed, however, that queer questions about the 'homosexual/heterosexual' opposition, or about the centrality of this opposition for modern notions of sexual identity, can actually have the effect of undermining the privileged status of 'heterosexuality' as well, a privileged status indicated within queer theory by use of the term 'heteronormativity'. One of the points made within queer theory (working in many cases under the influence of poststructuralism) is that dominant notions of 'heterosexuality' require for their existence notions of 'homosexuality', in relation to which notions of 'heterosexuality' are differentially defined (see, e.g., Fuss 1991). Thus, one of the most important potential effects of critical, queer questions about the 'homosexual/heterosexual' binary distinction is the way in which such questions interrogate the self-evidence of assumptions that are frequently made about *heterosexuality* (see, e.g., Halperin 1995: 43-48; Katz 1995; Jagose 1996: 16-19).

Moreover, while queer challenges to absolutist versions of the 'homosexual/heterosexual' distinction do stand in some tension with simplistic appeals to lesbian or gay identity—and hence in some tension, as well, with any simplistic appeal to a lesbian or gay 'social location' for purposes of biblical interpretation—in fact at least some of the complexities underscored by queer theorists are already implicitly acknowledged by the tendency to refer (as West, for example, does in this volume) not simply to lesbians and gay men but rather to lesbians, gay men, bisexuals and transgendered persons as 'queer'. The category of 'bisexuality', for example, while capable of being understood in a fairly rigid fashion as a third, distinct 'identity' comparable to 'gay' and 'straight', can also be conceptualized in a much more radical fashion so that it serves to challenge the self-evident status and boundaries of the other two categories (see, e.g., Garber 1995). Such a challenge is potentially important for biblical interpretation, for the biblical texts were arguably written in a context where the modern differentiation between 'homosexual' and 'heterosexual' as two distinct categories of persons had not yet arisen (cf. Boyarin 1995; Nissinen 1998). Thus a scenario such as that proposed by Jennings in this volume, in which male characters who are said explicitly to have sexual relations with women and to father children are nevertheless considered capable of entering into certain sorts of homoerotic relationships, will seem implausible to readers whose interpretative lenses are based on the modern 'homosexual/heterosexual' distinction. Such readers may find it difficult to imagine individuals whose sexual experiences include sexual relations with both men and women. Yet as Jennings correctly recognizes, evidence from other ancient societies indicates that same-sex and opposite-sex relations were by no means understood automatically to be mutually exclusive in the ancient world. In this case, paradoxically, a reading conversant with contemporary queer conversations may actually be more rather than less capable of achieving biblical commentary's traditional aim of allowing the biblical text to 'make its claims' without excessive interference from modern 'interpretative categories'.

Further complexities are introduced into static notions of sexual identity by the inclusion of 'transgendered' persons and practices under the queer rubric. The concepts of 'heterosexuality', 'homosexuality', and even to some extent 'bisexuality' are built on the idea that each one of us has, or should have, a clear biological sex and a coherent sense of one's own gender, for decisions as to whether one is 'heterosexual', 'homosexual', or 'bisexual' depend upon assumptions about one's own sex and gender as well as the sex and gender of one's preferred sexual partners. This comfortable picture is disturbed, however, by those situations in which culturally accepted indicators of sex and gender are ambiguous (say, in those surprisingly common cases in which a newborn infant cannot be easily classified as 'male' or 'female' [see Fausto-Sterling 2000; cf. Foucault 1980]) or when they are deliberately transgressed (say, in cases of sex-change operations, cross-dressing, or so-called 'gender identity disorder' [on the latter see especially Sedgwick 1993: 154-64; Spurlin 1998]). In part because careful attention to such 'transgendered' phenomena has the potential to upset the assumptions according to which sex, gender, sexual practice and sexual desire are most often organized in modern societies, queer theory's critical analysis of modern sexual systems and categories has been linked by many of its practitioners to critical analyses of sex and gender.

Thus the central concerns of queer theory often (though not always) overlap with central concerns of feminist studies, inasmuch as feminism, too, is devoted to the critical analysis of sex and gender. An important influence in this regard is the feminist critic Judith Butler, sometimes said to have been 'cited more persistently and pervasively than any other queer theorist' (Hennessy 1994: 94) but, with only a few important exceptions (e.g. Beal 1997), largely ignored by biblical scholarship. Butler's theory of 'gender performativity', discussed in more detail in my essay in this volume and appealed to by Lori Rowlett's essay as well, emphasizes the regulatory nature of binary notions of sex/gender and the fact that such binary notions have as one of their effects a privileging of heterosexual relations (Butler 1990; 1993). As Butler points out:

> 'Intelligible' genders are those which in some sense institute and maintain relations of coherence and continuity among sex, gender, sexual practice, and desire... The heterosexualization of desire requires and institutes the production of discrete and asymmetrical oppositions between 'feminine' and 'masculine', where these are understood as expressive attributes of 'male' and 'female'. The cultural matrix through which gender identity has become intelligible requires that certain kinds of 'identities' cannot 'exist'—that is, those in which gender does not follow from sex and those in which the practices of desire do not 'follow' from either sex or gender (Butler 1990: 17).

Since, however, these 'relations of coherence and continuity among sex, gender, sexual practice, and desire' are, in Butler's view at least, much less stable than dominant ideologies might lead one to believe, Butler challenges this complex of assumptions and practices (which she refers to as the 'heterosexual matrix') by problematizing not only the 'heterosexual/homosexual' binary but also the 'male/female' binaries of sex and gender upon which the 'heterosexual/homosexual' binary depends.

How might this strand of queer thinking impact biblical interpretation? Due in large part to the important work carried out by feminist and womanist biblical scholars, especially during the last twenty or thirty years, the critical analysis of biblical gender assumptions and representations is widely recognized today as one of the most exciting and productive trends in biblical scholarship. My own essay in this volume is premised upon agreement with those scholars who suggest that a critical gender analysis needs to be extended not only to biblical representations of women (which have understandably been at the center of most feminist studies) but also to biblical representations of men and of 'masculinity'. Thus I argue that the book of Hosea, which has long been subjected to a forceful feminist critique on the basis of the book's problematic sexual rhetoric and its representations of female characters, needs to be considered from the point of view of the book's assumptions about 'manhood' as well, including those assumptions about food, sex and masculinity which, I suggest, are used to characterize Hosea's God. At the same time, the work of Butler and others indicates that we should be cautious about overstating the coherence of the assumptions about sex and gender presupposed and promoted by the biblical texts, since such overstatement may contribute to the appearance of natural inevitability too often granted to heterosexual relations. A queer reading of the Bible's gender assumptions may indicate that even so thoroughly patriarchal a book as Hosea is not finally successful in its attempt to produce (borrowing Butler's language again) 'discrete and asymmetrical oppositions between "feminine" and "masculine", where these are understood as expressive attributes of "male" and "female"'.

Of course, critical questions about gender can also shift our attention back to the issue of social location inasmuch as not only texts but also readers are constituted in part by gender assumptions. This fact raises some important complications for the evaluation of queer commentary, for queer readers cannot by virtue of the label 'queer' escape their own implication in gender codes and structures even if queer theory makes our understanding of those codes and structures more complex. Thus Laurel Schneider, in her feminist theological response to the other essays in this volume, asks about the extent to which some of the queer readings of the Bible found here, especially those written by male authors, contribute to rather than critique the erasure and oppression of women already found in the Bible itself. As Schneider's trenchant questions indicate, the insistence by de Lauretis that queer theory pay close attention to the specificities of gender covered over by the conjunction in appeals to 'lesbian and gay' (and, perhaps now, covered over by appeals to 'queer' itself as a homogenizing term) still needs to be heard.

But queer theory's attempts to problematize normative approaches to sexuality extend beyond the critical analysis of such dichotomies as 'homosexual/heterosexual' and 'male/female'. Certain strands of queer theory work instead by taking as their point of departure alternative ways of organizing sexual practice that do not necessarily stress the gender of the sexual partners. Consider, for example, the controversial phenomenon that plays a central role in some of the contributions to this volume and is mentioned in passing by others: sadomasochism (S/M). If sadomasochism can rightly be characterized as 'queer' it is not because all of its participants necessarily identify with such identity categories as gay, lesbian, or bisexual (identity categories that, as we have seen, are sometimes grouped together under the rubric 'queer'). Still less is it the case that all lesbians, gay men and bisexuals identify with or participate in sadomasochism; on the contrary, sadomasochism tends to produce heated disagreements within gay and lesbian circles. The lesbian writer Pat Califia has pointed out in a provocative essay, however, that sadomasochistic sexual practices call into question the foundational status of 'sexual orientation' within much modern sexual discourse inasmuch as participants in such practices do include individuals who might in other contexts be identified as gay, lesbian, bisexual, or even heterosexual, but in various combinations with one another that have the effect of destabilizing those very identifications (Califia 1994: 183-89). Sadomasochism might usefully be characterized as 'queer', then, in part because it organizes sexual practice and bodily pleasure in ways that are quite different from, and hence contest, dominant approaches to sexuality with their attending normative notions about sexual identities, pleasures and power.

This sort of use of the term 'queer', extending as it does to persons and practices—for example, heterosexuals involved in S/M play—that cannot always be characterized meaningfully as gay, lesbian, bisexual or transgendered, helps to explain the appearance of such controversial phenomena as 'queer heterosexuals' (see, e.g., Thomas 2000). Because 'queer' is increasingly used not simply as an inclusive term for several specific sexual identity groups such as gay, lesbian and bisexual (though, as we have seen, such uses do continue to appear, including within this volume) but also as a way of signaling resistance to a whole range of social conventions of sexual normality (cf. Warner 1993; 1999; Halperin 1995), individuals who might generally be considered heterosexuals in certain contexts can be understood as participating in queer practice in other contexts to the extent that their sexual activities, desires, writings, political involvements, or other practices *challenge sexual normativity*. Not surprisingly, this understanding of 'queer' is not accepted by everyone, and even some of those writers who do use 'queer' in this sense express reservations about the possibility that such a notion of 'queer' might lead to insufficient attention to the specificities of lesbian, gay, bisexual or transgendered practices and experiences (see, e.g., Halperin 1995: 64-66). For our purposes here we can leave aside the complexities of this important debate and simply note, first, that such an understanding of 'queer' (as a general term of resistance to the sexually normal rather than a category of sexual identity) is increasingly common, if still contested, in queer theory; and, second, that such a use of 'queer' is perhaps presupposed by the inclusion of some of the essays in the present volume. Not all of the contributors to this volume would identify as 'gay' or 'lesbian', for example; and yet their essays serve as 'queer commentary' on the Bible inasmuch as they challenge conventional ways of bringing sexuality and the Bible into relation with one another.

And certainly it would have to be acknowledged that contemporary discourses on sadomasochism, though not entirely absent from previous biblical scholarship (see, e.g., Tarlin 1997; Boer 1999: 33-52), fall outside the conventional sets of interpretative lenses through which even the more adventurous biblical scholars generally read the biblical texts. But if readers of the Bible assume that issues associated with sadomasochism can safely be cordoned off from biblical interpretation, the contributions of Lori Rowlett and Roland Boer to this volume call such an assumption into question. Though written in different styles (about which more below) and focusing on different primary textual objects (Judges and the Deuteronomistic History in the case of Rowlett, the Pentateuch and, to a lesser degree, the Christian New Testament in the case of Boer), both pieces manage to expose ways in which the complex interplay among role definitions, power relations, pleasure, pain, dominance and submission that constitutes sadomasochism manifests itself in the Bible (at least according to a certain queer reading) not only in the relationships between particular human characters (e.g. Samson and Delilah) but also in the relationships between the central divine character Yhwh and the human characters with whom Yhwh interacts. For Rowlett and Boer, the dynamics of sadomasochism and the biblical covenant between Yhwh and Israel have some provocative, if disturbing, points of contact.

As Schneider's theological response to these essays indicates, readers who approach the Hebrew Bible out of a conviction that it contains, or a hope that it might contain, raw materials for theological construction may also have to take into account the implications of the dynamics of dominance and submission played out in multiple ways among biblical characters—including the biblical god(s)—to which Boer and Rowlett call our attention. Thus the conjunction between sadomasochism and biblical theology that begins to emerge toward the end of the contributions of Rowlett and Boer not only serves as an indication of the strange, and sometimes disturbing, couplings that can take place within queer commentary, but also calls into question any rigid distinction between 'theological' and 'non-theological' readings of the Bible. This distinction, though certainly not without value in the context of particular disputes (cf., e.g., Oden 1987; Davies 1995), may be another one of those binary oppositions that is in serious need of a deconstructive analysis. If one effect of 'queer' developments is an unsettling of prevailing assumptions about proper roles, practices, boundaries and relationships within sexuality, then this same queer tendency toward the unsettling of accepted distinctions might also undermine the boundary between theological and non-theological reading that is so heavily policed from both sides of the boundary in biblical studies. Queer readers, aware that normalizing approaches to sexuality are powerful today in both theological and non-theological circles, and that discourses which are ostensibly non-theological—legal discourses on sexuality, for example—continue to rely upon theological assumptions in both implicit and explicit ways (see, e.g., Jakobsen and Pellegrini 1999), are perhaps well positioned to carry out precisely such a critical analysis. It may thus be significant that several of the contributions to this volume, including not only those by Rowlett and Boer but also those by Jennings and myself, move beyond a queer analysis of the Bible's human characters to a queer reading of the biblical deity.

The contributions of Boer and Rowlett may also suggest that, in order to think about the possible development of 'queer commentary', it is necessary to reflect not only upon queer readers, and not only upon the questions and procedures that constitute queer reading, but also upon the possible shape(s) of queer writing. Boer, for example, rather than following any conventional format for the traditional academic essay, develops his argument by staging a sort of narrative dialogue among the biblical characters Yhwh and Moses as well as modern theorists who have dealt with sadomasochism such as Sigmund Freud, Jacques Lacan, Gilles Deleuze, Leopold von Sacher-Masoch and the Marquis de Sade. Such experimentation with academic writing is perhaps not so uncommon in today's 'postmodern' milieu, but Daniel Spencer perceptively notes in his response to Boer's contribution that in it 'queer form mirrors function'. After all, assumptions about the proper boundaries between, and roles of, academic and literary writing are no less susceptible to a queer destabilizing than are assumptions about proper boundaries and roles in sexual activity. As Michael Warner argues, ' "queer" gets a critical edge by defining itself against the normal rather than the heterosexual, and normal includes normal business in the academy' (Warner 1993: xxvi). Since 'experiments in critical voice and in the genre of the critical essay' have already been identified outside of biblical scholarship as characteristic of 'queer commentary' (Berlant and Warner 1995: 349) it is not surprising that several of the contributors to this volume engage in such experimentation.

For example, a similar resistance to the 'normal' conventions of biblical scholarship and a similar blurring of the lines between the 'literary' and the more conventionally 'academic' are also apparent in Michael Carden's contribution. Although Carden, in distinction from most of the authors collected here, focuses on one of the biblical texts that is often cited in opposition to homosexuality—specifically, the story of Sodom in Genesis—in fact he rightly refers to his piece as a 'reweaving' of 'some of the threads of the Sodom metatext' rather than, say, an exegesis or even a straightforward reading of the text of Genesis itself. One of the assumptions underlying Carden's mode of reading seems to be that we never simply approach 'the text of Genesis itself', but always read the Sodom story in relation to a series of various other texts. In that respect Carden's approach overlaps significantly with the approaches of at least some of those biblical scholars who argue that biblical interpretation can profitably be carried out in dialogue with contemporary theories of 'intertextuality' (see, e.g., Fewell 1992). For Carden the meaning of the Sodom story seems to be something that is constructed within the interrelations established among the biblical text, later readings of it, and contemporary readers such as Carden himself. Such meanings can be homophobic and misogynistic, as the history of interpretation of the Sodom traditions amply attests. Over against such homophobic and misogynistic readings, however, Carden juxtaposes some of those later readings of the Sodom story (such as certain Jewish traditions about Lot's daughters) that are in his view potentially useful for antihomophobic and feminist appropriations of the Sodom traditions.

Thus the intertextual relationships analyzed and/or constructed in Carden's reading result as much from his own ideological critique of religious homophobia as from an interest in reconstructing direct historical influences (cf. Beal 1992). Such a reader-oriented version of intertextual interpretation seems to be well suited to the task of queer commentary, inasmuch as 'queer' continues to call to mind unorthodox combinations and transgressive juxtapositions of things normally kept apart. As the North American gay writer Edmund White remarks in his biography of Proust (who was himself capable of constructing unconventional intertextual relations with the Sodom narrative, and who makes a brief appearance in Carden's essay), the 'heat' of 'creative energy' can be 'generated when two genres are rubbed against each other to form something entirely new' (White 1999: 81). The 'creative energy' released in Carden's piece results in part from the way in which he 'rubs' together such disparate genres of written discourse as biblical literature, midrash, medieval poetry and modern fundamentalist tracts in order to create a new form of biblical commentary.

Somewhat similar efforts at 'rubbing genres' together in a queer fashion are apparent in the early portions of Lori Rowlett's essay, where Rowlett asks not only about dynamics at work in the book of Judges and the Deuteronomistic History but also about the dynamics at work in later appropriations of these texts. In distinction from Carden, however, Rowlett moves in the direction taken by such scholars as J. Cheryl Exum and considers musical, and especially operatic, appropriations of the story of Samson and Delilah rather than simply the more traditional written appropriations (see Exum 1996: 175-237). In Rowlett's view attention to such appropriations confirms the instability of gender categories pointed out by Judith Butler, as referred to above. For our purposes at the moment, however, it is important to emphasize here that Rowlett's own contribution joins the contributions of Boer and Carden (as well as Liew's epistolary 'response' to these contributions) in destabilizing not simply the norms of gender and sexuality but also many of the academic norms that conventionally dictate the shape of biblical commentary.

IV

And so it should be obvious by now that 'queer commentary' on the Bible does not consist in the application of a single, 'queer' method to the biblical texts. On the one hand, the contributions to this volume are quite heterogeneous in comparison with one another; and, on the other hand, while the individual contributions gathered here are in many ways distinct (and sometimes radically so) from much previous biblical scholarship, numerous points of contact do clearly exist between some of these essays and some of the newer developments in biblical interpretation. At the same time, I have tried to point out that trends in contemporary queer theory make it difficult to define 'queer commentary' in a simplistic fashion as the production of readings by 'queer readers', at least so long as we understand the latter phrase to refer to some easily identified group of readers who can be firmly demarcated from other sorts of readers of the Bible. While certain shared experiences and social locations will probably continue to be identified more readily than others as 'queer', and while these shared experiences and social locations can in fact impact the practice of biblical interpretation (at least in my own view [cf. Stone 1997a] and the view of many, and perhaps all, of the contributors to this volume), nevertheless absolute and essential distinctions between 'queer readers' and 'non-queer readers' would seem to founder on the deconstruction of such binary oppositions as those between 'heterosexual' and 'homosexual', 'male' and 'female', and so forth.

Thus, rather than referring in any obvious way to a single method, a single subject matter (e.g. 'homosexuality in the Bible'), or a single set of readers who can be clearly and absolutely differentiated from all other readers, 'queer commentary on the Bible' might be better understood, in my own estimation at least, as a range of approaches to biblical interpretation that take as their point of departure a critical interrogation and active contestation of the many ways in which the Bible is and has been read to support heteronormative and normalizing configurations of sexual practices and sexual identities.

In conclusion, I would like to return briefly to the aforementioned essay by Lauren Berlant and Michael Warner from which the phrase 'queer commentary' has been borrowed. Berlant and Warner, faced with the challenge of describing queer projects for an audience of literary scholars but cognizant of the many difficulties involved in formulating such a description, eschew a single definition of 'queer' and point out instead that 'queer commentary has been animated by a sense of belonging to a discourse world that only partly exists yet'. Rather than emerging in an obvious way from a single site or with a single purpose, queer work 'aspires to create publics… Through a wide range of mongrelized genres and media, queer commentary allows a lot of unpredictability in the culture it brings into being' (Berlant and Warner 1995: 344).

The emphasis placed here by Berlant and Warner upon the 'public' dimension of queer commentary perhaps resonates with the call from some biblical scholars for a biblical scholarship sensitive to the 'public' dimensions of biblical interpretation (see, e.g., Schüssler Fiorenza 1999). But the assertion that queer commentary 'aspires to create publics' offers us as well a useful criterion against which the success of the queer readings contained in this volume might one day be evaluated. Such an assertion indicates that the value of queer intellectual work lies above all in its effects, in the spaces that it opens for voices previously unheard, and in the possibilities that it creates for a transformation of the practices, pleasures, desires and identities associated with sexuality. Readers of this volume may well disagree with one another over the plausibility, the relevance, the scholarly grounding, or even the propriety of both the individual readings found here and the collection as a whole. The value of queer commentary on the Bible, however, of which this volume should in my view be taken as an initial example, will hopefully be judged in the end by the extent to which it contributes to the difficult but pleasurable task of 'bringing a queerer world into being' (Berlant and Warner 1995: 344).

Part I

QUEER READINGS

YHWH AS ERASTES

Theodore W. Jennings Jr

Before embarking on this re-reading of the story of David and YHWH, it may be helpful to signal in advance some of the characteristics of the interpretive strategies that will be deployed. In the first place we may distinguish a 'queer reading' strategy from some of the closely allied strategies that it to a certain extent presupposes and sublates. The most common reading strategy is one that begins from the texts that have been deployed in aid of a homophobic prohibition or stigmatization of same-sex (usually male same-sex) relationships. The strategy often used in such re-readings is that of contesting the homophobic reading of these texts or, when that is not entirely successful, of contesting their relevance for contemporary debates concerning 'homosexuality'. From Bailey to Scroggs[1] this strategy has enjoyed significant gains resulting, for example, in the elimination of the story of Sodom from the arsenal of homophobic proscriptions of same-sex desire and practice and the contesting of the relevance of Leviticus or of presumed Pauline stigmatizations. This reading strategy remains, however, basically defensive in character.

A second strategy, until now rather underdeveloped, is that of discovering same-sex relationships that are positively valued in these texts. The material we will be considering, for example, has been mined for the relation between David and Jonathan as exemplifying a male same sex-relation[2] and others have found something similar in the

---

1. Derrick Sherwin Bailey's landmark study of *Homosexuality in the Western Christian Tradition* (London: Longmans, Green & Co., 1955) was primarily concerned with the emergence of the legal criminalization of same-sex practices but it paid significant attention to the biblical texts which were supposed to be the foundation of such laws. Robin Scroggs, *The New Testament and Homosexuality* (Minneapolis: Fortress Press, 1983), deals with Pauline texts.

2. Thus Tom Horner's *Jonathan Loved David* (Philadelphia: Westminster

story of Ruth and Naomi as an exemplar of lesbian love.[3] While much remains to be done with this 'gay-affirmative' (as opposed to a 'homophobic-defensive') reading strategy it also has built-in limitations with respect to the number of texts that come into view.

A 'queer reading' strategy, while dependent in complex ways on the possibility and the achievements of the previous strategies, need not limit itself to discovering same-sex relations in the text. For one thing it may be more inclusive of a variety of sexualities that are otherwise simply cast alongside one another (as gay, lesbian, bisexual, transgendered, in the contemporary listing) as well as taking into account other marginalized or non heteronormative sexualities (S&M, pederastic, prostitutional, promiscuous etc.) as perspectives from which to enter and interpret a text. While these readings may indeed seek to disclose dynamics within the texts that may otherwise be 'hidden from history' they also may simply seek to demonstrate how a text appears when viewed from such angles of vision as a contribution to the multiplication of such angles of vision. It is here not a question of what everyone should see but of what may be seen from this standpoint as one among many possible standpoints. It is not then a question of contesting homophobia directly or of legitimating same-sex practice or relationships through the discovery of canonical precedents. Instead it simply presupposes that queerness exists, at least in readers, and that this provides a way of illuminating the texts.

In the reading of a narrative text that will be pursued here the

Press, 1978) is the first to deal with this relationship in a theological context; David Greenberg's discussion in *The Construction of Homosexuality* (Chicago: University of Chicago Press, 1988) has a fine discussion of 'The Love of Warriors' (pp. 110-16). And Halperin's 'Heroes and their Pals', in *One Hundred Years of Homosexuality and Other Essays on Greek Love* (New York: Routledge, 1990, pp. 75-87), contains insightful and provocative discussion as well. All three of these books relate the David and Jonathan sagas to two other texts from antiquity that deal with the passionate love of two men for one another: the *Iliad* of Homer and the Babylonian *Gilgamesh Epic*. In addition Greenberg provides extensive cross-cultural parallels to the sorts of relationships which will be discussed here. More recently this reading has been more or less presupposed in Danna Nolan Fewell and David M. Gunn, *Gender, Power and Promise: The Subject of the Bible's First Story* (Nashville: Abingdon Press, 1993), pp. 148-51.

3.   See 'The Book of Ruth: Idyllic Revisionism', in Ilana Pardes, *Countertraditions in the Bible: A Feminist Approach* (Cambridge, MA: Harvard University Press, 1992), pp. 98-117.

question to be considered is not whether, for example, YHWH 'really is' a 'homosexual' or a 'pederast' or even a 'warrior chief', but is first about the character in the plot named YHWH[4] as this character is deployed particularly in relation to David. We are concerned to see how a certain homoeroticism operates in the development of this relationship.

But which kind of homoeroticism?

In a ground-breaking study Howard Eilberg-Schwartz has proposed that the relation between a male deity and a male (individual or collective) adherent is eroticized in such a way in biblical narrative that it may be seen as homoerotic.[5] Eilberg-Schwartz's point of entry into this analysis is dependent upon a Freudian perspective that privileges the father–son relationship. Accordingly he focuses upon the homoerotic aspects of the relationship between God and 'man' that are filtered through the father–son dynamic. The focal texts here are the narratives that depict the relation between Moses and God, but prophetic texts also play a role here, especially Ezek. 16 and 23.

Eilberg-Schwartz maintains that the overt homoeroticism of the relation between God and Israel is disguised or masked through an averting of the gaze from God's phallus/penis and through the feminization of God's human partner.

In this essay I will affirm the homoerotic character of the relation between the divine being and his male beloved. But I will seek to contest the restriction of this eroticism to the domain of an incestuous father–son relationship and propose instead of or alongside that relation another model of homoeroticism. I will suggest certain similarities to what has come to be known as a pederastic structure as well as parallels to the somewhat different structure of warrior eroticism

---

4. The question of the naming of this character is a vexed one. Calling this character 'God' or even 'the Lord' invokes an abstraction that distracts from the concreteness of narrative development of character. The tetragrammaton YHWH is consistent with the text, at least in Hebrew, but is protected from pronunciation by views of the holiness of the name (and the being thus named) that arise centuries later than the text. An alternative might be Adonai which may have been the name pronounced instead of YHWH and which is not similarly protected from pronunciation. When quoting the text in translation I have used 'the Lord'; otherwise I have moved between YHWH and its vocalization as Adonai. What is in any case to be kept in view is that we have to do here with a character in a narrative.

5. Howard Eilberg-Schwartz, *God's Phallus: And Other Problems for Men and Monotheism* (Boston: Beacon Press, 1994).

(which might be referred to, using Halperin's language, as 'Heroes and their Pals'). Accordingly, I will provisionally use the distinction between 'lover' (*erastes*) and 'beloved' (*eromenos*), borrowed from antiquity, to shed light on the relational dynamics to be discussed here—hence the title of this reading: 'YHWH as Erastes'. In order to develop this model I will attend to a narrative that Eilberg-Schwartz omits from his analysis, the story of the relationship between David and YHWH that is developed in connection with the (homoerotic) relations between David and Saul and David and Jonathan. The elaboration of this model will depend not on a psychoanalytic frame of reference but a cross-cultural one that is suggestive of parallel phenomena in warrior societies.

War Chiefs and their Boy Companions

We begin with some remarks about the cultural ambience of the saga concerning David. In general, it appears to be a saga written for men. In it women have only minor roles, as adjuncts to the male world. This is the reverse of the situation in the Tamar (Gen. 38) or Ruth stories. The male world is pre-eminently a world of battle and of court intrigue among warriors. It is a story for warriors and, especially, leaders of warriors.

One of the characteristic features of the culture of this warrior elite of Israel, especially as depicted in 1 Samuel, is that the primary companions of adult and young adult warriors are younger males. In these stories of men constantly on the march, in raid or skirmish or at camp, women seldom appear.[6] Instead the men, especially the dominant war leaders, always appear with their youthful boy companions.

We begin with Saul who is presented to us initially as 'a handsome young man' (9.2).[7] When we come actually to hear about this young man he is accompanied by a youth with whom he goes in search of his father's donkeys. The adventures of Saul and the youth lead to Saul's encounter with the venerable Samuel who will make him king of Israel. The handsome young man and his younger companion in adventure

---

6. In 1 Sam. 21.5 the absence of women in stories of men at war is made explicit: David avows that 'women have been kept from us when I go on an expedition'.

7. Except where otherwise specified and/or altered for emphasis I am using the NRSV.

serve as a kind of relational paradigm that will be played out in a variety of relationships including those between Jonathan and his armor bearer, between Saul and David (who becomes Saul's armor bearer), and between David and Jonathan (David will briefly appear also as Jonathan's armor bearer). In all cases the hero is accompanied or 'partnered' by a younger male companion.

In the first instance (the case of Saul and his 'youth') we seem to be dealing with a relationship between older and younger adolescents. Saul is sent by his father to take one of the 'boys' or 'lads' with him to find strayed donkeys (9.3). It is of some interest that we are several times reminded of the presence of the younger companion in the course of this journey (9.5, 7, 8, 22, 27; 10.14). The lad only disappears from the story with the coronation of Saul.

Indeed we may say that the lad serves the pivotal function in the story. For it is the boy who persuades Saul to inquire of the seer (who turns out to be Samuel) concerning the location of the donkeys and overcomes the difficulty in this encounter by producing the coin with which they approach the seer for advice (9.8). In spite of this the lad is excluded by Samuel (and later by Saul) from knowledge of Saul's royal destiny. In becoming king, Saul puts away his first youthful companion.

In this first episode Saul is not a warrior. Thus his young companion is not an armor bearer but one of the cowboys (or donkey-boys) on the modest 'ranch' of Saul's father, Kish. He is certainly no mute slave, but a true companion who manages to find a way to rescue the enterprise from failure and so to save the reputation of his older handsome companion.

Almost immediately we are introduced to Jonathan. In the meantime Saul has defeated the Ammonites (1 Sam. 11.11). Subsequently the battles will be fought by Jonathan. The first of these encounters is the battle of the pass of Michmash (ch. 14).

Here we are introduced to Jonathan and the 'young man who carried his armor' (14.1). It is clear from the narrative that the armor bearer is not simply a servant but a companion in the battle (14.6-7, 12-14). Between them they manage to kill about twenty Philistines of the garrison, provoking a general panic. Taking advantage of the panic (although acting with extraordinary caution) Saul finally commits his men to the battle. 'So the Lord gave Israel the battle that day' (14.23).

It is clear that Jonathan, like his father before him, has a young comrade with whom he undertakes the adventure that earns him praise. Because now we have to do with the adventures of warriors the comrade is no longer a donkey herder but an armor bearer. Yet the structure is similar. In both cases we have an apparently younger companion of somewhat lower status who nevertheless is a full partner in the adventures of the hero and who shares in the remembered glory of the hero. If the companion were only incidental either to the action or to the hero we would expect subsequent retelling to have erased the companion from memory. That this has not occurred suggests that the companion is a necessary part of the saga. Under what conditions might this be so? Certainly a pattern is emerging in which it is expected that the youthful hero be accompanied by a faithful 'sidekick' who, while younger and of lesser status, is nevertheless essential to the story. The social context within which these stories of heroic adventure are told seems to require this form of 'homosociality'.

Subsequently, in a section of the story we will consider again, David is chosen, at least in part for his beauty, to be Saul's boy companion and armor bearer (16.21-22). Even after David and Jonathan become friends, Jonathan is accompanied by a boy companion (ch. 20). In the final battle, Saul, who has of course lost David as his boy companion, has with him another armor bearer who refuses to help the king commit suicide when the latter is desperately wounded but, when Saul performs the deed for himself, does, in grief, fall upon his own sword (31.3-6; cf. 1 Chron. 9.4-5). Indeed this story echoes the first appearance of an armor bearer in the saga material, this time in Judg. 9 in the account of the death of Abimelech. The relation most closely parallels that of Saul and his last armor bearer for Abimelech also begs his armor bearer to slay him lest he die of the mortal blow caused by a woman crushing his skull with a millstone. The 'young man who carried his armor' in that case does comply with the last wish of his warchief hero (Judg. 9.54).

If the warrior hero is regularly accompanied by a youthful companion we should note that it is only of David that we never hear that he has taken such a young companion for himself. We will consider what we are to make of this later.

Are we to read this saga as entailing an erotic attachment between the heroes and their younger male companions? The saga itself does not speak of this directly. In order to 'flesh' this out, we would have to ask whether homosocial relationships between older and younger adolescents engaged in adventure may be thought to have an erotic and even an overtly sexual component. Here the answer we give would depend on at least two factors. The first has to do with what we suppose to be the case between older and younger adolescent male adventurers where women are absent. This may depend on one's particular view of psychodynamics. Do we regard such relationships to be characterized by an erotic component? And do we suppose that such relationships may include sexual practice?

In this latter connection another consideration comes into play, namely the cultural expectations or potentialities with respect to such relationships. Certainly we know of cultures within which it would be expected as a matter of course that such a relationship should find sexual expression. We also know of cultures in which sexual practice under such circumstances while not infrequent would be nevertheless interdicted. To which cultural sphere does the story of Saul, Jonathan and David correspond?

To a certain extent the answer one gives will depend upon the experience of the reader. Those who have had sexual experience under such circumstances or who are familiar with persons or cultures that take such experience for granted will be inclined to read the story as inclusive of sexual potentiality while those who are inclined to regard this as unthinkable will not notice the possibilities of such a reading or will even be outraged by its suggestion.

In my view there is nothing in the heroic saga material of Israel (Judges–2 Samuel) that precludes erotic or even sexual readings. It appears to me that a rather matter-of-fact attitude toward this would be most likely. If there were anxiety about this it would scarcely be necessary to outfit Saul with such a companion or to give the lad such an important role.

The stories we have thus far considered do not thematize the emotional attachment between the hero and his companion. They merely exhibit a structure that appears to have similarities to relational structures among young warriors that are familiar from other societies, many of which accept and expect the relationship to find sexual expression.

Is that what is happening here? We cannot say for sure without a detailed consideration of the relationships that are foregrounded in the narrative; those between David and his lovers: Saul, Jonathan and YHWH.

YHWH as War Chief

We may gain further clarity about the conventions which govern the relationship between warriors and their youthful companions by attending to the way in which YHWH is characterized in the saga.

Within this context YHWH is the pre-eminent warrior chieftain. The entire saga depends on the way in which YHWH is being displaced as the immediate warrior chief of Israel through the demand of the people for a 'king', for a war leader similar to that found in other nations (1 Sam. 8.5). Indeed YHWH himself interprets the desire of the Israelites for a warrior chief (king) to be a rejection of himself as their warrior chief (1 Sam. 8.7). The writer and reader/hearer of this saga regard YHWH as acting in accordance with the warrior code. Thus he is often harsh, insisting on blind obedience and utter loyalty, capricious, capable of apparent pettiness and clever strategy.

How does this warrior chieftain choose his youthful companions? In fact the basic structure of the saga depends on the choices which *this* warrior chief makes concerning who will be his youthful companion and armor carrier. He chooses two: first Saul and then, when Saul has displeased him, David. In so far as we can discern the motive for the choices, it is the astonishing physical beauty of the young men. This is always the first characteristic mentioned in the text. Thus when we are first introduced to Saul we are told:

> There was a man of Benjamin... He had a son whose name was Saul, a handsome young man. There was not a man among the people of Israel more handsome than he; he stood head and shoulders above everyone else (1 Sam. 9.1-2).

Saul has thus two related qualifications: his beauty and his imposing height.

The remarking upon the beauty of a male protagonist is something found in biblical literature only in two places outside the saga of David. The first is in the story of Joseph where it serves as the explanation of Potiphar's wife's infatuation with Joseph:

> Now Joseph was handsome and good looking. And after a time his master's wife cast her eyes on Joseph and said, 'lie with me' (Gen. 39.6-7).

The story of the attempted seduction occupies the entire chapter, results in Joseph's being imprisoned and leads to the interpretation of dreams which launches Joseph's career and thus is the hinge of the entire saga.

The only other text, apart from the David saga, in which male beauty is remarked upon in a protagonist is in the erotic poems of the Song of Songs. That is to say that the presentation of male beauty is offered to the eroticizing gaze. In two instances outside the David saga, this gaze is the gaze of women but in the David saga it is the gaze of (male) warrior chieftains (YHWH, Saul and Jonathan).[8]

Thus in the selection of David to replace Saul, seven sons of Jesse pass before Samuel. None of them are appropriate to YHWH, however, who disregards the height of Eliab (the height of Saul had apparently played a role in his earlier selection). YHWH claims that he does not look on outward appearances but at the heart (will) of the person (1 Sam. 16.7). However, when the last of Jesse's sons comes into the room we are told:

> Now he was ruddy, and had beautiful eyes, and was handsome. The Lord
> said [to Samuel], 'Rise and anoint him for this is the one' (1 Sam. 16.12).

Thus the selection of David as the boy companion of the main warrior chief, while it departs from the standards of beauty set by Saul, appears nonetheless to begin with his remarkable beauty.[9] The choice is never made on the basis of prior prowess. The first thing we know about Saul and David is their beauty. Now this certainly tells us that the hearers/ readers of this saga expect male beauty to be the initial criterion for the selection of youthful companions. To be sure other attributes are expected to follow: bravery and boldness is demonstrated by both Saul and David as it is by Jonathan's anonymous boy companion. Absolute loyalty appears also to be essential and we see how this is depicted in the apparent trustworthiness of Jonathan's companion in his assignations with David or in the final loyalty of Saul's last armor bearer. This

8.   Indirect evidence for this relationship between male beauty and the desire of other males comes from one of the servant songs of Isaiah. The astonishing thing about the one in whom YHWH delights here is precisely that from the standpoint of the powerful males (kings) of the earth this servant 'has nothing in his appearance that we should desire him' (Isa. 53.2). Somewhat more ambiguous in this regard is the presumed attraction of a (transgendered) Israel for the masculine youthful beauty of Assyrian cavalry officers (Ezek. 23.23).

9.   Roland Boer, in his *Knockin' on Heaven's Door: The Bible and Popular Culture* (New York: Routledge, 1999), notes in an intriguing paragraph devoted to this topic that '… one of the relationships that is most often neglected in readings of these chapters is that between Yahweh and David' and points to the suggestion that 'Yahweh responds, apparently, to his appearance' (p. 29). This

loyalty comes to most dramatic expression in the steadfast refusal of David to harm the man whose boy companion he had once been, even when Saul tries by every available means to kill David.

There appear to be two exceptions to this indication of male beauty as motivating YHWH's selection of a male companion in the subsequent part of the story of David that concerns his reign as king. Two of David's sons are said to be beautiful, yet they do not become the 'chosen' of YHWH. In 2 Samuel we are told of the remarkable beauty of David's third son, Absalom:

> Now in all Israel there was no one to be praised so much for his beauty as Absalom; from the sole of his foot to the crown of his head there was no blemish in him (2 Sam. 14.25).

And, at the end of the story of David, we are told of the beauty of his fourth son, Adonijah.

> He was also a very handsome man and he was born next after Absalom (1 Kgs 1.6).

Do these instances of male beauty contradict the interpretation of male beauty as signaling YHWH's choice of companion?

As it turns out, in both cases, what is going on is that the beauty of the younger male serves as an explanation for what indeed appears to be YHWH's choice of them over the aging David. In the case of Absalom what is prepared for by the remark concerning his beauty is that all Israel comes to suppose that he is indeed YHWH's chosen. Thus there ensues a full-scale uprising against David which results in David's flight from Jerusalem into the wilderness and which very nearly results in David's death and capture. Moreover it appears that the people of Israel are not in error in supposing that the beautiful young Absalom has been chosen by YHWH, for Absalom is the instrument for the fulfillment of YHWH's punishment of David for the death of Uriah, which death had been arranged to cover up Bathsheba's pregnancy resulting from David's seduction (rape) and adultery. In response to that crime YHWH had assured David that there would be severe internal strife in his household (2 Sam. 11.11). Absalom is the instrument for the accomplishment of that curse and is to that extent actually chosen by YHWH.

In the case of Adonijah his beauty is cited (together with his seniority as next after Absalom) as the ground of the plausibility for his determination to be king in place of the now elderly and frail David.

Adonijah's credentials for being chosen by YHWH seem to come down to his beauty (no other exploits of his are recounted) and this, indeed, seems enough to persuade both the high priest Abiathar and David's long-time general Joab. As it turns out Adonijah is accepted by the most influential in Israel as the next king but by a quick pre-emptive strike instigated by Bathsheba (with the collusion of Nathan), Solomon is anointed first.

Thus in what appear to be exceptions to the use of male beauty as signaling the choice of some one to be YHWH's boy companion, we find instead that this is precisely what makes it plausible to suppose, as Israel does, that YHWH has chosen them over his earlier but now aging favorite, David. As it turns out YHWH, who had spurned his first companion Saul in order to select David, has in the meantime himself learned the virtue of loyalty and remains loyal to David to the end.[10]

Given this rather cursory overview we may identify certain characteristics of the relation between the hero and his 'armor bearer'. First, as the name suggests, the armor bearer is the constant companion of the hero or warrior. While we often glimpse him in battle alongside the hero he must be present away from battle if he is to carry the arms or armor that, in battle, would be worn or employed by the warrior himself. He must then be supposed to be the constant companion of the warrior.

Further the youth is distinguished by an absolute loyalty to the warrior/hero. In two cases, that of Saul and that of Abimelech, this loyalty is demonstrated by a determination not to outlive the hero. From the youth's perspective the relationship is one of loyalty to the death.

---

10. We may also note that in this same saga we are four times told of the beauty of women characters. In at least three of the four cases what this beauty signals is overpowering physical attraction. It is her beauty that provokes David to lose his head over Bathsheba (2 Sam. 11.3). It is the beauty of Tamar, sister of Absalom, that drives Amnon, David's first son, to being so overcome with lust that he rapes her (13.1-14). It is the beauty of Abishag that leads to her selection to 'warm the bed' of the dying David (1 Kgs 1.1-4). The only exception appears to be the case of Tamar the daughter of Absalom (2 Sam. 14.27) but this may well be a displacement from Absalom's sister of the same name. Thus the connection between beauty and presumed erotic attachment applies equally to male and to female characters. But whether it is the male or the female who is beautiful in this saga, it is a male character who notices (or is expected to notice) and is drawn to (or is expected to be drawn to) the beautiful one.

This is, however, not necessarily true of the warrior's relation to the youth. Saul's sidekick disappears from the narrative only to be replaced later by David who is in turn replaced by at least one other (the one who dies at Saul's side). The same appears to be true of Jonathan as well who selects David to be his armor bearer in place of (or alongside) the one with whom he had gained glory in the battle of Michmash. Even as the relation with David deepens in intensity Jonathan has another armor bearer whom he can trust absolutely in the conspiracy to protect David from the wrath of Saul. YHWH too selects at least two such companions: Saul and David.

We may hazard here an analogy with marriage in that the husband/warrior may have more than one youth/wife while the youth/wife may have only one hero/husband. Indeed the theme of Saul's jealousy when his own son seems to supplant him as the lover of David provides one of the main driving plots of the narrative.

This analogy is in important respects misleading, however, since the youth is not in other respects 'feminized'.[11] In these narratives the youth is regularly noted for his boldness and bravery, sharing in the dangers and the adventures of the warrior, indeed sometimes outshining the hero in these masculine qualities. Moreover, if David is illustrative, the beloved youth may also exercise the functions of a husband to a wife without severing the relation to his warrior hero. Nevertheless the youth, we have seen, is selected, as are female consorts, at least to a significant degree because of his beauty, a beauty that awakens the desire and favor of the lover/hero.

The sort of homoerotic attachments we encounter in this text have some points of contact with what we find in other warrior cultures. In Greek terms the appropriate analogy is not so much Athenian pederasty but the attachments of male lovers that appear characteristic of Sparta[12] or the famous band of lovers of Thebes.[13] Something similar appears in accounts of Celtic warriors[14] and may even lie behind some of the homoerotic attachments of early feudal Europe.[15] One of the most

11. One should, however, exercise great caution in trying to identify what would count as 'feminization' given the remarkable exploits of Deborah and Jael (Judg. 5 and 6).

12. See, for example, Plutarch's life of Lycurgus.

13. See Plutarch's life of Pelopidus.

14. For an overview see Greenberg, *The Construction of Homosexuality*, p. 111.

15. Greenberg, *The Construction of Homosexuality*, pp. 242-98.

elaborately documented examples of homoeroticism in warrior cultures is found in Tokugawa Japan in accounts of the relationships between samurai and their boy companions.[16] In most of these cases both lover and beloved are warriors or warriors in training. The beloved is thus not a 'kept boy' but a partner in adventure distinguished by his beauty, boldness and loyalty. The context of these relationships means that the beloved need not be assimilated to the heterosexual model and is thus less likely to be 'feminized' than appears to be the case in more sedentary homoerotic cultures.

Thus far we have seen that the depiction of YHWH in this narrative places him within a context in which relationships between warriors and their younger companions appear to have a homoerotic character that is determined, in part, by considerations of the physical beauty of the younger companion. Thus the relation appears to be one mediated by some sort of homoerotic desire or that at least presupposes some of the features of homoerotic desire. But this suggestion remains somewhat abstract without attention to some of the episodes within which the relation between David and YHWH is played out.

Fancy Dancer[17]

In order to 'flesh out' the erotic character of the relationship between David and YHWH we may turn to one of the most remarkable episodes in the account of this relationship: that of David's shameless cavorting before Adonai and the ark .

The story of David's curious relation with the ark of the 'Lord of Hosts' occupies the whole of 2 Sam. 6.[18] But we will first concentrate our attention on the episode of 6.14 and its aftermath.

16. See *The Great Mirror of Male Love* by Ihara Saikaku (trans. Paul G. Schalow; Stanford: Stanford University Press, 1990), a seventeenth-century Japanese writer who composes his book as a collection of forty short stories, the first twenty of which deal with erotic attachments between samurai and their boy companions. For a discussion of a number of texts relating to this theme see Gary Leupp, *Male Colors: The Construction of Homosexuality in Tokugawa Japan* (Berkeley: University of California Press, 1995).

17. With apologies, and a salute, to Patricia Nell Warren.

18. I am indebted to the careful reading of this story and the one that follows (2 Sam. 7) provided by J.P. Fokkelman in his magisterial *Narrative Art and Poetry in the Books of Samuel*. III. *Throne and City* (Assen: Van Gorcum, 1990). He recognizes the highly personal character of the depicted roles of David and YHWH,

David danced before the Lord with all his might; David was girded with a linen ephod. So David and all the house of Israel brought up the ark of the Lord with shouting, and with the sound of the trumpet. As the ark of the Lord came into the city of David, Michal daughter of Saul looked out the window, and saw King David leaping and dancing before the Lord; and she despised him in her heart (6.14-16).

When the king has acted as priest to bless the people he comes home, where he is met by the enraged Michal:

But Michal the daughter of Saul came out to meet David and said, 'How the king of Israel honored himself today before the eyes of his servants' maids, as any vulgar fellow might shamelessly expose himself'. David said to Michal, 'It was in front of the Lord, who chose me in place of your father and all his household, to appoint me as prince over Israel, the people of the Lord, that I have cavorted before the Lord. I will make myself yet more contemptible than this, and I will be abased in my own eyes; but by the maids of whom you have spoken, by them I shall be held in honor'. And Michal the daughter of Saul had no child to the day of her death (6.20-23).

What are we to make of David's near-naked self-display before the physical presence of Adonai? Why is he dancing and cavorting? Why is he uncovered or naked? And why is Michal so enraged?

The significance of Michal's reaction and David's response in 2 Samuel is underscored by the omission of this interaction from the priestly retelling of this story of David and the ark in 1 Chron. 15. The Chronicler writes in a significantly different cultural and historical context, writing, it is supposed, several centuries after the composition of Samuel and in a society in which priests rather than warriors have the leading role. We may briefly note some of the other differences before returning to the interaction between David and Michal.

In the priestly story the Levites play a major role and David appears as their patron. It is because they were not in charge of the ark, for example, that YHWH 'burst forth' onto Uzzah to deadly effect (1 Chron. 15.13).[19] David is said to be wearing a robe (15.27) in addition to the ephod which is thus converted from an undergarment to an

---

noting that 'what meets the eye is that the king and God are on an equal footing' (p. 181) and this is made most clear by the move from titles (like king and God), to the proper names David and YHWH.

19. Unfortunately Fokkelman permits his own reading to be influenced by the Chronicler at this point (*Narrative Art and Poetry*, p. 189).

outer garment rather like a vestment. Although 1 Chron. 15.29 closely parallels 2 Sam. 6.16 it omits the salient feature that David's dancing and cavorting was 'before YHWH' thereby making it seem to be simply a quasi-liturgical act in company with the priests. Thus the highly personal character of David's dancing is greatly reduced. He is leaping and dancing, but fully clothed, accompanied by priests and not 'before the Lord'.

As a consequence Michal's earlier expressed disgust at David's act (still retained by the Chronicler) can no longer have any sense. For David is simply doing what the Levites do. The specific erotic charge of the story has been expunged. There is no claim that David has disgraced himself in the eyes of women nor that David's dance is a response to YHWH's having chosen him over YHWH's first 'beloved' Saul.

The cleaning up of this story by the Chronicler tells us what to look for in the saga of 2 Samuel.[20] And we shall see that this is most telling with respect to the omission altogether of Michal's remonstration with David and his reply. The account of 1 Chronicles serves as a kind of reverse highlighting of the salient details for our focus.

Michal is David's wife. But she is also, as the text reminds us, the daughter of Saul who had been David's first (human) lover. Moreover she is the sister of David's last and most intimate (human) lover, Jonathan. She had been given to David rather begrudgingly by Saul as a kind of trophy wife. And her love for David had been demonstrated by rescuing David from a jealous Saul's enraged attempt to assassinate David. Yet her role as David's protector had been taken by her own brother Jonathan who had supplanted both Saul and Michal as David's chief lover. Perhaps it is only for Jonathan's sake that David has reclaimed her as a wife though to the public she is especially known as Saul's daughter (as the narrator reminds us twice in the story) and thus as establishing a certain connection to Israel's first king.

20. That the Chronicler regularly cleans up the David saga is apparent, for example in the elimination of the whole David and Bathsheba story and the resultant trouble in David's household with respect to Absalom. In this case it is the erotic or sexual life of David that is 'cleaned up'. This even goes so far as to expunge Bathsheba from the role of mother of Solomon who becomes simply one of the sons 'born in Jerusalem'. Is it coincidence that the priestly class responsible for the Chronicles is also the class that finds both adultery and (certain forms of) same-sex sexual practice to be abominable (Lev. 18 and 20)?

To be sure Michal casts her scorn as a reminder of David's royal station, a station that she perhaps believes that she ensures. In any case his behavior seems to her to threaten his royal dignity and thus also her royal station.

But here is the rub. Michal had played second fiddle to David's erotic relationships to Saul and Jonathan. Now both are dead. But instead of having him at last for herself she has lost him to another even more powerful male before whom he shamelessly disports himself where everyone can see. David now has another male lover with whom she can never hope to compete. Her man, the king, is the shameless boy-toy of Adonai.[21]

Michal's outburst tells us a good deal about what David is doing here.[22] In her view he is dancing nakedly in front of the ark. Twice she emphasizes the claim that David has 'exposed himself': 'uncovering

---

21. Fokkelman also notices, though he does not develop, the aspect of sexuality that is evident in Michal's tirade: 'Michal…insinuates that his religious surrender to God is something quite different… We onlookers can take the clause to be a poorly-disguised sign of sexual jealousy' (*Narrative Art and Poetry*, p. 199). Fewell and Gunn also note that 'there is a sexual dimension to her scorn' (*Gender, Power and Promise*, p. 154) but do not take this any further in reading the relation between David and YHWH.

22. Michal's remonstration with David also opens up the possibility of a quite different reading than the one I am undertaking. For her point of view brings into question the entire phallocentric world that is on display in the queer reading I am attempting. Re-read through her eyes the homoeroticism of this phallocentric world is at the same time rather misogynist in the way it operates with respect to women in general and in particular in relation to her. As Fokkelman points out, her love for David had been deflected in the meantime to a man who in fact loved her and then, for reasons of state, she has been taken back by the man she had loved in her youth but who does not seem to love her any more now than before (Fokkelman does not note the displacement I have suggested by Jonathan). A feminist reading taking Michal as a point of departure would be a necessary complement to the queer reading I am suggesting and is pursued by the reflections of Fewell and Gunn (*Gender, Power and Promise*, pp. 153-55) and by J. Cheryl Exum, *Fragmented Women: Feminist (Sub)versions of Biblical Narratives* (Sheffield: Sheffield Academic Press; Philadelphia: Trinity Press International, 1993). At the same time the retrograde 'classism' of her remonstration itself (with its reference to slaves, female slaves and riffraff) would suggest the importance of a class critique of her position. The complementarity of and tensions among queer reading, feminist and class reading that I am suggesting emphasizes the importance of multiple readings and thus the non-absoluteness of the queer reading I am proposing.

himself...as any vulgar fellow might shamelessly uncover himself'. This emphasis upon David's having exposed himself in his dancing is, of course, what the Chronicler cannot permit us to see. That is why the chronicler has clad David in a robe as well as an ephod.

The uncovering of himself attributed to David is further 'exposed' as that which might excite the interest and perhaps fascinated amusement of the girls of the town. Michal's explanation of her despising of David exposes to the reader's eye the display of David's nakedness.

Moreover, David's reply that the girls of the town will honor him rather than despise him for this display suggests, given what we know of David's kingly promiscuity, that it is his genitals that are especially in view here. This is reinforced by the narrator's suggestion that Michal will remain childless after her outburst. What she has seen and despised will not be at her service to make her a mother. Michal has drawn our attention to David's nakedness and particularly to his genitals, more especially, his penis. It is this which Michal (and the narrator) have caused the reader to glimpse in his shameless cavorting.

David replies that the maids will not despise him but honor him, perhaps in spite, perhaps because, of what they have seen. But does it not seem that more is going on here? For David is not dancing to impress the girls of the town. He is, as he says, dancing before YHWH. Moreover he is not ashamed to be doing so.

Now why does David have to uncover himself in order to dance before Adonai? Surely this is not what any worshiper of the Lord does in 'liturgical dance'? Why this shameless display of the nude body?

We recall that the Lord has chosen his young male companions at least in significant part because of their physical beauty. It was this that seemed to motivate Adonai's favor, to awaken his desire and confirm his selection first of Saul and then of David. And now in the physical presence of Adonai (the ark) David displays his body to the One who first desired him for his beauty.

Now we may ask ourselves why David is thus displaying the desired body before the great lover. Certainly the idea of erotic dance in which the body of the one who wishes to be or is desired is well known in the literature of antiquity. To be sure it is almost always the female who displays herself in this way seeking to arouse the interest, the desire, the infatuation of the powerful male observer. Perhaps the most famous biblical example of this sort of behavior is the erotic dance of Salome whose nakedness is both veiled and revealed in the dance of the seven veils. In her case she was seeking (at her mother's behest) to inflame the passion of the king in order to secure his favor and so his compliance in the plot to assassinate John the baptizer.

Is something like that going on here? Surely things are more complex for in any case it is a male rather than a female who is here cavorting in erotic self-display before a more powerful male. Is David seeking to rekindle the old flame? It may be. But another dimension of this rather astonishing display comes to light when we consider the part of the narrative that leads up to this episode.

In the preceding narrative David had consulted Adonai as his war chief. And the result of this had been such destruction of the Philistines that David calls YHWH, 'the one who bursts forth' (like a bursting flood, 2 Sam. 5.20).

In consequence of this 'flood burst' David resolves to bring the ark to his town. This procession starts out with David and the men dancing before the Lord. But an untoward accident occurs. When the oxen pulling the cart on which the ark is perched stumble, the ark starts to fall. One of the men, Uzzah, reaches out to brace it and YHWH 'bursts out' again, this time killing the one who had inadvertently touched Adonai's physical embodiment.

David is furious with his ferocious lover and decides to leave the ark where it is. He returns to Jerusalem in a sulk and lets Adonai stew out on the farm, presumably to recover from this testosteronic tantrum. Three months later David hears that the place where Adonai's ark has been left is flourishing. The juxtaposition of a deadly 'bursting forth' with the unexpected bestowal of fertility and prosperity reads rather like a phallic fantasy and we will have to return to this dimension later.

Now there are many ways to read this but it looks like what has happened is that David's sulky withdrawal has taught Adonai a lesson.[23] For instead of bursting forth in murderous rage the ark gives bounty

---

23. Most readers interpret this story as a reminder of YHWH's sovereignty as one whom David cannot simply bring to the city at will. But this traditional reading strikes me as partial at best, wrong-headed at worst. After all, YHWH can't transport his own ark to Jerusalem. He has been abandoned on the farm of 'edom': that is, turned over to foreigners. If he doesn't show that he can be depended on, that is where he stays. Indeed given the earlier history of the ark and its ill effects on Philistines and Israelites alike it is clear that the One to whom it belongs is in great need of learning a bit of self-discipline if he hopes to be given a central place in the life of his people.

and blessing. It is then that David goes to get the ark, bring it to where he lives and dance naked before it.

The cavorting of David then is not so much seductive entreaty to rekindle an old flame but a kind of reward for Adonai's good behavior. Now that he is tamed the love between them can be consummated. And indeed in the ensuing narrative Adonai will basically wed himself to David (2 Sam. 7).

Another detail in this episode may serve to substantiate this reading. It concerns the act of cavorting. While dancing before the Lord is some-times spoken of in certain 'liturgical' contexts (and this is surely what the Chronicler intends the reader to see), the text associates it with a term that seems to refer to cavorting, disporting, gamboling.[24] This is certainly not a liturgical dance, at least not in any ordinary sense.

We meet with the image again in one of the songs of Isaiah (13.1-22). The song/oracle has to do, we are told, with the destruction of Babylon. The picture of the devastation of the apex of culture and civilization is remarkable. Its climaxing feature is that nothing remotely domestic or civilized will take refuge in its ruins; not nomads, not sheep—only the wildest of beasts. Hyenas and jackals prowl its ruins; howling creatures. And there 'goat demons will cavort' (v. 21). Goat demons? What is it that is cavorting in this wildest and most uncivilized of places? Goat demons. Another oracle of Isaiah to similar effect has jackals and other fauna inhabiting the ruins of a former citadel of civilization together with Lillith (the storm demon) and the same goat demons: cavorting and howling goat demons in places of wildest devastation (Isa. 34.14).

Here I believe we must think of the satyr figures that inhabit also the ancient Greek and Roman imaginarium. Their goat-like legs and cavorting habits image forth a wild and untamed eroticism. They are the contrary of culture and its 'discontents'. They are if you like unrepressed id.

This appears to comport as well with another appearance of these satyrs/goat demons. In the instructions for offering sacrifice found in Lev. 17 we are told that Moses is to tell Aaron to carefully dash all the blood of the sacrifice on the altar and to burn all the fat from the meat 'so that they may no longer offer their sacrifices to goat-demons, to whom they prostitute themselves' (Lev. 17.7). Presumably fat and

24. Fokkelman reads the description of David's dancing as follows: 'Pointing to the hands and feet of David, the participles are a merismus for the ruler in a total movement which stands for total surrender' (*Narrative Art and Poetry*, p. 196).

blood either were offerings to the goat demons or were regarded as intoxicating the people into prostituting themselves with the goat demons. To be sure 'prostituting oneself' may be largely metaphorical in the sense of turning to other gods. But it does also suggest offering oneself promiscuously to service others sexually; precisely the sort of behavior a priest might suspect of those who cavort with satyrs.

I am not going to suggest that David is worshiping a goat demon or is himself transposed into one even though satyrs were worshiped by shepherds and carried pipes and lyres for music and dancing and even if David had been a shepherd and also had carried a lyre for making music in the fields. What this chain of associations does suggest, however, is the shamelessly erotic character of the cavorting which the narrator ascribes to David and of which his royal wife accuses him.

David's reply to his wife's accusation is rather extraordinary. In the first place he underscores that the one whose gaze he sought in his dance was the Lord. It was YHWH he sought to entertain or delight with his cavorting.

He further explains that the motive for doing so has to do with the fact that this YHWH has chosen him. It is because YHWH is his lover, the one who has picked him above all others, that David directs his cavorting to his gaze. Moreover David does not resist pointing out that YHWH's choice of him occurred despite the fact that YHWH had previously chosen another as his favorite and companion. That other of course was Saul, Michal's father. In spite of YHWH's previously having favored Saul he has subsequently chosen David. It appears that David is rather flaunting the being beloved over Saul.

It is only then that David admits that his shameless cavorting before YHWH might possibly be regarded as shameless. 'I will make myself even more contemptible than this; and I will be abased in my own eyes' (2 Sam. 6.22). How, we may wonder, does David intend to be even more shameless than he has already been in his naked cavorting before his great lover?

The KJV speaks of David 'playing' before YHWH but what David seems to be saying is that this was only 'foreplay'. He intends to 'go all the way'. We shall have to see whether or in what way this suggested consummation will be the subject of narration but first we must pursue another clue in the text concerning an ephod and its relation to the ark.

The Ark and the Ephod

And now to the ephod. Certainly in Michal's view David might as well
have been completely naked in his satyr-like cavorting. But earlier we
were told he was wearing a linen ephod, apparently a short linen apron
that covers the genitals (while at the same time perhaps calling
attention to them and so exposing them).

But while David's ephod may both reveal and conceal his genitals,
as I have suggested, we are led in an interesting direction if we pursue
another ephod. I mean not one that belongs to David but one that
belongs to Adonai.

We encounter a narrative concerning the divine ephod in Judg. 8
where one is made of gold by Gideon and placed in his town of
Ophrah. The priestly editor sniffs that 'all Israel prostituted themselves
to it there, and it became a snare to Gideon and to his family' (Judg.
8.27). Notwithstanding the priestly displeasure it appears that the Lord
was not in the least offended by Israel 'prostituting' themselves with
this ephod for 'the land had rest forty years in the days of Gideon'
(8.28).

We should not, however, overlook that the promiscuous sexuality
hinted at in the term 'prostituted themselves' is also attributed to the
relation of Israel to the 'goat demons' whose cavorting has resembled
the capering of David before the Lord. Here it is not the ark but the
ephod that draws the apparently shameful behavior of Israelite males.

The Lord's ephod shows up again in another strange story later in
Judges in which a young man named Micah makes an image for the
Lord out of silver that he had previously stolen from his mother. This
image we are told had the form of an 'ephod and teraphim'.[25] In a story
that occupies ch. 18 the Danites conspire to take possession of Micah's
metal ephod (and the young Levite he had conscripted to replace his
son as priest for the shrine of the ephod). By means of the stolen ephod
the Danites are successful in their attempt to take over the land of a

---

25. At a guess the teraphim is what an ephod covers. At any rate it may be
supposed to have something of a phallic shape since it serves to substitute more or
less convincingly for the body of a man (when covered) as part of the ruse used by
Michal to help David escape from Saul. The shape suggested is long and
cylindrical. And it has a head to which goat hair (!) may be affixed to complete the
ruse. That is, it is a herm.

quiet and unsuspecting people and there 'they maintained as their own Micah's idol that he had made, as long as the house of God was at Schechem' (18.31).

The point of alluding to this strange tale is to notice once again that the Lord's ephod is a potent representation of the Lord. It seems to represent the phallic prowess and potency of God and indeed brings success and bounty to those who possess it. It masks and reveals, represents and embodies the phallic power of the Lord.

This focus on YHWH's loincloth or whatever it is has a remarkable appearance in one of the symbolic actions of the prophet Jeremiah (13.1-11). He is told to take his own loincloth with which his loins are covered, and hide it in the cleft of a rock by the river. When he is told to recover it he discovers, unsurprisingly, that it is spoiled. Now what YHWH says is that just as this loincloth clings to the loins of the wearer so also should Judah cling to the loins of YHWH (13.11). But that which clings to YHWH's loins (Judah/Jerusalem) has been ruined and so should be thrown away. From this image I wish particularly to emphasize the image of clinging, that is, the intimacy between the loins (genitals) and the loincloth. And that Judah should cling to that to which YWYH's loincloth clings—his phallus.

The ephod, we have noticed, is ambiguous: it both hides and focuses attention upon the genitals of the wearer. Here we may think of something like a loincloth or breechcloth, a g-string or jockstrap. Such a piece of apparel may serve to decently cover as well as indecently draw attention to the male genitalia. In the case of YHWH's 'jock-strap', what happens when it serves not as a piece of apparel but as an item that represents its wearer? What happens when it becomes a fetish in other words? And as such is cast in hard and shiny metal like the ephods made by Gideon or Micah. How does the carrying around of a large metallic jockstrap represent YHWH?

Now imagine that it is this object that is adored. That it is that with which the men of Israel are said to prostitute themselves. That it is what one consults to derive battle plans to defeat more powerful foes. The Lord's ephod is a potent fetish of the divine phallus.

God's ephod, as it happens, plays an important role in the David saga as well. It first appears in a battle scene in which it is carried by the great-grandson of Eli (1 Sam. 14.3). It is now the ephod associated with Shiloh rather than Schechem. But it is nevertheless carried into battle with the same hope that it will not only represent but somehow *be* the potency of the Lord on the side of the outnumbered Israelites. What is remarkable is that a few verses later we are told that it is not an ephod but the ark that is carried by the Israelites into battle (v. 18).[26]

This conflation of ark and ephod is not without significance. For much later, when David is hounded by a jealous Saul, he is brought the ephod of God with whom he enters into conversation about how to escape the threat of Saul (1 Sam. 23.6, 9). In dire straits again for the same cause David again calls Abiathar to bring the ephod to talk with (1 Sam. 30.7). Later David will engage in precisely the same behavior, sitting before the ark in order to have conversation with the Lord.

Now what I want to suggest is that the ark and the ephod have the same function. They make physically present the hyper-masculine presence of the Lord. They both disguise and disclose the phallic potency of Adonai. The function of the ark as phallic representation of the divine has already been at work in the story of the ark that lends to YHWH the nickname 'perez'. The ark before which David dances is the sheathed phallus of his lover.

That the ark functions as an ephod or phallic sheath is further illustrated in the earlier history of the ark. We recall that in 1 Samuel the ark, rather than protecting Israel against their enemies as expected, had in fact been captured by the Philistines. Now there is a great deal that is intriguing about the history of the ark among the Philistines that would reward a 'queer' reading but the episode that most dramatically substantiates the view that the ark embodies the phallic potency of YHWH is that concerning YHWH in the house of Dagon. The Philistines transport the ark to their city of Ashdod. There then follows this curious episode:

> then the Philistines took the ark of God and brought it into the house of Dagon and placed it beside Dagon. When the people of Ashdod rose early the next day, there was Dagon, fallen on his face to the ground before the ark of the Lord. So they took Dagon and put him back in his place. But when they rose early on the next morning, Dagon had fallen on his face to the ground before the ark of the Lord, and the head of Dagon and both his hands were lying cut off upon the threshold; only the trunk of Dagon was left to him (1 Sam. 5.2-5).

The ark has been placed in the house or sanctuary of a fertility god of the Philistines as a trophy of their victory and a sign of the humiliation

---

26. The LXX corrects the reference to the ark here to a more consistent 'ephod'.

of YHWH. But instead of the submission of YHWH to Dagon we have the representation of Dagon's submission to YHWH; he is face down, on the ground. Now the first occasion might be read as the voluntary submission of Dagon to YHWH and so perhaps as a cultic act of prostration. But the second occasion makes clear that Dagon's submission is not voluntary but is accomplished with great violence, resulting in his dismemberment.

What is the character of this forced submission that the ark exacts of Dagon? It seems quite likely that the narrative represents Dagon as having been raped by the ark. Indeed in this saga material we already have the association of rape and dismemberment in the accounts that end the book of Judges concerning the Levite's concubine. Thus the god of phallic power, instead of dominating YHWH, has himself been dominated: forced into head-down submission to the violent potency of the ark.

The theme of phallic assault may actually continue in the tale of YHWH's stay among the Philistines. Peter Ackroyd notes that the affliction of 'boils' or 'tumors' that scourges the Philistines in the subsequent episodes may also be understood as hemorrhoids. That YHWH afflicts the Philistines, both young and old (1 Sam. 5.9; cf. Gen. 19.4), with the marks of anal rape gives added emphasis to their own seers' warnings about being 'made sport of' by YHWH (1 Sam. 6.6).[27]

This is a tale that 'makes sense' in a narrative world in which the domination of aliens is regularly represented as enacted through forcible gang rape. This is the world within which the story of Sodom (Gen. 19) is possible as well as that of the account of the crime of the Benjaminites in Judg. 19. The idea of phallic aggression as manifestation of male dominance is well known in the ancient world (as it is in contemporary prisons). Indeed it is not unknown to occur among the gods as the Egyptian tale of Seth and Horus makes clear. In that tale too Seth seeks to demonstrate his dominance of Horus through anal rape and very nearly succeeds save for a trick played by Horus that includes dismemberment (his own hand which had caught the semen)

27. Peter Ackroyd, *The First Book of Samuel* (Cambridge: Cambridge University Press, 1971), p. 55, noting that 'The Hebrew text itself offers an alternative at certain points in the narrative, the latter word being thought improper for public reading.' This is confirmed by Everett Fox in his notes to his translation of the books of Samuel, *Give us a King* (New York: Schocken, 1999), p. 24: 'The written text has "hemorrhoids"; scribal tradition has substituted "tumors" here.'

and that winds up getting his semen into Seth who then appears to be feminized (made pregnant indeed) by Horus.[28]

Now I am not suggesting that this tale licenses male homosexual rape as an expression of dominance. Even in the tale of YHWH and Dagon we see that there is a significant role reversal. For the ark of the alien and vulnerable YHWH is presumably in Dagon's house in order to be submissive to Dagon. Instead of submitting to Dagon's phallic superiority, however, it is Dagon who must forcibly submit.

However, those who use the story of Sodom to condemn what two millennia later will be called 'sodomy'[29] should reflect on the curious story of Dagon's forced submission. Is the Lord also a 'sodomite'?

This brief excursion into the earlier history of the ark serves to make clear that it is to be understood, like the ephod, as the physical embodiment of YHWH's phallic potency.

That then sheds light on what has brought David to dance there and to dance in just this way. The Lord we recall had burst forth on David's enemies, like a torrential stream. But the Lord's potency had also burst forth on the innocent Uzzah. Now David's sulk had brought his unpredictable lover to a kind of contrition and so the Lord/ark/ephod is welcomed by the cavorting and dancing, almost naked, beloved. The phallus is friendly, and so one may caper before it in welcome and perhaps even prepare oneself to be more shameless.

In the homoerotically suffused relation between David and YHWH the maleness of both characters seems essential. Both have 'ephods'. In both cases it serves both to conceal and expose: David's ephod, Adonai's ark (posing as an ephod, or is it the other way around?). David's maleness is coyly draped in linen. Adonai's is impressively sheathed in the ark. One is lover, the other beloved. But it is the lover, the erastes, who has had to learn to behave himself if he is to be near his beloved, trusted by his beloved, ecstatically welcomed by the beloved. For if in this tale Adonai is the top and David (as usual) plays

28. See 'The Contendings of Horus and Seth', in William Kelly Simpson (ed.), *The Literature of Ancient Egypt: An Anthology of Stories, Instructions, and Poetry* (New Haven: Yale University Press, 1973), pp. 108-26. References to this story in studies of 'homosexuality' normally fail to report that the victim of anal rape here actually comes out on top. Even more rare is the recognition of the bawdy character of the tale which seems to 'spoof' the gods.

29. For the development of the idea of sodomy see Mark D. Jordan, *The Invention of Sodomy in Christian Theology* (Chicago: University of Chicago Press, 1997).

the role of the bottom, it is by no means the case that the top is always in control or that the bottom is simply dominated. This is not, after all, rape. It is love.

Holy Union?

The sixth chapter of 2 Samuel ended with David's indication that if Michal thinks he has thus far been shameless with YHWH it is his intention to be even more shameless. This assertion is counterposed by the narrator's suggestion that David's relation with Michal will not be consummated. What this strange juxtaposition leads us to expect is that the relation between David and YHWH, in contrast to that between David and Michal, *will* be consummated. And the register within which we are to expect the consummation is specifically erotic, even sexual.

Now it is the case that this consummation will not be narrated in specifically sexual terms. But this is not because the sexual consummation of a relation between YHWH and his beloved is necessarily unthinkable. The theme of the (sexual) consummation of the relationship between YHWH and his beloved is by no means alien to the literature of Israel.

The prophet Jeremiah, who speaks both in celebration of and in dismay at the intimacy of YHWH's relation to himself, does in fact use the image of sexual seduction and even rape to complain of the way in which YHWH has treated him (Jer. 20.7). And later Ezekiel will use the image of YHWH's sexual consummation of his betrothal to Israel in a remarkable passage of almost pornographic character (16.8). In the case of Ezekiel the image will depend upon a transgendering of Israel into a lovely female in order to make the sexual imagery work. But there is no suggestion of Jeremiah's having been transgendered (although he is forbidden to have a wife and children).[30]

Moreover, that the divine being may be thought of as capable of a sexual consummation of relationship lies behind the notion of the relationship between Mary and God in Luke's account of the conception of Jesus. Since the being 'overshadowed by the power of the Most High' results in conception (itself about the only public demonstration of sexual consummation of male–female relationships available) one must

---

30. That Jeremiah is not transgendered by the sexual aggressiveness of YHWH may owe to the way in which YHWH is figured in the discourse of Jeremiah not as a husband but as a warrior (Jer. 20.11, 12).

reckon with the possibility of imagining something like sexual consummation as the essential basis for Luke's narrative. Thus readers who make something of the narrative concerning the 'virgin birth' of Jesus should not be surprised that YHWH may be depicted in other contexts as sexually consummating a relationship.

The narrative of ch. 7 of 2 Samuel will not provide a quasi-pornographic description of consummation of the homoerotically charged relationship between YHWH and David. But we will see that it does depend in important respects upon the suggestion of such a consummation. The narrative in fact has something of the function I have ascribed to an ephod. It both conceals and so draws attention to such a consummation.

The entirety of ch. 7 concerns this consummation or what takes the place of sexual consummation. The story begins with a kind of attempted role reversal. It is David who proposes to build his lover a house of cedar like the one in which he lives. Building a house for a conjugal partner and/or the partner's divinity is something that will get Solomon in trouble later (1 Kgs 11). On one level this building of a house seems a kind of 'reward' for YHWH. It is also a kind of domestication. In any case it may also be a reversal in that it is the act of a husband for a wife. This apparent reversal of roles appears as something of a continuation of the way in which David has apparently caused YHWH to behave himself by leaving the ark temporarily in alien territory after the outburst against Uzzah.

The provision of a house for YHWH wins the initial approval of Nathan who is, however, accosted by YHWH in the night with a message for David. The message is at least double in character. It begins with a reminder that YHWH has been quite content to live as a warrior in a tent as he has moved about with his people. YHWH will not live in a house, at least not while David is alive. He will maintain his freedom, living as a warrior in a camp.

Thus YHWH corrects Nathan who had agreed to David's original impulse and provides an alternative: It is YHWH who will build David a house; not the other way around. This negotiation of roles is quite intriguing to behold. It is affectionate, at least on the surface. But it is also making clear just who is the top here and who the bottom; who is the lover and who the beloved.[31]

---

31. Fokkelman remarks that 'David is merely to take up the position of receiver' (*Narrative Art and Poetry*, p. 211).

To make this clear YHWH reminds David, through Nathan's oneiric seance, that it is he, YHWH, who has the initiative in the relationship. He took David from the field, from following sheep, and made him a prince. That is, it is not for David to take YHWH from the field (tent) but YHWH has already done this for David. Moreover he has been steadfast in being with David wherever he goes. He has been with David as the warrior who has defeated David's enemies (let's be clear who is the warrior and who the armor bearer).

Now this discourse is both stern and affectionate. Throughout YHWH refers to David as 'my servant', a term otherwise used by YHWH only of Abraham and of Moses.[32] It reasserts the role of YHWH as the initiating subject and as the loving possessor of David. David is being gently reminded that he does not have to be the active subject but may rely confidently on YHWH to carry this role in their relationship.

Now this reminder of the dynamics obtaining in the relation between hero and armor bearer also brings to mind one of the features of this relation I have previously noted, namely the freedom of the warrior to choose more than one or successive armor bearers.

This possibility had already been invoked by David in his reply to Michal to the effect that though YHWH had first chosen Saul, he had subsequently chosen David to replace Saul as his favorite. This recollection is a double-edged sword since it both places David above Saul and suggests the tenuousness of YHWH's selection of favored companion. At the very brink of consummation a nagging doubt rises to the surface. Is this also why David wanted to house/domesticate YHWH? To make sure of the faithfulness of his rather unpredictable lover?

In any case YHWH, while refusing the gift (bribe) of a cedar house, does seek to meet this doubt, bringing it into the open and seeking to dispel it. He promises that he will not take his steadfast love from David as he had earlier done with Saul (2 Sam. 7.15). YHWH is promising lifetime faithfulness, binding himself to David for life. It is something like a marriage vow, or at least, as we now say, a holy union.

Now the specific form of this faithfulness, this steadfast love of YHWH for David, will take a rather surprising form. It will have to do with YHWH's relation to David's offspring, that is, to David's son. YHWH promises, 'I will be a father to him and he shall be a son to me'

---

32. Noted by Fokkelman who also notes that the term 'sounds intimate' (*Narrative Art and Poetry*, p. 214) and remarks upon 'the highly personal tone' of the discourse (p. 215).

(7.14). It is significantly not the case that YHWH is or will be a father to David. The model of homoerotic relationship that we are displaying here is quite different from that which Eilberg-Schwartz sees between Moses and God or Israel and God. The erotic character of the relation to David is not explained in terms of a paternal relation between David and YHWH but a paternal relation between YHWH and David's son.

Put perhaps too briefly David's son will have two fathers: David and YHWH. This calls to mind the way in which, in contemporary society, the 'normalcy' of same-sex relations is offered to view in grammar school: 'Solomon has two daddies'.

What is particularly striking here is that the relationship that YHWH proposes concerning David's son is the sort of relationship that David adopts to Jonathan's son Mephibosheth. Indeed this latter relationship seems to bracket the whole episode. We first meet with Jonathan's crippled son in 2 Sam. 4.4 with the quasi-adoption of Mephibosheth coming in the narrative of ch. 9. Indeed the relation between David and Mephibosheth continues far into the narrative 19.24-30, seeming to reach a certain conclusion in 21.7.

While an argument for the erotic relationship between David and Jonathan cannot here be developed but only presupposed, what is striking is that the erotic and perhaps sexual relation between David and Jonathan takes the form of a relationship between David and Jonathan's son after Jonathan's death. This is precisely what YHWH suggests concerning his relationship with David's (yet unborn) son after David's death.[33]

The relationship between human males thus parallels and interacts with the erotics of the relation between David and YHWH. We will therefore have to note the intertwining of these erotic relationships.

But first we must turn to David's response to the avowal or betrothal proposed by YHWH. David responds with alacrity. Immediately he places himself 'before the Lord': that is, in the same relation as in his wild dance. But here the posture is not one of dancing but of sitting before the Lord, that is, before the ark. Now all is decorous and in a certain way ceremonial although by no means cultic in character. David immediately presents himself before his lover in his lover's tent.

His reply indicates that he is more than content to be the beloved

33. Actually the narrative has already mentioned Solomon as one of the sons born in Jerusalem (5.14) prior not only to the relation with the ark but also in advance of the account of David's affair with Bathsheba.

rather than the lover. There is no attempt to return to the earlier plan. Rather the words of David are of total consent.

What may be most remarkable given YHWH's earlier ways of behaving is that this consent has not been produced by YHWH's fearsome power but by his offering and assurance of 'steadfast love'.

David picks up the term that YHWH had used ('my servant') and in speaking to YHWH calls himself repeatedly 'your servant'. And this is counterposed with the appellation of his lover as 'my lord'.[34] This is not the first time the reader of the Samuel saga will have encountered this terminology. It is precisely that which David has used in relation to his human lover Jonathan at the point of greatest intimacy between them (1 Sam. 20.7, 8). The terminology has thus been prepared in the narrative to be read as the words not only of vows of love between two males but as pointing to a love that lasts beyond death. If the love of David and Jonathan prefigures that of David and YHWH in terms of faithfulness and intimacy what transpires in the speech of David to YHWH is an intensification of what had transpired between himself and Jonathan.

The relationship between David and YHWH is thus consummated in a kind of 'marriage' that borrows its terms from the homoerotically charged relationship of David and Jonathan. Whatever it is that David had in mind about being even more shameless has been covered by this avowal of steadfast love and its unconditional acceptance by David. Certainly it is the case that this relationship will cover David not so much with shame as with honor. For the relation that YHWH initiates and consummates with David is not simply a private matter between these two principals but is also one that implicates and in a way includes the whole of Israel.

It is this relation therefore that stands behind and makes thinkable the development in Hosea, Jeremiah and Ezekiel of the image of Israel as YHWH's beloved. What will change in that further development of this motif, however, is that Israel will be explicitly portrayed as a wife: that is, will be transgendered. This will occur not so much in order to hide the relation between two ostensibly male subjects but in order to account for Israel's promiscuity in seeking other lovers. That is, the problem explored in the transgendering of Israel is not the

34. Fokkelman notes that the word used here (*adonay*) is unique to Samuel (*Narrative Art and Poetry*, p. 237).

transgendering as such but the unfaithfulness of Israel: Israel's search for other male lovers. Nor will YHWH escape unscathed from this transgendered metaphor for it will also call into question YHWH's own masculine competence for he will be the cuckolded husband. But the exploration of those themes takes us far from the relation we have been uncovering between YHWH and David.

What is perhaps most striking about the narrative we have been examining is not the homoeroticism it exhibits but the transformation that it portrays in the character of YHWH. In the early stages of this narrative YHWH is characterized by an almost uncontrolled phallic aggression. At the beginning of 1 Samuel he is certainly rather undependable, arbitrary. It is there that he abandons his own people in their need yet proceeds symbolically to rape not only the god Dagon but also Dagon's people, the Philistines. Even when he is returned to Israel he strikes out against his own people when their prying eyes seem to invade the 'privates' of the ark (1 Sam. 6.19).

In the ensuing narrative he chooses Saul as his companion but is ready to abandon him almost at once in favor of the beautiful David. Now one of the most notable characteristics of David in relation to his human lovers is an abiding loyalty. His love is indeed steadfast love not only toward Jonathan but also toward Saul. It is this that seems somehow to 'win over' YHWH. This does not occur without certain setbacks along the way. In the episode with Uzzah YHWH seemed to be up to his old tricks of breaking out in testosteronic rage against his own people. But David's fury and sulk brings him around and he is welcomed with the wild abandon of his beloved. And when David almost forgets himself and appears ready to change roles YHWH woos him back to being the beloved through the promise of fidelity to David and to his house.

The story of this relationship does not end here. David and YHWH do not live happily ever after. The marriage they have contracted will be a remarkably stormy one characterized not only by David's high-handedness with respect to Bathsheba and her husband Uriah and its sorry aftermath in David's own 'house'. YHWH will even seem to turn against David and his own people, tempting David to conduct a census that will be punished by plague (2 Sam. 24). In spite of all the outrages and provocations, however, YHWH will not withdraw his steadfast love from David, nor will David ever finally rebel against his lover. The relation may grow cold or distant but it will not be repudiated by

either of them. In consequence, in the further history of Israel it will
not be YHWH's faithfulness that will be in question but Israel's. And
even when things seem broken beyond repair YHWH will not finally
abandon his people. And some will remember that this perhaps is true
'for David's sake'. For in the saga of Israel it is in the relationship to
David that YHWH seems to learn what it is to love 'all the way'.

Concluding Reflections

In what follows I will indicate some of the features of the narrative that
offer themselves for thought concerning male same-sex relationships.

YHWH and Zeus

If, as I have been suggesting, the relationship between YHWH and
David may be understood in terms of a certain homoeroticism then we
are immediately brought up against the question of the relationship
between this saga and the various accounts of homoerotic attachment
between the gods and humans that are found in Greek myth and legend.
While most of the male deities of the Greek world come to be outfitted
with accounts of relationships to beautiful young human males,[35] the
accounts of the relation between Zeus and Ganymede, first found in
Homer (*Iliad* 20.233-35), comes to be elaborated as a paradigm of pederasty perhaps most famously in Plato's *Phaedrus* but also in a large
number of texts from both classical and hellenistic Greek literature.
Indeed so conventional does this paradigm become that it may be
spoofed in (pseudo) Lucian and (in the Latin form of Ganymede's
name) come to designate as 'catamites' the 'passive' partners of male
same-sex relationships. The Renaissance recovers this tale of desire,
seduction and abduction and elaborates it in narrative, poetic and plastic
art.[36] Although there are a number of other accounts of the love of a
god for a mortal, this one has come to have a decided prominence in
the Western imagination.

It is therefore useful to notice a few elements of similarity and also
of contrast between the legend of Zeus's abduction of the beautiful

---

35. See Christine Downing, *Myths and Mysteries of Same-Sex Love* (New York:
Continuum/Crossroad, 1989), pp. 146-67; and W.A. Percy III, *Pederasty and Pedagogy in Archaic Greece* (Urbana: University of Illinois Press, 1996), pp. 53-58.

36. See James M. Saslow, *Ganymede in the Renaissance* (New Haven: Yale
University Press, 1986).

Ganymede and the saga of the relationship between YHWH and the beautiful David. As this characterization reminds us, both relationships appear to be motivated by the extraordinary beauty of the young mortal. As it happens both of these young mortals are described as shepherds and in both cases their being desired and favored by the divine character means that they leave behind the paternal home. In both cases it is the male divinity who is the initiator of the relationship and who acts upon the desire incited by the beauty of the mortal. Moreover in both cases a permanent relationship between the (divine) lover and the (human) beloved is thereby initiated. In both cases a permanent status difference between lover and beloved also characterizes the relationship. David will become 'my servant David' while Ganymede becomes the cup-bearer (as opposed to armor bearer) of Zeus. Both relationships therefore correspond to models of age or class distinctions within male same-sex relationships and are, in that sense, 'pederastic' or asymmetrical in structure.

Within this remarkable context of shared characteristics, however, we may notice certain important contrasts. Of course in many accounts and depictions of the relationship between Zeus and Ganymede what comes to the fore is the scene of abduction. That Zeus takes the form of a raptor (an eagle) makes the relationship describable as rape rather than 'love'.[37] However, several of the retellings of this episode downplay this aspect of the relationship in order to assimilate it to the conventions of pederastic friendship (most obviously in Plato's *Phaedrus*). As we have had occasion to note, David is by no means merely a passive partner in this relationship but also an actor, even if not the initiator.

Of even greater moment in distinguishing the saga of David and YHWH from the tale of Zeus and Ganymede is that YHWH does not extricate his beloved from the world of mortals. David remains a character in the social and political history of humanity. He remains an earthling and in his ongoing life in society he has other (human) lovers (Saul and Jonathan), has wives and children, adventures and catastrophes, grows old and dies. It is as human, all too human, that David is

---

37. It is this aspect of the story that leads Aristides in his *Apology* to apply the term 'arsenokoitai' from Paul to the tale of Zeus thereby giving us the first and I believe decisive clue to the meaning of this term in the pauline corpus. See William Petersen, 'On the Study of "Homosexuality" in Patristic Sources', *Studia Patristica* XX (Leuven: Peeters Press, 1989), p. 284.

the beloved of YHWH and his being the beloved does not make him divine or even quasi-divine.

To a significant degree this also bears upon the difference between Zeus and YHWH. For Zeus is a member (albeit the pre-eminent member) of an aristocratic society of gods. His social life and his emotional and political existence are largely confined to relations to other divine beings with only occasional sallies into the world of mortals. YHWH on the other hand is a rather antisocial divinity (at least as far as other gods are concerned). Virtually his entire social, emotional and political life is lived out with human beings. He has little or nothing to do with other gods save to incite humans to revolt against their presumed dominion. He is in that sense something of a class traitor and decidedly a loner.

Thus the YHWH of our narratives does not even have a female consort (like Hera), nor divine offspring, nor divine companions, or drinking partners. And this means that if he is to be conceived of as having an erotic life at all it is with mere mortals. And since it is the human world with which he seems to be entirely preoccupied there is no sense in which he is tempted to take his beloved from the earth but rather makes him a partner or companion in his historical engagements.

A second difference, closely connected to the first, has to do with the significance for other humans of YHWH's relation to a human beloved. In the case of Zeus and Ganymede the relationship appears to have few consequences for other humans. That Ganymede is beloved of Zeus implies nothing concerning Zeus's relationship to Ganymede's place or people of origin (usually Crete). Ganymede the beloved is simply a singularly beautiful youth, not a representative of his people as a whole.

In the case of YHWH and David, however, their relationship is deeply intertwined with the relation of both to the people of Israel. David's extraordinary beauty is what brings him into the center of the historical drama of YHWH and his people. Thus David as beloved is, to a significant degree, an epitome and paradigm for YHWH's relation to Israel.

This is played out even in the moments of greatest intensity in the relation between David and YHWH. Even when he dances before the face or eyes of YHWH, David is not alone but has around him the people (probably especially the men) of Israel. The betrothal scene of 2 Sam. 7 is filled with references to David's relation to Israel and to the way in which the relation of YHWH to David assimilates features of

YHWH's relation to Israel. And this is also true of the curious episodes of famine (2 Sam. 21) and plague (2 Sam. 24) that play out after the 'honeymoon' phase of the relationship between David and YHWH has moved on to something quite different. In the story of David and YHWH we may say that 'the personal *is* the political'.

Now this means that David as the male beloved of a male YHWH configures the relationship of Israel, Judah and Jerusalem to the same deity. Thus the homoerotic dimensions of the relationship between David and YHWH are, to a significant degree, transferred to the relationship between Israel and YHWH. Since, as I have suggested, David is, in contemporary parlance, set up as the 'bottom' to YHWH's 'top' this will have potentially crucial consequences for the distinctive features of Israelite and Jewish (and perhaps Christian) masculinity. Indeed I believe that this goes a long way toward explaining the distinctive characteristics of Jewish masculinity suggested by Boyarin.[38]

The View from the Bottom
In order to make this more clear let us explore briefly the position of David as 'bottom'. I have said that in the saga David is always the beloved of a more central male character. He is chosen by Saul and subsequently by Jonathan as 'armor bearer' just as he has been chosen by YHWH. But David himself never has such a younger male companion. He is permanently typecast as the eromenos.

Yet the saga concerns itself essentially with David. To be sure his lovers are always implicated in his adventures but he remains the foregrounded character of the narrative. As a consequence this narrative does not depict homoerotic relationships primarily from the point of view of the erastes or lover but primarily from the point of view of the eromenos or beloved. Now this is very different from what we find in classical and Greco-Roman literature where we are everywhere confronted with the point of view of the lover. In that case it is with the lover of youths that we are concerned. But the youths themselves are generally the object of desire not its subject. In fact there is a considerable body of opinion that precludes the beloved both from desire and from pleasure.

---

38. Daniel Boyarin, *Unheroic Conduct: The Rise of Heterosexuality and the Invention of the Jewish Man* (Berkeley: University of California Press, 1997).

Indeed it is this exclusive attention to the erastes as subject that makes the occasional occurrence of an eromenos as agent of desire so startling. Above all, in Plato's *Symposium* the protestation of the young Alcibiades of desire (and attempted seduction) in relation to Socrates is so remarkable simply because it breaks the taboo of considering the beloved as an agent at all. And one wonders if it is not precisely this irruption of subjectivity in the place of the eromenos that accounts for the development of Alcibiades' character as a cautionary tale (see Plutarch's *Lives*).

In contrast David, precisely as beloved, has a fully developed subjectivity. Especially in relation to YHWH but already in relation to Jonathan and even Saul it is David's response to his lover that is prominently displayed and narrated. David is not simply the beloved who receives, he is also a subject. He spares Saul's life; he adopts Jonathan's son. And in relation to YHWH the answering subjectivity of David decidedly complicates the narrative of YHWH's love for him. We have noticed, for example, in the episode of the ark that David seems to seek to teach YHWH a lesson in control before he will admit him into his place of residence and only then orgiastically celebrate the delayed arrival of his lover. The scene of betrothal is also one in which David appears to seek to overtake YHWH's initiative (by seeking to build him a house) and so has to be reminded about just who is the initiator (and so the 'top') in this relationship. Yet this is by no means a mere 'power struggle' since David is beloved, favored and betrothed to YHWH precisely as 'bottom'.

Now it seems to me that this development of David as a subject results in much greater psychological complexity in the depiction of homoerotic passion. The view from the bottom that is at work here contrasts sharply with the view from the top characteristic of Greco-Roman homoerotic romance.

It is moreover the privileging of this role of being the male beloved of a male erastes which will have far-reaching implications for the attitude toward male homoeroticism in the history of Israel and indeed of Christianity. If there is anything to Anders Nygren's attempt to distinguish Greek eros from Christian agape[39] (which unlike Nygren I would attribute to Israel as well) then it may be precisely this differ-

39. Anders Nygren, *Agape and Eros* (trans. Philip S. Watson; New York: Harper & Row, 1963).

ence: that between being a subject who desires another, and being a subject who is aware of being desired and favored by another.

A Question of Gender

One is tempted to speak of the feminization of the beloved by the male lover in highly gendered settings and this has been often remarked upon as the hidden dynamic and dilemma of Greek pederastic relations. But feminization in a strong sense is necessary only when the maleness of the beloved is an inconvenient detail that must be suppressed. In that case the homoerotic aspect of the relation is actually repressed in favor of a heterosexual model. But if the homoerotic character of the relationship is more prominent then the maleness of either partner is not itself the problem but is an essential aspect of the attraction. In the homoerotically suffused relation between David and YHWH the maleness of both characters seems essential.

As a hypothesis I would suggest that it is precisely the warrior character of the social reality portrayed in this text that prevents the masculinity of the beloved from being brought into question. In a homosocial context such as this, masculinity is not strongly dependent upon one's relationships with women but is acted out among males in terms of boldness and loyalty. As a result there is less likelihood that the relationship of lover and beloved be transposed upon and read in terms of the relationship of male to female.

However, in more 'domestic' settings, that is, where the household provides the basic paradigms of relationship, then there may be a stronger tendency to try to read homoerotic relationships in terms of heteroerotic ones (or even incestuous ones). In this case the beloved comes to have a somewhat unstable gender identity. And this is certainly observable in the anxieties concerning homoerotic relationships that K.J. Dover has explored in classical Greece (especially Athens in time of peace).[40]

In terms of the Hebrew Bible we may see something of this occurring in the transgendering of Israel in Hosea, in Jer. 2–3 and in Ezek. 18 and 23. And this may also lie behind the possibility of introducing the prohibition of 'lying with another male as if you were a female' in the late priestly law code of Leviticus.

---

40. K.J. Dover, *Greek Homosexuality* (Cambridge, MA: Harvard University Press, 2nd edn, 1989 [1978]).

In any case I do not believe it is helpful to read the homoeroticism of this relationship as existing on a scale of 'more or less' masculine or, even worse, as entailing feminization. For this essentializes binary distinctions between male and female as well as casting feminization simply as a depletion of masculinity.[41]

Within the limits of the androcentric, phallocentric, militaristic, perhaps misogynistic and classist world of this narrative we may also find a helpful clue for exceeding the ill effects of a binary opposition of male and female and so a way to value the distinct masculinity of males in love (and thus the distinctive feminism of two women in love).

The Erotics of Faith

We began by noticing that Eilberg-Schwartz had suggested a certain homoerotics in the relation between God and Israel. I have sought to suggest a different model of homoeroticism that also is to be read in the texts of Israel. But I want to conclude by simply remarking that what seems to me to be remarkable is not the homoeroticism that may be read in the text but that the relation between the divine and the adherent may be read as erotic at all.

Of course one may suppose that, since eroticism is an important and indeed essential aspect of human consciousness and relationship, it is only natural that this might find some place in the relationship between the believer and the divine. And while I certainly agree that eroticism is a major force in human experience and that it cannot simply be put aside in representing religion it does not seem to be true that the erotic plays an equal role in all representations of the relationship between the worshiper and the divine.

Certainly it is not the case that the basic relation, for example, obtaining between the Olympic deities and their worshipers was typically represented as erotic in character. When this did seem to occur (as in the Dionysian rites) this was a radical departure from what had gone before or what was otherwise typical. Instead the gods of Greece and Rome seem to live out their domestic, erotic and social life quite apart from humanity. It is as if their relation to human beings is figured rather like that of the court to a distant peasantry who are

41. One of the most insistent forms of this 'binary' opposition of masculine and feminine may be found in the Roman world. See Craig A. Williams, *Roman Homosexuality: Ideologies of Masculinity in Classical Antiquity* (Oxford: Oxford University Press, 1999), for an analysis, especially pp. 125-59.

obliged to provide taxes (sacrifices) and occasional services (and avoid insulting their touchy cultural superiors) but are otherwise pretty much left to their own devices.

But as we have noted, YHWH's emotional and social life is directed entirely to human beings. In so far as YHWH is represented as a person (and even a male) then the erotic finds expression not in relation to a consort but in relation to the humans he has chosen as his companions, friends and lovers.

The erotic engagement of YHWH with Israel (and the believer) provokes an answering erotics of faith. It is this that may account for the rather troubled relation between faith and sexuality that has haunted Christianity perhaps far more than Judaism. But that would take us far afield from the erotics of the narrative we have been considering. However, at least in this narrative the erotic character of the relation between YHWH and David (and, by extension, Israel) does not serve to inhibit the erotic life of the human characters. David does after all have his own 'love life' which is complexly but not oppositionally related to the homoerotics of his relation to YHWH. There may therefore be far more to learn from this narrative than space permits us to explore here.

YAHWEH AS TOP: A LOST TARGUM

Roland Boer

Queer Sinai

In the beginning was the Word, which is to say, the signifier. Without the
signifier at the beginning, it is impossible for the drive to be articulated
as historical. And this is all it takes to introduce the dimension of the *ex
nihilo* into the structure of the analytic field (Lacan 1992: 213).

Somewhere on Mount Sinai, in a cozy corner away from the volcanic
ash, smoke and oppressive heat, sits a figure. The chair is somewhat
ornate, with delicate embroidery on the upholstery, finely carved legs
and back rest; the small table at which he sits is similarly finished.
Made from 'acacia wood', it is but 'two cubits long, one cubit wide,
and a cubit and a half high' (Exod. 25.23), more of a coffee table than,
say, a dinner table, with scarcely enough room for the assorted pots and
cups and plates that crowd upon it at the moment. Cheap it is not, for it
is overlaid 'with pure gold' (Exod. 25.24), with a rim of gold around its
edge, bearing tracings of pomegranates, desert roses and scarabs
around its edge. Shade comes from a tasseled sun umbrella, decorated
with a tapestry of 'devouring fire' (Exod. 24.17), that envelopes table
and chairs, as well as the 'pavement of sapphire stone' beneath (Exod.
24.10). Tea has been poured from the finest gold-leaf teapot, into cups
of floral china, delicate patterns in gold running throughout; these
various 'plates and dishes', 'flagons and bowls' are precisely for 'drink
offerings' such as this (Exod. 25.29). Some flat bread, unleavened, 'the
bread of the presence' (Exod. 25.30), lies on the plate in the center,
awaiting a visitor. In the process of adding sugar and milk, this figure
appears slightly built, dark hair carefully curled, blow dried, sprayed
and gathered in a loose ponytail, ear rings dangling on either side of a
face made up in cool, icy colors. His moustache (no beard of course) is
neatly trimmed to a flourish. Manicured hands hold daintily but firmly
onto the cup, from which he sips with obvious pleasure. Although we

might be dying to catch a glimpse of his body—is it lean and muscled, flabby, wasted?—it is entombed in a vast fur coat, from his neck to his ankles, although a knee does poke out from his crossed legs. As he sips, another person appears, sweaty, grim, an already elderly male with long white beard and strong nose.

'Sit down, sit down, Moses, take a load off your feet', says the first.

'Thanks', puffs Moses. 'Shalom.'

'Shalom, indeed, my dear, although it's usually mine to give.'

'Big fucking mountain you've got here, Yahweh. What's wrong with the plain, or an occasional anthill?'

'Must impress the other gods, dear, can't let appearances slip… Some tea?' asks Yahweh, the teapot hovering for a moment over the second cup, a quizzical, and carefully plucked, eyebrow raised to a question mark.

'Yeah, thanks.'

'Sugar? Milk?'

'I like mine straight, unadulterated.'

'That's my man', flutters Yahweh, stirring his own tea again and taking a sip.

'Well', continues Yahweh, 'we need to have a chat, since I want you to make me a beautiful tent, a tabernacle where you and your Israelites can worship me.'

'Great, just what we need…' begins Moses.

Yahweh's face clouds over; Moses breathlessly adjusts. 'No really, we'd love to make you…a tent. But what happened to those commandments, the laws, the statutes?'

'A mere side matter, Moses. What I'm really interested in is that tent. This is going to take a while, "forty days and forty nights" (Exod. 24.18) to be precise, so settle in and listen, since I need to tell you everything "concerning the pattern of the tabernacle and of all its furniture"' (Exod. 25.9).

And so Yahweh speaks to Moses of the tabernacle he wants, beginning with the ark of the covenant, moving on to its cover replete with golden cherubim, another table, the golden lampstand, the curtains, frames, altar and court. Yahweh, it turns out, has a fondness for gold, carefully wrought woodwork, fine linen, woven curtains and tapestries. As Moses rolls up some dried desert leaf in papyrus, and lights his home-made cigar from a flaming bush nearby, he is overcome with déjà vu. Now where did I do this before, he thinks, unconsciously undoing his sandal straps.

' "…three cups shaped like almond blossoms, each with calyx and petals, on one branch, and three cups, shaped like almond blossoms, each with calyx and petals, for the other branch—so for the six branches going out of the lampstand" ' (Exod. 25.33), continues Yahweh, snapping Moses out of his reverie. It is the golden lampstand, Moses realizes, full of flowers and blossoms and petals. Moses draws back the strong smoke into his lungs, drifting off yet again. Yahweh sips his tea, wrinkles his nose at the smoke, and continues.

' "Moreover you shall make the tabernacle with ten curtains of fine twisted linen, and blue, purple, and crimson yarns; you shall make them with cherubim skillfully worked into them" ' (Exod. 26.1). Now he has Moses' attention: interior design has always been my forte, Moses ponders. His fingers itch for needle and thread, for 'embroidery with needlework' (Exod. 26.36).

'How will I join the curtains together?' he asks.

' "You shall make fifty clasps of gold, and join the curtains to one another with the clasps, so that the tabernacle may be one whole" ' (Exod. 26.6), answers Yahweh.

The details roll on, endlessly, measurements, adjustments, materials—nothing of the design of the tabernacle is left to chance. Fine twisted linen is to be everywhere, blue, purple and crimson yarns, hammered gold, golden rings and clasps, acacia wood poles and frames.

'Where am I going to get this stuff from?' asks an attentive Moses, seeing for the first time how attractive and sensual Yahweh really is.

' "Tell the Israelites to make for me an offering: from all whose hearts prompt them to give you shall receive the offering for me…gold, silver, and bronze, blue, purple, and crimson yarns and fine linen, goats' hair, tanned rams' skins, fine leather, acacia wood, oil for the lamps, spices for the anointing oil and for the fragrant incense, onyx stones and gems to be set in the ephod and for the breastpiece" ' (Exod. 25.2-7), replies Yahweh, 'they're generous bastards, these Israelites.'

'But my favorite has to be the pretty frock for Aaron, the chief priest, to wear.' Forgetting his tea in its floral cup, Yahweh becomes excited, his eyes flaming and intense; earrings quiver and locks dance about as he speaks.

' "You shall speak to all who have ability, whom I have endowed with skill, that they make Aaron's vestments to consecrate him for my priesthood. These are the vestments that they shall make: a breastpiece, an ephod, a robe, a checkered tunic, a turban, and a sash. When they make these sacred vestments for your brother Aaron and his sons to serve me as priests, they shall use gold, blue, purple, and crimson yarns, and fine linen"' (Exod. 28.3-5). Moses listens intently, taking notes, wondering why he also doesn't get such a wonderful wardrobe, full of colors and gold and gems (Exod. 28.6-30). His jealousy rises to a crescendo with the robe of the ephod.

' "You shall make the robe of the ephod all of blue. It shall have an opening for the head in the middle of it, with a woven binding around the opening, like the opening in a coat of mail, so that it may not be torn. On its lower hem you shall make pomegranates of blue, purple, and crimson yarns, all around the lower hem with bells of gold between them all around—a golden bell and a pomegranate alternating all around the lower hem of the robe"' (Exod. 28.31-34).

Even Yahweh is now drooling at his own description. Moses is overcome.

'What an outfit! What a frock!' he cries out. Bells of gold and pomegranates all around the bottom, with fine needlework in blue, crimson and red throughout. 'Why is Aaron so special?' he demands.

'Aaron shall wear it when he ministers, and its sound shall be heard when he goes into the holy place before the Lord, and when he comes out, so that he may not die', Yahweh replies.

'So, you like this clothing so much you'll zap him if he doesn't wear it?'

'That's the story.'

All this talk of tingling clothing, pomegranates and bells and hems, has made Moses horny; he is already at the half husky, dying for a look beneath those furs that Yahweh insists on wearing on this unbearably hot mountain. I'm sure he's got a great, pert, upright butt, he asserts. But Yahweh remains seated, for now...

Sadomasochism: An Oral Tradition

Sadism and masochism occupy a special position among the perversions, since the contrast between activity and passivity which lies behind them is among the universal characteristics of sexual life (Freud 1977: 72).

Roland, with whose portrait I ought to begin...and in him that part which differentiates men from our sex was of such length and exorbitant circumference, that not only had I never laid eyes upon anything comparable, but was even absolutely convinced Nature had never fashioned another as prodigious; I could scarcely surround it with both hands, and its length matched that of my forearm. To this physique Roland joined all the vices ... (Justine, in Sade 1991: 671).

It has pleased Nature so to make us that we attain happiness only by way of pain (Madame de Saint-Ange, in Sade 1991: 202).

'OK, Yahweh', says Moses after recovering his composure, 'what happened to the thundering deity, the volcano God breathing fire and smoke, the destroying divinity who threatens to wipe out the whole people if they but touch this mountain?' (Exod. 19.12).

'Well, Moses, right now I feel like wiping them out again, since they are worshiping some golden calf, a replica of me, damn them, the fucking little assholes.' Moses quite likes assholes, and wonders whether Yahweh does as well.

'Just now', he said, 'I thought interior design was your thing...'

Through the smoke a number of figures emerge. Aaron, Nadab, Abihu, the seventy elders (Exod. 24.9), thinks Moses, but as they draw near they take on a somewhat different appearance.

'Sigmund', says Yahweh, 'pull up a chair. You too Donatien, Leopold, Jacques and Gilles. What a nice group. Tea everyone?' Yahweh takes their orders and Moses realizes what all the other cups and plates are for. When they are settled and comfortable, introductions made, where needed, especially for Moses who is a little nonplused, Yahweh continues.

'Perhaps Donatien and Leopold shouldn't sit next to each other, yes, that's right, just move around a little, Donatien, but do sit still and stop your incessant babble. Now, the question for our discussion for the next few days—Moses has another thirty-nine to go—is whether the Bible is a masochistic text or a sadistic one.'

'So, Yahweh', says Gilles Deleuze, 'are you as much a top as a purveyor of high camp? The question for me, however, is whether you are a sadist or masochist.'

'Well, you know, sadomasochism—which for me is a single phenomenon with different parts, about which we'll have to ask Sigmund a little more in a few moments—is for many the end run of pornography, for it combines explicitly the dynamics of unequal power, pain and sex that are so assiduously sought for, it is commonly argued, in pornography itself. The power of such a critique lies in the moral coding assumed with these terms and its connection with gender: that is, power, pain and sex are understood to represent the relation between male and female, the heterosexual relation that belongs down the road somewhat in the twentieth century. But what if the gender relation is not only historicized but also problematized in a queer fashion, if the willed dynamics of power are gay, lesbian, bisexual and transgender rather than merely heterosexual? And what if the moral coding of the key terms is negated or reversed? Power, sex and pain become either neutral or positive terms for one's sexual fantasy—mine, for instance. Is not all fucking some negotiation, an exploitation even, of the imbalance of power between the subjects of the act itself?'

'I agree absolutely!' ejaculates Leopold von Sacher-Masoch, 'as Severin says to Wanda in my *Venus in Furs*, "It is because we are opposites—indeed almost enemies—that my love for you is part hatred, part fear. But in such relations one person must be the hammer, the other, the anvil. I choose to be the anvil: I cannot be happy if I must look down on the woman I love. I want to be able to worship a woman, and I can only do so if she is cruel to me"' (Sacher-Masoch 1991: 171-72).

'My question remains', says Gilles, 'what is your practice? What acts do you prefer? Surely it's not just talk.'[1]

1.   What about you, someone will ask: are you not replicating the same relation, or do you engage in S/M? In a fashion that repeats the Deleuzian inversion of the Freudian relation between fantasy and reality (fantasy, for Freud, compensates for, provides an ideal, primary, expression of real life), I have found that my 'real' life has followed my writing. Scenes, images, events, both fictional and theoretical, that I have produced in my writing have subsequently happened to me, without any conscious agency on my part. It is not that I have based my writing on autobiographical experiences: autobiography follows the written text! I leave it to the reader's imagination to conjure up such scenes. It is, then, with some trepidation and anticipation that I write this paper. Too often, it seems, I end up in S/M relationships, often with a written contract, a covenant even, a commitment, but at times no more than a nod and a smile. The problem with the latter, of course, is that the dimensions of top and bottom need to be worked out as you go—a situation fraught with dangers, as everyone knows. There is of course Stephen Moore, a primary S/M, one whom I can't help read, but am I the bottom, I wonder, or is he? I want so much to submit myself to him, to beg and crawl and lick and suck. But can I? And then there is another S/M relationship, with a top that must remain unnamed, masked, in shadow behind the leather mask and body armor. In this relationship, to which I was held for many years, there was a contract in which I was clearly the bottom and the Other was the top, a cruelly religious covenant, dripping with the blood of Jesus and the saints and martyrs of the Christian tradition, which made it even more excruciating. That is one covenant I was immensely pleased to break, for it had long since ceased to provide satisfaction.

'Why don't we ask Sigmund before answering that question?' suggests Yahweh.

'It seems to me', says Dr Freud, puffing incessantly on his eternal cigar, finely clipped beard wagging as he reverts to his native Austrian German, 'you owe the common parlance of sadomasochism to me, although the term has about the same status as a discourse liberally sprinkled with "fuck" at, say, a middle-class dinner party, a political campaign speech or a religious gathering (church service, perhaps, or sacred meal). I admit that I took up both sadism and masochism from Krafft-Ebing, although I specified sadism as "cases in which satisfaction is entirely conditional on the humiliation and maltreatment of the object" and masochism as "that in which satisfaction is conditional upon suffering physical or mental pain at the hands of the sexual object" (Freud 1977: 71). For me, there is a "sadistic component in the sexual instinct. As we know, it can make itself independent and can, in the form of a perversion, dominate an individual's entire sexual activity" (Freud 1984b: 327). In fact, sadism is what I call a death instinct, that tendency towards death that we find in all organisms, from the most simple protozoa to the most complex beings. These death instincts can also be called "ego-instincts" (316), and they exercise pressure towards death, the preferred final state of an organism if it is allowed to follow its normal path. The problem, of course, is that sadism has been tied up with the sexual instincts, with eros, the opponent of the death instincts, that which leads to a prolongation of life. Sadism gets here, it seems to me, by being separated off, going its own way for a while and thereby becoming separated from the ego, to whom the death instincts normally apply. It then returns with its direction now firmly oriented not towards the subject, but towards the object, the sexual partner, who must now be overpowered as part of sex itself.

'As far as masochism is concerned, however, I changed my mind in light of the preceding argument. At first I argued that masochism is derived from a primary sadism, that it is a prime example of the vicissitudes of the instincts, of which there are four: reversal into its opposite, turning round upon the subjects's own self, repression and sublimation (Freud 1984a: 123). The first breaks down into two, "a *change* from *activity to passivity*, and *a reversal of its content*" (124). Sadism and masochism belong to the first subdivision, since "masochism is actually sadism turned upon the subject's own ego"

(124). The point of all of this is that the aim of sadism remains the same, the infliction of pain, sexual torture, what changes is the object of that torture, either the other (sadism) or the ego (masochism). It is a shift from active to passive, from masculinity to femininity (Freud 1977: 73), that entails three steps: sadism (inflicting pain on another); replacing the object of pain with oneself (a passive shift); the creation of another person, who now becomes the subject inflicting pain (masochism proper) (Freud 1984a: 125-6l see also 1977: 70-73; 1979: 180).'

'That new subject is the top, isn't it?' asks Yahweh.

'We called it that after Sigmund finished his work', replies Gilles, 'but then you changed your argument, didn't you Sigmund?'

'At first I argued that "a primary masochism, not derived from sadism in the manner I have described, seems not to be met with" (Freud 1984a: 125). But then, if you follow my argument above, I felt that if sadism, a death instinct, can shift from the ego to the object (for death instincts focus on the ego), then the opposite may also happen, namely the shift from the ego to the object, from masochism as primary to sadism. "Masochism, the turning around of the instinct on the subject's own ego, would in that case be a return to an earlier phase of the instinct's history, a regression" (Freud 1984b: 328). By the time I got to *The Economic Problem of Masochism* (1984c) I assumed that there is a primary masochism, and the masochism I described earlier, the one that turns the sadistic impulse in on the subject, is then a secondary masochism (Freud 1984c: 419). It all derives from the conflict between eros and thanatos, the libido, or sex drive, and the death drive. The precise way in which the libido negates the death drive is to direct it outwards, onto external objects, where it becomes what is known as the will to power or the instinct for mastery. The part of this externalized instinct that is connected with sexual fantasy is sadism. However, there is another portion of the death drive that isn't projected outwards; it remains inner-directed, and when connected with sex a close link is established between sexual stimulation and destruction. This is primary, erotogenic masochism (see Freud 1984c: 418). In other words, we get what I call fusions between the death and sex drives in both sadism and masochism, for here the libido and the death drive become inextricably linked.'

'Are there not two other types of masochism?' asks Gilles Deleuze.

'*Ja, ja*, what I call feminine and moral masochism, although both are derived from the primary erotogenic masochism, the experience of sexual pleasure in pain and through pain. Feminine masochism is that in which the subject wants to be castrated, copulated with and to give birth—all signified by fantasies and acts of gagging, binding, painful beatings, whippings and so on. Moral masochism is based in the suffering produced by guilt, and not always obviously connected with sexuality.'

How can talking about sex be so untitillating, thinks Moses to himself. God, I hope the others are just a little bit more sexy. He can't help but thinking that sadism is a decidedly masculine business for Sigmund, and masochism distinctly feminine (see Freud 1979: 184). He notices Gilles fidgeting about; in fact, Gilles hasn't sat still since he got here. And then he looks so startled, surprised to see us all here.

'I'm going to disagree with you, Sigmund', says Gilles, 'although of course you haven't had the chance to read my "Coldness and Cruelty" essay before now. I'll let you have a copy before we all go back to our graves.'

'Yes', returns Sigmund, 'I've read it. Ever since *Anti-Oedipus* (1977), both you and Guattari have been identified as explicitly anti-psychoanalytic, anti-Freudian (I would suggest that it is still very Freudian). Such a stance has demanded a return at different times to take me on again and again.'

'But I want to hear what Jacques has to say before we get to my work', says Gilles, 'for although you pursue some new lines of argument, binding together certain ideas to Sigmund's arguments, you don't fundamentally disagree with him, do you?'

'No, of course', says Jacques Lacan, 'I always said that I was going back to reread Freud, to interpret him again for our years. Yet, even though I assumed, with the later Freud, "the fundamental character of masochism in the economy of the instincts" (Lacan 1992: 14), in the end I found masochism a "marginal phenomenon", a desire to reduce oneself "to this thing that is treated like an object, to this slave whom one trades back and forth and whom one shares" (Lacan 1992: 239). After all, I don't think Leopold has quite the stature of the Marquis as a writer.' At this Sade takes on a gleeful air, whereas Leopold merely sulks, a grim look on his face, avoiding Sade's excited gaze.

With his shock of white hair and habit of talking in riddles, Jacques appears quite sexy to Moses. Perhaps because of Jacques' fame as a seducer, Moses is struck by an urgent desire to suck his cock.

'I am much more interested in Sade, to whom my *The Ethics of*

Psychoanalysis may be read as a response. Given that we are seated here at the seat of the Law, of Torah, sipping tea with Yahweh, the law-giver himself, and Moses, I want to begin with the Law (since the aforesaid book is also a sustained discussion of Kant). Indeed, it seems to me that the Law, the prohibition, is precisely what excites desire: the possibility of transgression, of stepping past censorship is what Sade is all about, it seems to me. Thus, in the commandment against coveting one's neighbour's house, ox, male and female servants, wife, and other possessions in Exod. 20/Deut. 5, Law and the desire to transgress come hand in hand. So also in the dialectic of sin and law in Rom. 7 (although here I replace sin with "the Thing" [*das Ding*]): "The dialectical relationship between desire and the Law causes our desire to flare up only in relation to the Law, through which it becomes the desire for death" (Lacan 1992: 84). In fact, the very nature of Law is that it is constituted by its transgression: breaking the Law is the basis of its existence, as may be seen in a number of ways. For instance, transgression allows the Law to come into play, or officers of the Law are above the Law, and then there is the symbiotic relation between law enforcement and corruption. And this is where desire comes into play, for the desire of which I speak in relation to the Law is that which seeks to break the Law in order to attain its fulfillment. To twist the dialectic a little further, it is therefore this excess, the "challenge to the gallows" that produces enjoyment, that is precisely obedience to the Law, the fulfillment of one's Duty where that involves excess (see Zizek 1991: 239).'

'But how does this relate to perverse sex?' asks Moses, his mouth slightly dry. Yahweh looks on with a knowing smile.

'I've always been infatuated with Donatien, the Marquis, here, even though he does yabber incessantly, and his work is a "sepulchral mound"—the cunt as a grave, we might say—since for me his work is the fulfillment of Kant. For in Sade's narratives the combination of Law, desire, transgression and disgust takes place through perversity: "One doesn't have to read very far for this collection of horrors to engender incredulity and disgust in us, and it is only fleetingly, in a brief flash, that such images may cause something strange to vibrate in us which we call perverse desire, insofar as the darker side of natural Eros enters into it" (Lacan 1992: 232). And how is perversity, the strange vibration of a darker Eros, realized? Through pain: "Kant is of the same opinion as Sade. For in order to reach *das Ding* absolutely, to open the flood gates of desire, what does Sade show us on the horizon?

In essence, pain. The other's pain as well as the pain of the subject himself, for on occasions they are simply one and the same thing" (Lacan 1992: 80). It is, then, pain that opens "the flood gates of desire", that releases perverse desire. The first quiverings and ripples of desire become the waves of a perverse flood released by pain.'

'So, Sade is much more important for you than even for Sigmund', suggests Gilles, still looking startled but highly alert.

'Yes, so much so that I feel he completes the watershed work begun by Kant. In fact, in my "Kant with Sade" I trace, by means of both diagrams and written text, the twist of the Sadean fantasy (Lacan 1990: 62-65). From here I draw the conclusion that what begins as the sadist inflicting harm on the subject, and in that way finding pleasure (this is the "Will-to-Enjoy"), ends up construing the sadist as subject of that harm (for Sade this was his repeated imprisonment, arranged by his mother-in-law as well as the revolutionary government after 1789, and eventual commitment to the Charenton asylum by Napoleon, where he stayed until his death). According to my formulae, the sadist as subject (S) becomes the barred subject, $. Here, let me draw it for you in this sand' (Lacan 1990: 62, 65):

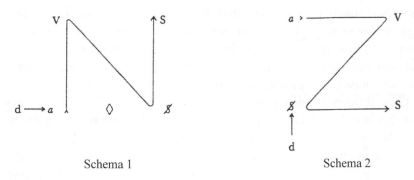

Schema 1   Schema 2

'Oh, I remember that time', says Donatien, 'apart from my equine wife, it was her infernal mother, Mme de Montreuil, that kept me behind bars. Much better was Mme Quesnet, my companion for the last fifteen years of my life. She was a "decent, kindly, matronly person, sweet and good and with a keen mind" (Sade 1991: 102).'

After studying Jacques' designs, Gilles interjects, 'But that is, in the end, what Sigmund was arguing, except that he called the end result masochism: for Sigmund, sadism turned in on the subject produces (secondary) masochism; for you sadism inevitably turns in on the subject, which merely reinforces the close relation between sadism and masochism, especially when we remember that Sigmund even argued that sadism and masochism often appear in the same person (Freud 1977: 73). And you just said that the pain of the other and the subject are one and the same thing.'

'Don't you agree?' asks Jacques.

Before he can answer, Donatien launches himself into the discussion. The years in prison have not been kind to him, for the lack of exercise, apart from the occasional walk, has left him very fat, so that he has difficulty sitting in the chair. And yet, prison has led to one of the most remarkable collections of literature in Europe, even if only a fraction remains.

'What a nice little gathering; a pity there's no women', he begins.

'The Hebrew Bible is like that', observes Moses.

'But still, there's seven of us, a holy number I do believe, or perhaps a signal to tell me how long I have to go in prison. Before we talk any further, I need to fuck. Why don't we arrange ourselves thus: one lies on his back, Jacques, you perhaps; and then another sits on his cock— yes, you, Sigmund, take it easy on the entry but then you'll need to slide up and down for a bit—and a third sucks Sigmund's cock, such a handsome, uncircumcised one that it is, although it does resemble a cigar in some ways. Gilles, that seems the best thing for you, while Leopold fucks your ass. That leaves me to masturbate Gilles, and Yahweh and Moses to whip us all, but especially Leopold and I. Make sure you draw blood please, you scoundrels, you libertines.'

There follows a series of exclamations and groans, whippings, curses and shouts—'holy fuck', 'hurt me, you bastard', 'glory be', 'you divine asshole', 'Oh, Jesus!'—that it would be rather tedious to repeat here, although one may find them repeatedly in Sade's work. All too quickly, it seems, everyone has gotten their rocks off, so to speak, in their own way, so they settle down to some more tea.

'I'm quite flattered', resumes Sade, 'as Leopold here should be as well, that Dr Freud has used my name to describe a whole sexual condition, although I wouldn't call it a perversion. For me it is but natural, the way Nature made us, whether libertine or no: one likes the cunt, the temple of Venus, the other the dark altar of the ass; one likes to suck and swallow cum, the other shit or blood; one likes to beat and injure, the other to be beaten and injured; one likes children, another old people; and some even like to murder. For the whole moral code of our so-called society assumes the existence of a God, of one who rules and who will give judgment at the end of our lives. For me, this God does not exist, is but a figment of our imagination, or worse still, made up by priests so that they could exploit the common people.'

Yahweh looks rather amused at the argument, although there are a good number of atheists present, apart from Sade—Sigmund, Gilles, Jacques, and probably Leopold. If it comes to a vote, Yahweh thinks, my position might be shaky.

'Yet', replies Gilles, 'don't you elevate Nature to the same position as the God whom you have done away with?'

'Nature is but a blind force', replies Sade, warming up to his topic, 'not a God. All we need to do is consider Jesus, the founder of this basest of religions. "Has there ever existed a rowdy scoundrel more worthy of public indignation?! What is he but a leprous Jew who, born of a slut and a soldier in the world's meanest stews, dared fob himself off for the spokesman of him who, they say, created the universe! ... it is through hocus-pocus, and puns that God's envoy announces himself to the world; it is in the elegant society of manual laborers, artisans, streetwalkers that Heaven's minister comes to manifest his grandeur; it is by drunken carousing with these, bedding with those, that God's friend, God himself, comes to bend the toughened sinner to his laws... Fanaticism gets minds in its grip, women shriek, fools scrape and scuffle, imbeciles believe, and lo! the most contemptible of beings, the most maladroit quacksalver, the clumsiest imposter ever to have made his entrance, there he is: behold! God, there's God's little boy, his papa's peer; and now all his dreams are consecrated! and now all his epigrams are become dogmas! and all his blunders mysteries!" (Sade 1991 [*Justine*]: 514-15; see also 1991 [*Philosophy in the Bedroom*]: 212-13). Jesus is nothing but a smutty fellow, scoundrel, low fellow, imbecile and imposter.'

Even Yahweh blanches for a moment, although the Christian focus of Sade's polemic is problematic in itself. So Sade draws his attack to Yahweh.

' "But picture, in your own terms, this frightful God you preach: he has but one son, begot of some passing strange commerce; for, as man doth *fuck*, so he hath willed that his Lord *fucketh* too..." ' (Sade 1991 [*Philosophy in the Bedroom*]: 213).

'What have you got against me?' bristles Yahweh, feeling the hot blood rush to his face.

'He is "[a] horrible God, this God of yours" ', says Sade, somehow missing Yahweh's presence, ' "a monster! Is there a criminal more worthy of our hatred and our implacable vengeance than he!" ' (Sade 1991: 211).

'It seems as though we are getting close to the main issue', interjects Gilles, before a full-scale fight breaks out between Yahweh and Sade, although it would be an odd one, with them swinging at cross purposes, missing one another as they look elsewhere for their foe. 'The question for me is whether sadism and atheism are inextricably connected.'

'Of course they are', explodes Sade, 'for if you allow Nature to determine how we are (see Sade 1991: 209-11, 274-75, and in many other places), then there is no room for a God.' Sigmund and Jacques also assent that sadism and atheism must go together.

'Well, I tend to disagree', broke in Gilles, anxious to move along, for once Sade gets going, he is very difficult to stop, as any reader of his works knows. Episode follows episode, cocks become more fantastically large with each fiend, the women more and more beautiful, and the pain more unbearable, until the story itself breaks down, collapsing in on itself. 'It is true that your works are something of a watershed in European literature, providing, among other things, a virtually complete list of sexual practices—even Sigmund didn't have to look too far for them—apart from fisting and erotic vomiting. And it is true as well that you, Donatien, set the agenda for a whole new form of reflection on sex and literature, specifically the connection between pleasure and pain. For you sexual pleasure is obtained through the infliction of sexual pain on the victims of your stories—mostly women—with all the ambivalence that this has left subsequent readers. But, apart from providing some dimensions of French thinking with a basic term that designates pleasure beyond pain—*jouissance*—you also provided a whole new way of thinking about sex that was simultaneously libertine and materialist as well as profoundly insightful about the nature of sex itself. I am thinking here of the inevitable play of power in any sexual relationship, the use of sex as a negotiable item in such a relationship, a tool in the struggles of human interaction, but particularly of the willed dynamics of power in sex. Yet I disagree with two points in the argument thus far: that sadism and masochism go together; and that sadism is atheistic.'

At this Yahweh sits up, intrigued that this blathering blasphemer might actually believe in him. He gathers his furs more tightly about, although he is conscious that for some time now Leopold, that silent, dark German, has been casting longing glances in his direction, surreptitiously feeling his furs.

'We might compare sadomasochism to a fever', recommences Gilles, although Moses is now solidly dozing, dreaming of the ass he has just whipped. ' "[N]o doctor would treat a fever as though it were a definite symptom of a specific disease; he views it rather as an indeterminate syndrome common to a number of possible diseases. The same is true of sadomasochism: it is a syndrome of perversion in general which must be broken down to make way for a different diagnosis" (Deleuze 1991: 132-33). And it turns out that sadism and masochism are two very different practices, two perversions with "irreducibly specific symptoms". To begin with, sadism is speculative and demonstrative, showing the full range of sexual practices in unceasing succession, whereas masochism is dialectical and allows the imagination full play (sadism cuts out the imagination, is determinately real). And then, sadism works always with the negative, with pure negation, whereas masochism makes use of disavowal and suspension, perpetually putting off the moment of satiation. Third, sadism works through "quantitative reiteration", endless repetition, whereas masochism is characterized by qualitative suspension, seeking postponement, pause, marble tableaux with still figures, paintings. Next, sadism has its own specific masochism (the sadist likes to be beaten), and masochism its own sadism (the torturer created by the masochist), and yet it seems to me that these forms of reverse sadism and masochism, that confuse Sigmund so much, are working at different wavelengths. Fifth, sadism gets rid of, negates the mother and elevates the father (one argument for sadism's theism), while masochism "disavows the mother and abolishes the father". Both the fetish and fantasy are used in very different ways in both perversions. Given its liking for stillness, suspension, there is an aestheticism in masochism that is not found in sadism, with its frenzied movement, the inability for the moment to be more than fleeting. Further, sadism is institutional, seeking a libertine institution although finding only the prison, being part of the building of the new republic after being released from the Bastille, whereas masochism is contractual, constructing contracts for each specific relation. For sadism the superego and identification are primary (another argument for sadism's theism), while in masochism the ego and idealization are primary. Tenth, the processes of desexualization and resexualization are utterly distinct, and finally, sadism is characterized by apathy, masochism by coldness' (see Deleuze 1991: 134).

By this time, not only Moses sleeps, for only Jacques remains awake to follow a fascinating argument. Maybe I should just whip them to keep them awake, Gilles thinks to himself; so, taking up Moses' whip, Gilles soundly whacks them all a few times across the back. Simultaneously furious and excited, they awake, although it is not only Leopold who enjoys it.

'Let's see how all this works in thinking about whether Yahweh here exists or not', blurts an irate Gilles, although his arm enjoyed the workout. 'Take the function of the dream, for instance: in sadism, the function of the dream, and thereby of fantasy, is to produce the real; the purpose is action. Sade's "own erotic dream consists in projecting the unreal dynamic of his sensuous enjoyment on to characters who are not dreaming but acting ... Therefore the more this eroticism is *dreamt*, the more it requires a fiction from which dreams are excluded and where debauchery is fully actualized" (Blanchot 1963: 35, as cited by Deleuze 1991: 72). For Sade, then, the dream functions to negate dreaming, to deny its presence. Further, the dream becomes an instrument that must affect the objective world; its purpose is to enhance the eventual disruption of the acts of lust and violence (see Deleuze 1991: 72-73). Of course, all of this was written in prison, but Sade longed for his release, for the ability to put into action his texts, even if only as plays, which he was allowed to do for a time in the Charenton asylum, until even these were banned as being too dangerous for the inmates. So, on the question of God, the dreamed-for annihilation of God functions to effect his negation, and yet the drive for the real itself necessitates God's existence, *if we place God in the position of the sadist*. That God is a sadist underlies Sade's polemic. God is a monster, impostor, criminal and fucker; Jesus a libertine and quacksalver. And for Sade, the sadist is very much a real person, however much created by Donatien's own writing.

'By contrast', continues Gilles, 'if we take up the issue of fantasy again, we see that in masochism "it consists in neutralizing the real and containing the ideal within the fantasy" (Deleuze 1991: 73). The ideal and the real are absorbed into the suspended fantasy out of which Masoch does not wish to emerge. Thus, with regard to God, he must remain a fantasy, a construction of the masochist, a projection beyond. This is especially so when we fix God in the position of the torturer created by the masochist: ultimately, the torturer—here God—is the creation of the masochist, necessary for her or his own fantasy, but a construction nevertheless. Other elements solidify my argument: the sadist's concern with the superego, the elevation of the father, and the analytic procedure—all these require God as sadist; whereas masochism's resistance to the real, the mythical and imaginary mode of the text, the dominance of the ego and abolition of the father all point to the atheism of masochism, by which I mean that God, the torturer, is constructed in the symbolic world of his or her perversion.'

'But that's not entirely your argument', objects an omniscient Yahweh.

'You're right', admits Gilles, 'it comes from the reading of my work by a perverse and wanton antipodean biblical scholar.'

'Biblical studies will do that to you', says Yahweh, who is now uncertain as to whether he wants to be a real sadist or an imaginary masochist's torturer, and is concerned by Leopold's silent but intense gaze on his furs. 'Why don't we let Leopold speak? As for me, what I am interested in, apart from the pleasurable reception of pain for which masochism is the designator, is the question of the contract, the covenant between bottom and top, as well as some of the practices characteristic of masochism—binding, whips, chains, blood, bursting bladders, obedience, silence, in short, entire submission.'

Mary in Furs

The Lord hath smitten him by the hand of a woman (Jdt. 16.7, epigraph to *Venus in Furs*, Sacher-Masoch 1991: 143).

Now, therefore, the wording runs: *'I am being beaten by my father'*. It is of an unmistakably masochistic character (Freud 1979: 170).

… acts of the kind attributed to a certain Angela de Foligno, who joyfully lapped up the waters in which she had just washed the feet of lepers—I will spare you the details, such as the fact that a piece of skin stuck in her throat, etc.—or to the blessed Marie Allacoque, who, with no less a reward in spiritual uplift, ate the excrement of a sick man. The power of conviction of these no doubt edifying facts would vary quite a lot if the excrement in question were that of a beautiful girl or if it were a question of eating the come of a forward from your rugby team (Lacan 1992: 188).

'I have no particular need to set up a gang-bang, as Donatien here is already keen to do again', begins Leopold von Sacher-Masoch, 'since for me what counts is atmosphere and suggestion, and so I don't need Donatien's willed obscenity.'

'What kind of atmosphere?' asks Yahweh.

'Well, let me quote Gilles, for a moment, since he captures it best: "The settings in Masoch, with their heavy tapestries, their cluttered intimacy, their boudoirs and closets, create a chiaroscuro where the only things that emerge are suspended gestures and suspended suffering"' (Deleuze 1991: 34).

'Oh, then you would really like my tabernacle that Moses here is about to build, full of curtains, tapestries, acacia furniture covered in gold, and lovely frocks for the priests to wear', enthuses Yahweh, warming rather to this enigmatic figure, a professor no less and novelist.

'Indeed, you must show me around when it is done, Moses', suggests Leopold.

'I guess so', replies Moses, somewhat uncertainly now, suspended for a moment, thinking about what these tabernacle plans might actually mean.

'I do like the Bible so much', continues Leopold, 'for, as Annie Sprinkle says, "the Holy Bible is so erotic. I sure hope they don't ban it" (Sprinkle 1998: 8). Cain and Christ, who bears the mark of Cain, are both heroes for me, characters who suffer at the hands of God, whose sign is the same mark—X or +. Cain is a favorite, for, apart from the importance of crime in nature and history that he signifies, he is also the favorite of his mother, Eve, a tiller of the soil. In fact, he killed his father's favorite, Abel, thereby eliminating the image of the father and elevating his mother, Eve. This crime is precisely my kind of thing, even with the punishment, the mark, inflicted by that other Father, Yahweh here, that threatens my fantasy.'

'Can't we take this back earlier into the story?' says Moses with an authorial eye. 'Isn't the story of the fall itself like this? The father being beaten here, Adam, is the image of Yahweh, who is the ultimate target of the beating. For Eve brings Adam into subservience to her by enticing him to eat from the tree of good and evil, with the result that they are thrown out of the garden.'

'There we find Adam, grinding away, tilling the soil, under the heel and whip of Eve', notes Gilles. 'Leopold has a wonderful post-Eden scene, which I will quote in full (read "Eve" for "Wanda"):

They [Wanda and three young African women] led me to the vineyard that lay along the south side of the garden. Maize had been planted between the vines and a few dry heads were still standing: a plough had been left there.

The blackamoors tied me to a stake and amused themselves by pricking me with golden hairpins. But this did not last long, for Wanda appeared with her ermine toque, her hands in the pockets of her jacket. She told them to untie me and fasten my hands behind my back. Then she had a yoke laid on my shoulders and I was harnessed to the plough.

The black demons pushed me on to the field; one drove the plough, the other led me on a leash, and the third goaded me with the whip, while Venus in Furs stood by, watching the scene' (Sacher-Masoch 1991: 232).

'It gives Christ's "Come unto me all ye who labor and are heavy laden..." a new meaning', notes Sade.

'With that', continues Leopold, 'let me return to the other one of my pair Cain/Christ. For Christ also is an image of the Father, who is destroyed, although for me it is his mother, Mary, who puts him on the cross and thereby eliminates the Father. Now, it is Christ's resurrection that enables the second birth, the new ideal self of both Christ and Cain, which is not in the image of the Father, but born of the woman alone. You might, as Gilles does, describe my work as Christological (Deleuze 1991: 97), for this image of untold suffering and the resurrection of a new self pervades my work.'

'Is the passion narrative of Christ then a foundational masochistic text?' asks an incredulous Sade, feeling the focus shift away from him.

'Indeed it is', interposes Gilles, 'for not only is suffering valorized as never before, but it is willed suffering, in total submission. Further, it is a suffering and submission that becomes the model for all believers who follow. They must imitate Christ, *imitatio Christi*, who is the basis of a new covenant.'

Yahweh is not too sure that he is keen on such an interpretation, but then Leopold did write in a Europe steeped in Christianity. 'Anything from the Hebrew Bible, apart from Cain?' he asks.

'I do love the story of Samson and Delilah, which recurs in *Venus in Furs*. The room rented by Wanda and Severin in Florence has a painting of Delilah and Samson on the ceiling (see Sacher-Masoch 1991: 268). I like to see myself, through Severin (who becomes Gregor, Wanda's slave), as Samson, beaten and betrayed: "Even Samson, the hero, the giant, put himself into the hands of Delilah who had already betrayed him once, only to be betrayed yet again. And when he was captured and blinded by the Philistines, he kept his brave and loving eyes fixed upon the fair traitress until the very end" (Sacher-Masoch 1991: 155). And then, when Wanda and Severin secure their masochistic contract, I look at the painting, taking in its complete license with the biblical text: "Delilah, an opulent creature with flaming red hair, reclines half-naked on a red ottoman, a sable cloak about her shoulders. She smiles and leans towards Samson, who has been bound and thrown at her feet by the Philistines. Her teasing, coquettish smile seems the very summit of cruelty; with half-closed eyes she gazes at Samson, while he regards her longingly, crazed with love. Already his enemy has laid a knee on his chest and is about to blind him with the white-hot sword" (Sacher-Masoch 1991: 221). Of course, the picture comes into its own when Wanda, my Delilah, betrays Severin and produces "the Greek" from behind the curtain, who mercilessly beats Severin (Sacher-Masoch 1991: 268).'

'But what of Gilles' borrowed argument that you are an atheist?' asks Sade, still put out by the suggestion that he actually believes in God.

'I'm not sure yet. You could argue that my removal of the Father, God, in the stories of Cain and Christ, is enough to justify such an argument, but Gilles wants to enter a different boudoir, following this antipodean pervert, and the problem with his argument is that the torturer, whom he suggests is God, is in my texts a woman, always.'

'So there's no room at all for a divine torturer?' queries Yahweh, nonplussed.

'Some have suggested that behind the female torturer may be found the father. Yet for me the father is not hidden in the beating female, but in the figure being beaten. As Gilles writes, "*It is not a child but a father that is being beaten*. The masochist thus liberates himself in preparation for a rebirth in which the father will have no part" (Deleuze 1991: 65-66). And that rebirth is what I have already mentioned, the resurrection of the New Man who is not in the image of the Father. Yet the situation is more complex than this, for in my work there are in fact three mothers—you will understand by now that the torturess is of course the mother: the uterine mother and the Oedipal mother are both bad mothers, ones to be transcended, and their place is subsumed by the oral mother. She is the good mother, the one who transplants the father and ensures the rebirth of the male in her image: Eve and Mary, in other words.'

'What's this uterine, Oedipal and oral mother shit?' asks Moses.

' "Masoch's three women correspond to three fundamental mother images: the first is the primitive, uterine, hetaeric mother, mother of the cloaca and the swamps; the second is the Oedipal mother, the image of the beloved, who becomes linked with the sadistic father as victim or as accomplice; and in between these two, the oral mother, mother of the steppe, who nurtures and brings death" ' (Deleuze 1991: 55), interposes Gilles.

'For me they are the mother herself, the wife chosen in the image of the mother and mother Earth who swallows up the man at death', adds Sigmund.

'So the oral mother is in the end Eve and Mary, who have also been uterine and Oedipal, but now absorb these into themselves', says Moses, with a hint of understanding.

'Exactly', says Leopold, 'she's the torturer in my books and life.'

'So, how can she also be the God whom this antipodean suggests is there?' asks Moses.

'Well', says Yahweh, 'this antipodean argues that the torturer created by the masochist must be a divine figure, and that there is a slippage from the Christian God (not quite my kind of thing, I might add) to the female torturer of masochism.'

'And what brings him to such a conclusion?' quizzes a quizzical Moses again.

'A debilitating and soul-destroying experience of the abuse of power, as far I can recall', rejoins Yahweh.

'Well, tell us; what does he argue?' adds an impatient Gilles.

'He feels that in Leopold's writings it is finally God who is effaced by the torturing woman. We may begin with the simple observation that the male masochists in Masoch's stories always worship their female torturers. Thus, in *Venus in Furs*, Severin worships Wanda as a god, as Venus from Mount Olympus. He worships her (both Wanda and statues of Venus), is her slave, loves her, is beaten by her, etc.—all features of my relation with Israelites in the Hebrew Bible, at least. Listen to Severin speak of his affection for the statue of Venus:

> It is enough to say that she is beautiful and that I love her madly, passionately, with feverish intensity, as one can only love a woman who responds to one with a petrified smile, ever calm and unchanging. I adore her absolutely... Often at night I pay a visit to my cold, cruel beloved; clasping her knees, I press my face against her cold pedestal and worship her (Sacher-Masoch 1991: 153).

> At times I would steal into my father's library, as if to enjoy a forbidden pleasure, and would gaze upon a plaster statue of Venus. I would kneel before her and recite the prayers I had been taught, the Lord's Prayer, the Hail Mary and the Creed... I prostrated myself before her and kissed her feet in the way I had seen my fellow countrymen kiss the feet of the dead Savior (Sacher-Masoch 1991: 173).

'Is there not an extraordinary slippage here, from Venus to the Christian God?' asks Yahweh with a look of distaste when he says the word 'Christian'. 'To Venus, the goddess of love, Severin, the character in Masoch's novel, says "Our father, who art in heaven...", moving then to "Hail Mary, mother of Jesus". Who is Masoch's character worshipping? Venus, God, Mary, or perhaps Psyche or Astarte (see Sacher-Masoch 1991: 164)? Venus in furs might just as well be Mary in furs, or, for that matter, Wanda in furs, for Severin worships the flesh-and-blood Wanda (the name taken on by Masoch's wife in an extraordinary process of identification) as though she were Venus (and, I suggest, Mary, Psyche or myself).'

'But you still haven't really established a slippage, a glistening slide, a silky channel from Venus/Wanda to God', objects Moses, tightening the screws.

'Well', rejoins Leopold, 'I think the role of Judith and Holofernes is the crux, for here a smiting Yahweh and beating woman merge into one. Let's read from my novel, *Venus in Furs*, again:

> I breakfasted under the arbor, reading the book of Judith. I could not help envying the heathen Holofernes who came to such a bloody end, beheaded by a regal lady.
> 'The Lord hath smitten him by the hand of a woman'.
> The sentence made a deep impression on me. 'How unchivalrous those Jews are', I thought. As for their God, he might choose his words better when speaking of the fair sex.
> 'The Lord hath smitten him by the hand of a woman'. What must I do for him to smite *me*?' (emphasis in original; Sacher-Masoch 1991: 155).

'You don't merely mean that Judith is Yahweh's agent here, do you?' asks a nervous Sigmund, for he could see his argument about the father lying behind the torturing woman of Masoch's work being turned on its head.

'No', jumps in Leopold, 'ultimately my desire is to be beaten by a woman, a goddess, who stands behind God. In answer to my question—what must I do for him to smite me?—my answer is: find your own Venus, your own goddess, who will beat me in his place.'

'In other words', comes in Gilles, 'when Yahweh beats you, it is in fact your goddess, the oral mother, who beats you. The Lord's hand is a woman's hand, wielding the whip, tightening the rack.'

'So', resigns Sigmund, 'behind the father lies the torturing woman, or, to put it in Gilles' terms, borrowed from me, there is a "symbolic transfer or redistribution of all paternal functions to the threefold feminine figure" (Deleuze 1991: 61). This is the masochistic vision of the death of God: the female(s) kill God, take his paternal functions and then kill and resurrect the son in their image (see Deleuze 1991: 131).'

'But this isn't all that this perverse individual from the antipodes argues', pipes in Yahweh, showing a lovely manicured hand, nails all done up in an eerie, ice-cold blue. He was, however, starting to fade, his voice hardly discernible.

'What's that?' asks Sigmund, straining to hear what Yahweh is saying.

'I think he wants to say', says Moses in a representative role, 'that just as the torturing woman is constructed by the masochist, made by him in the image of himself, so also Yahweh, the torturing God of the masochist, is also very much a construct.'

'But does that make him any less real?' questions Gilles, as Yahweh gains some substance again.

'Is not a construct unreal?' returns Sigmund, and Yahweh fades again. In his place begins to appear a madonna, Mary herself.

'The imaginary is as real as the elusive real', comes in Jacques, producing Yahweh in his chair once again; Mary fades a little.

'But I always create my torturers from an existing woman, as with Wanda, who says to Severin: "Dangerous tendencies were lurking in me, and you were the one who awakened them; if I now take pleasure in hurting and tormenting you, it is entirely your fault. You have made me what I am, and you are so weak and unmanly that you are now blaming me"' (Sacher-Masoch 1991: 260).

While Yahweh slips away and Mary appears more firmly, Moses takes the discussion in a new direction. 'Surely you can't find masochism in the Bible', he asserts.

'We already have the setting, in the tabernacle, with its tapestries and curtains and the enclosed, stifling atmosphere', observes Leopold. 'And then the central tableau, atop the torture table, as it were, is the contract, the covenant, between top and bottom.'

'A covenant!' interjects Moses, who has just signed and sealed one with Yahweh on behalf of the Israelites, 'Why is that masochistic?'

'The covenant or contract is the "ideal form of the love relationship and its necessary precondition"' (Deleuze 1991: 75), says Gilles, quoting himself. 'Masoch wrote about it, lived it out in his own relationships with women; in short, assured that it is fundamental to any masochistic relationship.'

'But isn't the primary form of the covenant in Western thought found in the Bible, repeatedly?' asks Moses, in the process of reassessing whether he is indeed a masochist. 'What does the masochist contract involve?'

'Submission to the will of the "top"', recites Leopold, 'the taking on a new name and a new identity, sometimes a time limit, at others none, complete obedience to the "top", punishment for the lack of obedience, in whatever form is appropriate, reward for obedience...'

'But that', jumps in Moses, 'is just what Yahweh and I agreed upon: we (the people) are to obey his law, for which we will be rewarded with land, prosperity and long life. Disobedience brings punishment. And, you know, apart from other societies in the ancient Near East, who also drew up contracts, mostly after warfare, the covenant has, after all, a long pedigree in Christian theology (not my forte, I must admit), structuring the twofold canon itself of old and new covenant (and thereby simultaneously recognizing and annulling the Jewish and Muslim claims to the Hebrew Bible). Its basic nature remains, an arrangement, a contract between God and human beings, with mutual obligations and duties for each party. Closer to my preferred arena— the Hebrew Bible—the most well-known example is the Deuteronomistic perception of covenant, traceable in Deuteronomy through to Kings most directly, but appearing elsewhere, such as the work of the prophet Jeremiah. This schema is basically the same as the one Yahweh and I just signed: if the people obey God's law, worshiping no other gods and marrying no one but Israelites, then God will bless them with the land, long life, wealth and many children. If they do not obey, then punishment will follow, eventually, in the form of no land, children, money and a short, painful life. According to this form of the covenant, God, or Yahweh, has set up a dual path, one for obedience, the other for disobedience: all it takes is the response of the people. One might also think of the Noachic or Abrahamic or Davidic covenants: in the last of these, a permanent regime is established; a king will remain on the throne of Judah forever, and yet if the king does disobey, as was to happen frequently, then Yahweh does not remove him, but "when he commits iniquity, I will chastise him with the rod of men, with the stripes of the sons of men" (2 Sam. 7.14)'.

'Sounds like ideal masochistic covenant to me', says Leopold. 'Is there also a provision for death as punishment?'

'Yes, in some cases, death.'

'Christianity has a death as the basis of the new contract at its very heart', adds Sade.

'Some masochist contracts have death as the final punishment as well, should the top decree it', Leopold rejoins. 'In the harsher contract between Wanda and I, death is an option (see Sacher-Masoch 1991: 279). Indeed death, which is the only way to end a contract at times, is part of the very harsh contracts that I drew up later in life, where nothing was left to me, all my will power was ceded. I became entirely the tool of my top, after I had educated her sufficiently.'

'Sounds like Calvinism', pipes up a quiet Sade, who has some experience of Huguenots. 'In its Calvinist form, the covenant is a very one-sided business, with human beings unable to do anything for themselves, given as they are to total depravity, utter knavery. Radically removed from the good, we humans must rely totally on God, whose unconditional grace provides us with salvation, if, and it is a big if, we (now a much more restricted we) belong to the elect, to those predestined for salvation, heaven, eternal bliss, what have you. God's grace was manifested through an old covenant—the Law of the Old Testament—and then, when that didn't quite do the job, through a new covenant in Jesus Christ. The essence of this covenant is that God's wrath for our sins, the inevitable result of our depravity, would lead to our utter annihilation, nuked, as it were, out of existence, were it not for Jesus, that lewd fellow, who steps in between and takes the blast for us. He is then our substitute, submitting to God's destroying anger, so that we escape what is due to us. Under this arrangement, all we can do is reverently love the Lord—if we are of the elect—and seek to do his will whenever and wherever we can. As for the lost... Well, you see what a swindle this system is!'

'These contracts have been made not only with God, but also with the devil, for in the Middle Ages one might either be possessed by the devil or form a pact of alliance with him. What Donatien here espouses can be understood as institutionalized possession, whereas Leopold's work operates with a contracted alliance (see Deleuze 1991: 20-21).'

'But who sets up the contract?' edges Sigmund back into the discussion.

'The top... I mean, Yahweh', affirms Moses.

'No, it is in fact the bottom', contradicts Leopold.

'But did I not receive the covenant and law from Yahweh?' replies Moses with another question. 'Was it not "written with the finger of God?"' (Exod. 31.18).

'Well no', responds a faint Yahweh, 'you gave it to me to sign, after some persuasion. I'm actually not so keen on it myself.'

'What do you say Gilles?' asks Moses, his world turning upside down, just as Sigmund's had earlier.

' "The masochistic contract implies not only the necessity of the victim's consent, but his ability to persuade, and his pedagogical and judicial efforts to train his torturer"', replies the self-quoting Gilles (Deleuze 1991: 75). 'In fact, you might also argue that the contract's function is to block the reality and hallucination of the father's aggressive return (see Deleuze 1991: 65), for the contract is between the oral mother and masochist.'

'So', concludes a distraught Moses, 'now I have constructed a covenant with Yahweh which actually keeps him permanently at the edge, out of the picture, for the contract is really with the oral mother, with Eve, Mary...'

'Afraid so', rejoins Leopold, 'but there's more'—Moses groans—'for the function of the contract is to provide not Yahweh, or God, with the symbolic power of the Law, but the mother figure.'

'The Law is, to quote Slavoj Zizek, the "ultimate perversion"', explains Gilles, 'for in masochism the punishment for disobedience of the Law is the source of enjoyment. The Law (and note, among other things, the dominance of imperatives in both the tables of the law in the Hebrew Bible and masochism [Deleuze 1991: 34-35]) is converted from forbidding the satisfaction of desire by the threat of punishment to ordering the satisfaction of the desire that follows punishment. The punishment itself is not the source of pleasure, but pleasure is made possible by and follows the punishment.'

'But that's what I argued a little earlier', expostulates Jacques.

'That means', grinds out Moses, 'that the people, as bottoms, will deliberately disobey the Law in order to set in train the punishment that is outwardly avoided but unconsciously wished for, so that they might gain pleasure. As just now, they have made their golden calves so that

Yahweh will punish them. And that, finally, is what the disobedience of Adam and Eve is all about: this setting, this law about eating from the tree of good and evil, which is a masochistic one I suppose, is structured so that disobedience is the only possible option.'

'The ultimate desire of the masochist', finishes Jacques, 'the *che vuoi?*—what is it that you really want?—is to be punished for disobedience, to transgress and find pleasure.'

'Isn't this what the story of Jesus' passion is all about?' says the Christocentric Leopold. 'The bottom, a believer, Jesus himself, an Israelite, relies upon every word of God to live, expects, even desires, punishment, for any misdemeanor (according to the terms of the contract) will bring about its own retribution in its own time. So also Jesus takes on the role of bottom, punished for the elect, so that they can continue to be bottoms. Under the old scheme, God would have run out of bottoms quite quickly, given a predilection for killing them off.'

Moses rises to his feet and grasps the two vast tablets of the law and smashes them upon the rocks. 'What did you do that for?' whispers a faint Yahweh.

'Not only did I write them, but now they also produce disobedience so that you can punish us.'

'I'll just have to punish you anyway.'

'Hold on, you two, settle down!' intervenes Sigmund. 'If the punishment of the Law is the gateway to pleasure, but not the pleasure itself (such a mockery of the Law explains why sadistic and masochistic sex has the strongest legal penalties), then isn't pleasure held off, suspended, kept waiting?'

'Is that why', asks Yahweh with a dawning realization, 'the porn pictures and films of what they call S/M always focus on the bound figure, tied up, gagged, labia splayed, penises constricted? And they always look like they've been there for hours, in the same posture. Nary a meat shot or cum shot to be seen.'

'That's because the climax is precisely the suspense, not consummation', offers Gilles. '"Waiting and suspense are the essential characteristics of the masochistic experience. Hence the ritual scenes of hanging, crucifixion and other forms of physical suspension in Masoch's novels"' (Deleuze 1991: 70-71).

'So Christ himself is a masochist!' exclaims Sade. 'What do those lengthy gospel stories all lead up to? After the chief priests apprehend Jesus, Pilate questions him, releases Barabbas, sends him to Herod (according to Lk. 23.6-12), has him scourged, and after Jesus carries his cross up onto the hill, with the help of Simon of Cyrene, what do we get? A man hanging there, hour after hour, suspended, limp. To be sure, he is prodded occasionally by a soldier, but he mainly hangs. No wonder so many crucifixes choose precisely this moment! I must agree, Christ is a masochist and Christianity is masochistic.'

'And Golgotha is the ultimate B&D den', mutters Leopold.

'Yes indeed', replies Gilles, 'but what needs to be stressed is that masochism is a state of waiting, in two forms. There is an interminable waiting for pleasure and an interminable, extreme expectation of pain (see Deleuze 1991: 71). And this is why Masoch is so interested in art, especially the plastic arts, for they suspend movement, arrest it, hold it still, eternal, frozen. "The whip or the sword that never strikes, the fur that never discloses the flesh, the heel that is forever descending on the victim, are the expression, beyond all movement, of a profound state of waiting closer to the sources of life and death"' (Sacher-Masoch 1991: 70).

'That sounds like a commentary on the Akedah', says Moses, breaking the stillness. 'For in Gen. 22 the climax, the moment of high tension and extreme satisfaction, is when Abraham suspends the knife over bound Isaac's motionless neck, ready to strike, to slash, to watch the life-blood spurt out of him over the altar. Don't we have here the primal scene, with apologies to Sigmund, of masochistic suspension. In a different, and perhaps earlier, version of the story, the immediate satisfaction of the Akedah, the obvious sexual release, is the killing of Isaac. But, as you said, the high point, the climax is suspension, the held moment. Another possibility is the release of Isaac and his substitution by the ram in the bushes, but this is only a letdown.'

'Indeed', joins in Leopold, 'I know the story well, like most in the Hebrew Bible, and the high moment is when the flame is about to be set to the kindling, the fire about to lick the still warm body, the knife arcing down to slice the youthful neck. Countless artists have chosen precisely this moment for their etchings, drawings, statues and paintings, and rightly so. But does not the whole story work with this suspense? The first command of Yahweh—"Take your son, your only son Isaac, whom you love, and go to the land of Moriah, and offer him there as a burnt offering upon one of the mountains of which I shall tell you" (Gen. 22.2)—sets the waiting in place. What will happen, we wonder: will he kill him? They set out, with two young men, in silence for two whole days! For only on the third day does Abraham speak, upon seeing the mountain (vv. 4-5). Oh, how I wish I was Isaac from that moment on, made to carry the wood in place of the ass left behind, a beast of burden for Abraham! And then more suspense, more waiting. In reply to Isaac's question—"where is the lamb?" (Gen. 22.7)—Abraham merely replies, "God will provide himself the lamb for a burnt offering, my son" (v. 8). In silence again Abraham builds an altar, arranges the wood, binds Isaac and lays him on the altar. As he takes "the knife to slaughter his son" (v. 10) the angel intervenes, the knife a fraction away from the neck, as their talk stays the hand that would slay the son (vv. 11-12).'

'I always thought the angel was crucial to the story, despite what the critics say', whispers Yahweh, or is that Mary?

'The angel and Abraham do talk a lot, don't they? Even after the ram has been found and slaughtered and so on, they sit down for a longer chat', observes Moses.

'And in the end, instead of Isaac's blood, it is his seed, or sperm that dominates, with descendant after descendant following' (Gen. 22.20-24), adds Leopold.

'I'm not so sure', says a troubled Gilles, 'for what we have here is a very male thing—Yahweh, Abraham, Isaac, even the two young men at either end of the story. Not a woman to be found, nor even the effacement of the father.'

'But did you not just argue that behind Yahweh, in fact even through Yahweh, acts the oral mother?' asks Sigmund, who always has an interest in these things.

'You know, Sigmund may have something here', says Moses, leaning forward, keenly interested. 'Gen. 22.1-3 is prefigured by 16.2, where Abram hearkens "to the voice of Sarai" in the same way that he obeys Yahweh in Gen. 22. And then Gen. 22 may be read as a response to the laughter of both Abraham (17.17) and Sarah (18.12) at the news of the conception of Isaac, as well as the pregnancy and birth (21.1-7), with Sarah's curious words: "Who would have said to Abraham that Sarah would suckle children? Yet I have borne him a son in his old age" (21.7).'

'Do you mean', asks Gilles, 'that Abraham does the bidding of Sarah in setting out either to kill Isaac, as an earlier stream of the tradition has him do, or, as the story now is, to replace him with the ram, the furry or woolly animal?'

'Especially', says Sigmund, 'if we see Sarah, the three-mothers-in-one (uterine, Oedipal and oral), behind Yahweh. Abraham then listens to the Sarah behind Yahweh all along in order to do away with the son who is in the image of the father and replace him with one who is in the image of the mother.'

'But how is the ram the image of the mother?' cries out an exasperated Sade.

'At this point we need to think for a moment about the central role of the furry animal in masochism', suggests Gilles. 'We might compare the ram in the bushes to the hunting scenes in Masoch's novels, in which the ideal woman (in Gen. 22 it is Yahweh/Sarah) hunts a bear or a wolf or another furry beast in order to obtain its fur. The outcome is not quite what we would expect, for this is the story of the oral mother overcoming the primitive prostitute mother, the one who gives birth—since a basic drive of masochism is to transfer the functions of the bad mothers (primitive and Oedipal) onto the good oral mother—with the final aim of rebirth, of a second birth in which *the father has no part* (see Deleuze 1991: 61). So what we have here is the production of a ram, caught in the bushes, cornered, whose death signals the death of the primitive mother, so that not only can Yahweh/Sarah assume her mantle, but also Isaac can be reborn without Abraham's involvement.'

'Oh my God, now I'm lost', resigns Moses.

'But it does explain the ever-present furs in my novels', observes Leopold, 'for the oral mother always wears them, as a sign of her assuming all the female roles.'

'And they are also part of the function of fetishes', adds Gilles, 'which for you are furs, shoes, whips and even the odd helmets your women wear. "The fetish is the object of the fantasy, the fantasized object par excellence"' (Deleuze 1991: 72). But I'm afraid this question about the role of the fetish will have to wait for another discussion, since I understand that the perverse antipodean is writing something on fetishism at the moment.'

A few heads now turn in Yahweh's direction, looking upon his furs, fantastic calf-length boots, manicured hands, beautifully done hair, the whips hanging from his chair, with the same eyes as Leopold and Gilles. For Sade, the whip, crown of thorns, coat, nails and cross of the passion narrative take on a new look as well. However, it is becoming very difficult to distinguish Yahweh from the oral mother, Sarah, Eve, Mary, behind that hair and fur coat.

Revelation

At the sight of her lying on the red velvet cushions, her precious body peeping out between the folds of sable, I realized how powerfully sensuality and lust are aroused by flesh that is only partly revealed (Sacher-Masoch 1991: 239).

With all eyes upon her, this divine figure stands up, the lines of distinction completely blurred. 'Why is there always such an easy fit between things such as masochism and the Bible? Is it possible that the Bible, in its very patterns, themes, relationships, the divine-human structure, preconditions any sexual relation (for masochism is sexual from beginning to end) that comes out of the West, or at least where the Bible has a deep and lasting cultural influence? So, it turns out that the basic features of masochism appear first in the Bible: fetishes, fantasy, imagination, covenant, law, beating, whipping, binding, construction of the torturer, atmosphere, suspension, waiting, and even the oral mother.'

Turning to go, the figure staggers in a cleft of the rock and the fur coat slips for a moment from the shoulders to reveal a slender, muscled and well-toned back, but above all the most glorious, divine ass anyone, even Donatien, in all his wide experience, has ever seen. It is beautifully rounded, shapely, upright, firm, with a soft sensuous movement as (s)he walks away. Gilles glimpses a breast, Sigmund thinks he sees a phallus. All too soon a hand moves down to grasp the fur and cover the back again. They miss the face this last time, but the ass made their own faces shine for days afterwards (see Exod. 33.21-23; 34.29).

Violent Femmes and S/M: Queering Samson and Delilah

Lori Rowlett

Although the story of Samson and Delilah can be read in a number of different ways, stereotypical role assumptions are usually made about the two main characters. According to the established paradigms of biblical studies, Samson is seen as the flawed, tragic Man of God, with Delilah as the evil foreign temptress. As Danna Nolan Fewell notes, commentators usually consider her 'the *femme fatale par excellence*' (Fewell 1998: 79, emphasis in original). However, what happens when the story is read through a glass queerly? The pattern of domination by the exotic Other in a tale of bondage and degradation emerges as a stock S/M scenario. Delilah is the femme dominatrix, teasing and tormenting Samson, who has all the characteristics of a 'butch bottom'. (The role-play terms butch and femme may apply to anyone, male, female or other, in any combination.) The constant give and take between the two lovers resembles S/M role-play, complete with ritual questions, hair fetishism and other power games. Delilah does not trick him into saying or doing anything. Samson deliberately relinquishes control to the dominatrix who repeatedly subjects him to humiliation and bondage. The story therefore can be read in terms of the ritual codes of S/M games. Other codes come into play as well: issues of gender, political identity and power are interwoven with a deeper question of divine control and relinquishment of control, raising the possibility that the structure of the book of Judges places Yahweh in a rotating game of S/M.

Gender in Samson and Delilah

The genders of the two characters in the Bible are apparently static. One is a man and the other a woman. The process of gender identification in other versions of the Samson and Delilah story is never quite so simple.

The earliest musical versions (other than a few madrigal songs sung by males) of the Samson and Delilah story were oratorios written during the era when the great divas were male castrati, which set up the expectation of imaginative identification across gender lines. Benedetto Ferrari (a seventeenth-century Italian composer) wrote an oratorio, *Sansone*, but, unfortunately, very little survives of the earliest performance history. Handel wrote his *Samson* oratorio late in life, and while castrati were used extensively in his operas, none were used in his oratorios (Smithers 1977). However, musical performance was and still is often a gender-bending masquerade (Rosselli 1992). Many operas popular today have 'trouser roles' in which a woman singer portrays a young man. In an earlier era such roles could be played by a boy pretending to be a woman pretending to be a boy.

As women came to be cast in female parts, due to increasing acceptance of women as public performers, opera developed toward the kind of romantic melodrama seen in Saint-Saëns' *Samson et Dalila*, with libretto by Ferdinand Lemaire (Scherer 1998). The overripe emotional treatment gives it a campy flavor, very much like a drag performance. As Umberto Eco points out in 'The Myth of Superman' (Eco 1981), the message of a text may be expressed at the outset in terms of a fixed code, but it is caught by divers groups of receivers and deciphered on the basis of other codes. The sense of the message often undergoes filtration or distortion in the process, which completely alters its 'pragmatic' function. Grand opera, like musical comedy, is often received by a gay male audience through a code of camp sensibility which involves no small measure of identification with the femme characters.

A role like the Saint-Saëns' Dalila is already full of hyperbolic female characteristics, like a drag performance. As Judith Butler makes clear, all gender is like drag in that gender, even in heterosexual contexts, is constantly being performed (Butler 1993: 125-26). Drag is not a secondary imitation of an original set of gender norms, which are stable and in some way 'natural'. Instead, hegemonic heterosexuality requires a constant and repeated effort to imitate its own idealizations (even by heterosexuals). The illusion of naturalness is achieved through constant repetition, but heterosexuality's attempts to become its own idealizations can never be fully or finally achieved. Not only is constant performance of gender norms required to maintain the illusion, but an elaborate structure of pathologizing practices and normalizing sciences is needed to consecrate its claim. Drag, according to Butler, reflects on the imitative structure by which heterosexualized gender produces itself, disputing its claim to naturalness.

No one has ever accused grand opera of naturalness in any case. Already a complex code in which every aspect of character is conveyed by a set of conventions well known to its fans, opera invites identification with the stylized performance of the femme. Although both male and female characters are likely to pour out their hearts in an aria, female opera characters are especially made to operate in the sphere of romantic relationships. The focus on love as sphere of influence is a way of performing gender, along with the hyperfeminine wigs, make-up, gestures and costumes. Therefore power usually has to be confined to this sphere for female characters, whether they are victims or victimizers. They are not always the more vulnerable partner, as the Samson opera demonstrates. Samson is the more vulnerable, but he can act out his power in various contexts. For Delilah, the romantic sphere is where her power finds an outlet, as is typical for the diva roles. John Crum, in a review of several books on the queer reception of opera (Crum 1996), says that during the era of the closet (by which he means mainly the pre-Stonewall era), gay males identified with the opera diva because she suffered and yet she was powerful. I would argue that the diva is still a figure of great importance for identification because of her role(s) as powerful femme and expressive outlet for strong emotion.

Identification with a gender, Butler maintains, is always an ambivalent process, which involves identifying with a set of norms 'that are and are not realizable' at the same time. There is always a cost in every identification because it implies the loss of other possible identifications. The identification of (at least some) gay men with opera divas provides a way of vicariously participating in overdetermined gendered emotion, emoting 'as a woman', while at the same time allowing a man to 'reverse and resignify' (to use Butler's terms) the performance as camp.

The overdetermined gender characteristics given to Delilah are not limited to opera. Milton's closet play *Samson Agonistes* (Milton 1963) employs a set of seventeenth-century gender descriptors built into Delilah's words. Unlike her biblical counterpart, Milton's Dalila (as Milton spells her name) attempts a reconciliation with Samson in which she presents her self-defense as a speech. In it she blames her woman's 'frailty' and 'weakness' which make her 'inquisitive, importune of secrets, then with like infirmity to publish them'. Hope Parisi points out that these are faults assumed to be specifically female (Parisi 1994). Parisi goes on to contextualize Dalila's deference to male opinion and her reticence to speak as conventions of femininity in the seventeenth century, a period in which women's speech was problematic. Women were to remain silent, at least in public life. Romance was one area, however, in which they were allowed a voice, so Dalila speaks in terms of love. Love, she says, caused her to do what she did. The use of feminine clichés in the characterization of Dalila constitutes another example of 'gender performance' in Butler's terms, although Milton's play was never performed in an actual theater. Closet plays, by definition, were only meant to be read, not performed. Nevertheless, Milton's Dalila, while not necessarily a woman on the stage, provides another example (albeit a two-dimensional one) of the performance of gender. She is a woman (on the printed page) performing herself female by her impersonation of a hyperfeminine ideal.

When the biblical Samson and Delilah story is read through the lens of its literary and musical performance history, we end up with a butch bottom and a dominatrix femme of either indeterminate gender or gender so overdetermined as to verge on the camp sensibility of gender impersonation. The sexes could easily be further altered by transposing the Samson role into the contralto range for an all-female cast, but no one has yet done so. It would be fascinating with an all-male cast too, like the controversial *Swan Lake* ballet in 1999.

Male and female are, as Butler says, unstable categories. Similarly, butch and femme, in gay and (especially) lesbian aesthetics, are intentionally fluid roles, meant to be played with, not meant to be immutable categories. Either one can be male or female, or some other interstitial category. Relations of dominance and submission in S/M are likewise fluid. As Foucault says, there are roles, but the roles can always be reversed. Even when roles are stabilized, S/M is a strategic game in which power structures are creatively acted out for the purpose of bodily pleasure. Some S/M practices produce intense sexual pleasure while bypassing the genitals themselves. Because S/M involves the eroticization of body parts other than (exclusively) the genitals, it represents what David Halperin calls a remapping of the body's erotic sites (Halperin 1995: 88). Therefore, any role may be played by any person, regardless of genital configuration.

S/M Play

Although Delilah is popularly thought of as a temptress and deceiver, she is remarkably straightforward in the biblical account. As Fewell notes, Delilah asks directly for what she wants. It is Samson who deceives her by giving her false information about the source of his strength and how to subdue him. She does not 'tempt' the information out of him either. Instead, Samson gives it willingly when he grows tired of their bondage play and tired of her asking. Perhaps he is merely tired of winning the bondage game and is willing to take it up to the next level, knowing it to be a dangerous move, yet desiring it.

Danger and lure of the unknown may be what attracted Samson to foreign women in the first place (Crenshaw 1978). According to the Deuteronomistic History, the problem with non-Israelite women as wives is not their sexual ways, but their religion. The assumption is that they bring their non-monotheistic practices into the community, where they become a source of pollution. Nevertheless, the mystery of the forbidden may have been attractive to him in all three of his liaisons with foreign women, because the unknown always includes an element of danger. One wonders too whether part of the attraction might be power. The Philistines were the ones with political power. Does Samson want to match wits with them? Or, more likely, does he harbor a deep desire to be dominated by a woman from the powerful group, a woman who represents power itself?

Judging from the structure of Samson's game with Delilah, he desires her as dominatrix. Fewell, a perceptive critic, recognizes the 'game' element of the Samson and Delilah story: 'He submits to her willingly, as if it were some kind of game', and then later, 'He is indeed playing games with her' (Fewell 1998: 79). Fewell does not follow up the implications of the sexual game of dominance and submission, however. Samson submits willingly to Delilah so she can tie him up, a classic bondage game. When he tires of winning every time, he delves into an act of deeper submission. In modern S/M, both partners have a codeword to stop the game to keep it safe, but part of the allure is being on the edge of danger. As John Preston points out in his article on the gay male leather scene (Preston 1996), 'overcodification' makes the game too safe, too predictable, and that makes it unsexy: 'For me, S/M had all been about living on the edge, being on the very cusp, being an outlaw: roles were something to be tried on, mocked, challenged'

(Preston 1996: 176). When Samson takes the game to the next level, he is seeking a new challenge.

The dominating partner in S/M sometimes plays a parental role. Preston describes what he calls the 'daddy thing' as a fetish with an element of truth underneath: 'Daddy has some lessons he can show a good boy who wants to learn. He knows how to put a bottom through a rite of passage... Daddy knows where the edge is...' (Preston 1996: 185). In S/M with a female top, the parental role may be a mother-figure. Delilah in the Samson story has strong motherly overtones, another fact noticed by Fewell:

> He transfers his allegiance from his real mother to his substitute lover-mother. Not only does he reveal the secret known only to himself and his mother, but he entrusts himself to Delilah as a child might trust his mother. As he sleeps upon Delilah's lap (some texts read, 'between her knees'), he loses his manly hair and his manly strength (Fewell 1998: 79).

Shaving hair is also a classic element of S/M play, although the modern reader has no way of knowing how long it has been so. In the biblical story, Samson's hair had to remain uncut because of the Nazirite vow, in which his mother said that no razor would touch his head. His strength departs from him as divine favor departs from him for breaking this vow. What is usually not remarked upon in discussions of Samson's manly strength being bound up with his long hair is the fetish aspect of hair shaving. Having the power to make someone submit to the removal of his hair, or to remove his own hair, whether of the genitals, body or head, is the prerogative of the top. Having the power to command someone not to is a dominating move also. Since Samson's mother was the one who made the original vow dedicating him as a Nazirite, she and Delilah are in competition to be the top, a competition Delilah wins. However, Yahweh is the real top, since the vow was ultimately made to Yahweh.

The one sense in which Delilah acts as deceiver of Samson, as she is so often accused by critics of doing, is in quitting the S/M game. Instead of continuing to keep him on the edge of danger, she at that point abandons him and the sex play. She disappears from the story altogether, leaving him in other hands, divine as well as human. First the Philistines have their way with him, then Yahweh does.

Theological Application of the Pattern

On a deeper level, the S/M reading of Samson and Delilah lays bare the underlying power relations of the book of Judges, which is a constituent part of the Deuteronomistic History. The cycle of stories in Judges centers on various heroes with divinely bestowed powers. As Eco has pointed out, superhuman heroes often operate within the confines of a 'closed text', so that a series of events repeats according to a set scheme. The hero's extraordinary powers are brought to bear on petty localized manifestations of evil which always resurface, only to be vanquished again and again on a small scale. The same divinely bestowed powers could presumably end the underlying evil once and for all, but instead, like S/M role-play, the scenario always begins again at the same point.

Human heroes, according to Eco, are 'consumed' by the action of the story, which brings death or some other denouement to the human characters and eventual closure to the text. With Superman and other superhuman characters, however, events become cyclical. While the individual human Judges, who act as Yahweh's surrogates in the biblical stories, eventually die, Yahweh is the one character who never does. Furthermore, he is, like all superheroes, invincible. Why, then, is Yahweh limited to violent small-scale victories, again and again, over local opponents?

Yahweh, in the S/M pattern, alternates between being a top (deploying power) and being a bottom (relinquishing power), toying with the ancient Israelites, who (by definition) are not gods and therefore have considerably less power in the game. Yahweh emerges as a sadistic character in the Deuteronomistic Historian's (henceforth called DH) schema in Judges because he/she has the power to do 'good' on a grand scale, but chooses to dole it out in small doses and then pull back, letting people be overcome by 'evil'.

'What is good?' Eco asks in his analysis of the Superman stories. Because Superman is 'practically omnipotent', he should have in front of him an enormous field of action for doing good:

> From a man who could produce work and wealth in astronomic dimensions in a few seconds, one could expect the most bewildering political, economic, and technological upheavals in the world. From the solution of hunger problems to the tilling of uninhabited regions, from the destruction of inhuman systems (if we read Superman into the 'spirit of Dallas',

why does he not go to liberate six hundred million Chinese from the yoke of Mao?), Superman could exercise good on a cosmic level, or on a galactic level, and furnish us in the meantime with a definition that through fantastic amplification could clarify precise ethical lines everywhere (Eco 1981: 122-23).

The question then becomes what is the 'evil' in the book of Judges and what is the 'good'. In the DH's frame around each episode, 'doing evil in the sight of Yahweh' always consists of taking part in Canaanite or Philistine religious practices. In other words, religious diversity is the problem. The good is a rigid monotheism that must be reinstated and reinforced by means of physical violence. The same supernatural power could eliminate the need for violence by establishing permanent peace and justice, thereby short-circuiting the cycle of dominance and submission. However, the DH's Yahweh makes no attempt to end the violence. Instead, to use Eco's words, the closed text remains static. The accomplishment of only partial or temporary acts mirrors the author/compiler's sense of order, a concept of order that pervades the cultural model in which he lives, and which involves the frequent deployment of violent action. The violence of the cycle in Judges is therefore useful because it is exactly the same power strategy that the DH wants to legitimate in his own context.

In his article on Superman, Eco discusses the way that an iterative scheme 'sustains and expresses a world'. The world has the same configuration as the structure which expresses it: If we examine the ideological contents of the Superman stories, says Eco, we find not only that the content sustains itself through the structure, but that, on the other hand, the stories help define their expressive structure as 'the circular static conveyance of a pedagogic message which is substantially immobilistic' (Eco 1981: 122). In Superman, evil is defined only as crimes against private property. In his little town, Superman constantly has to battle evil incarnate: organized crime, usually in the form of bank and mail-train robbers. At the same time, he expends huge amounts of energy organizing parochial benefit performances in order to collect money for orphans and indigents, when presumably the same energies could be employed directly to produce riches or to modify the larger situation. The point, Eco argues, is that since evil in Superman's moral world assumes only the form of crimes against private property, good assumes only the form of private charity. Eco describes the moral structure as civic consciousness completely split from political consciousness, and he says that the narrative structure helps to keep political consciousness from developing (Eco 1981: 122-24). Therefore, the capitalist politics of the context, mid-twentieth-century America, not only remain unchallenged but are continually, and ritualistically, reiterated in the content of, and by the iterative structure of, Superman.

Superman's petty actions for (narrowly defined) good and against evil constitute a cyclical pattern to express and impose societal norms, just as gender, drag and S/M rituals are repeating cycles. Likewise, the cycle of divine power assertion is a stylized repetition of acts in the text of Judges. In all of these cases, the illusion of a stable essence is structured by repeated acts that approximate the ideal of a substantial ground of identity. If acts and attributes which produce cultural signification are performative, then identity is revealed to be an illusion, in this case, an illusion created by the DH by a series of redundant displays. No lasting effects result, necessitating more cyclical violence. Divine power is revealed to be a regulatory fiction which the DH can deploy to keep the people of his own political context in line (or, dare we say, in bondage?).

What then is the historical context of the DH? I have argued extensively elsewhere that the first edition of the history was most likely compiled, using a plethora of older traditions, during the Josianic period, when the Jerusalem monarchy was attempting to reassert itself in the wake of Assyrian collapse (Rowlett 1996). Political and religious power were being consolidated in the capital city and the lines of hierarchy were being re-established with one place of worship, the temple in Jerusalem. The rhetoric of monotheism was essential to Josianic power. It depended upon the idea of one king under one deity (who gave him his authority), with one religious power structure subordinate to both. Competing shrines, with their own lines of power, would not be tolerated because they constituted a threat to the regime. The pre-monarchic heroes in the DH serve as models for later kingly behavior. They succeed to the extent that they maintain the monotheistic hierarchy and fail when they deviate from it.

Other scholars have recently argued that the Josianic date is too early for the DH's compilation, and that the DH is most likely post-exilic. For purposes of the present article, rather than reiterate my own lengthy arguments, I would point out that the same type of power consolidation was taking place in the exilic context, so my observations would apply to that situation as well. When the exiles returned and began the process of rebuilding their temple and their religio-political structure, they were not impeded by their new overlords, the Persians, who kept their distance. Josiah's era may have been considered a model to emulate by those establishing power in Second Temple period Jerusalem, which would account for the idealized picture of Josiah in the DH if that were the case. Either way, the governing authorities in Jerusalem were deploying a rhetoric of violence in an unstable situation. Because monotheism was essential to the line of hierarchical authority being put forward in power centralization, religious diversity was made the identifiable evil. It represented competing loyalties and dispersion of power. Consequently, it had to be repeatedly vanquished in a cycle of recurrence.

Conclusion

Reading the Samson and Delilah story through an S/M lens reveals a power structure replicated at several levels. The titillating play of Samson and Delilah mirrors the cat-and-mouse game Yahweh plays with the Israelites, which in turn serves the political purpose of the DH, the author/compiler who constructed the story. Queering Samson and Delilah, viewing them as role players without fixed identities or essences, calls into question by analogy the stability of the divine/ human dichotomy as well. If Yahweh has enormous divine powers, sufficient to establish his or her will globally many times over, then why does he or she allocate just enough of it to various heroes to keep the cycle of violence going? Perhaps he or she derives pleasure from the game, or perhaps the sadistic pleasure belongs to his or her (literary) creator, the DH.

LOVERS AND RAISIN CAKES:
FOOD, SEX AND DIVINE INSECURITY IN HOSEA

Ken Stone

I

Toward the beginning of a discussion of food and sex written several years ago, the cultural anthropologist Donald Pollock modifies a now-famous statement by Claude Lévi-Strauss in order to argue that food and sex are 'each "good to think" the other' (Pollock 1985: 25; cf. Lévi-Strauss 1963: 89).[1] Pollock's assertion is but one example of a recurring anthropological concern with structural, metaphorical and other relations between, on the one hand, eating, diet and food produc-tion; and, on the other hand, sexual activity, identity and reproduction (see, e.g., McKnight 1973; Meigs 1984; Gregor 1985; Counihan 1999). Such anthropological comparisons between food and sex prove difficult to resist for a reader of biblical texts such as myself, interested as I am in anthropological readings of the Hebrew Bible in general and of biblical discourses on gender and sexual practice in particular.[2] What might happen if we used this fertile comparison between food and sex as a lens for reading biblical texts? Could careful attention to the appearance of food and sex in a range of biblical texts (as well as in later interpretations of biblical texts) shed light on those texts, on the cultures that produced those texts, or on the subjects and practices involved in the reception of those texts? Might the relation between food and sex be 'good to think' biblical interpretation?

Such a question has been asked within biblical studies only on rare

---

1. An earlier version of this paper was read at a session of the Reading, Theory and the Bible Section at the 1999 Society of Biblical Literature meeting in Boston.

2. Throughout much of this paper I will assume, but not repeat, the reflections I have engaged in elsewhere (Stone 1996) about the nature and goals of an 'anthro-pological reading' of biblical discourses on gender and sexual practice.

occasions (by, e.g., Eilberg-Schwartz 1990; Fewell and Gunn 1993; Rashkow 2000). Indeed, the relevance of links between food and sex in the Bible has been questioned even by some of those scholars who detect such links elsewhere (cf. Douglas 1975: 262). Moreover, the conjunction between food and sex may seem odd to many contemporary readers of the Bible because of a widespread tendency to assume that sexual matters are inherently more significant than food matters. Such assumptions about the greater gravity of sexual matters in comparison with other human phenomena such as food (assumptions referred to critically by Gayle Rubin as a 'fallacy of misplaced scale' [Rubin 1984: 278-79]) no doubt help to explain the fact that contemporary questions about biblical views on sex far outweigh questions about biblical views on food, in terms of both the amount and the heat of discussion generated. Sex is a matter about which Christian denominations, for example, argue and threaten to split. Practices associated with food and eating, on the other hand, while still treated with great seriousness within some streams of Judaism or within marginal religious groups such as the Adventists, are often considered by Christians to be trivial matters that can safely be left to individual choice.

Yet one could suggest, not only on the basis of anthropological studies but also on the basis of readings of classical texts (see, e.g., Foucault 1985: 50-52; Nussbaum 1990) and texts from the postbiblical history of Christianity (see, e.g., Grimm 1996; Shaw 1998), that questions about food have often been a matter of much greater concern than they are for many readers of the Bible, at least in the West, at present. Indeed, it has to be recognized that for many people around the world, food—and especially its scarcity—continues to be as significant as, if not more significant than, sex. The fact that more attention is given to sex than to food in much of the contemporary West cannot finally be understood without attention to such realities as global and local inequalities in the distribution of resources. At the same time, I would not want to underestimate the weight given to sexual matters even in contexts where the struggle for daily sustenance is severe. Indeed, there is some cross-cultural evidence which indicates that, in times and places where food is scarce, food supplies can be manipulated in order to gain sexual access (see Counihan 1999: 9).

What I wish to stress here, in any case, is that a preoccupation with sexual matters and a relative lack of concern about food in many contemporary contexts shapes the ways in which certain question—for example, questions about homosexuality—are put to the biblical texts while other questions—for example, questions about food practices and food symbolism—are more often ignored. Rather than simply reversing this emphasis, however, and focusing upon food instead of sex, I prefer to follow the recommendation of Pollock and others that we think about food and sex in terms of their variable but ubiquitous interrelations. Such an approach, which follows a recent trend toward thinking about 'sexuality' in terms of complex relations among disparate phenomena rather than as a single, clearly demarcated area of human behavior and psychology (cf. Stone 2000a), may help us to dislodge many of the assumptions about sexuality that impact our reading of the Bible and structure contemporary debates on the Bible and sexual ethics.

In the present paper, then, I want to experiment with this approach in the context of a reading of the book of Hosea, a biblical text with which I have long sought a palatable relationship. Leaving aside many of the difficulties—sometimes interesting, sometimes less so—that have traditionally vexed academic readers of Hosea, I will focus primarily on issues that arise from the curious conjunction, in this book, of language about food and language about sex.

In order to proceed, however, I will also need to consider the question of gender, since our experiences of both food and sex are often shaped by beliefs and practices having to do with gender. These interrelations among food, sex and gender have been examined in detail in recent years, above all under the impact of feminist scholarship, which has led the way in exploring such topics as the problematic relationship of women to the preparation and consumption of food (see, e.g., Coward 1985; Lawrence 1987; DeVault 1991; Bordo 1993; Malson 1998) or the contested role of sexuality as a source, for women, of both 'pleasure and danger' (Vance 1984). But as crucial as these considerations are for the questions I am raising, I especially want to problematize here the interrelations among food, sex and *manhood*. For those interrelations, I will argue, help to constitute key but troubling components of Hosea's 'theology' in the strict sense of that term as 'speech about God'.

Of course, after more than a decade of compelling feminist and womanist scholarship on Hosea (e.g. Setel 1985; Yee 1992; Frymer-Kensky 1992: 144-52; Weems 1989; 1995; Brenner 1995: 40-241; Sherwood 1996; Exum 1996: 101-28; Bird 1997a: 219-36), one could reasonably object that attention to food, sex and *manhood* in Hosea carries with it the risk of extending the marginalization of women long carried out by both the text and its readers. While I take this objection seriously, my own, rather queer, relation to norms of 'manhood' leads me to agree with those feminist scholars (e.g. Bach 1993: 192-93; Sherwood 1996: 302) who suggest that one important role for male biblical scholars working in the wake of feminism is to analyze critically the ideologies of masculinity constructed by biblical texts and their readers. While such critical analyses have indeed started to make their appearance (see, e.g., Clines 1995: 212-43), my own opinion is that much work remains to be done and that gay male readers of the Bible such as myself may have a particular contribution to make here. Such a contribution need not be seen in opposition either to feminist work on masculinity (e.g. Bordo 1999) or to other feminist goals, for in spite of the important caution put forward by some queer theorists (e.g. Rubin 1984; Sedgwick 1990) about the practice of simply reducing questions of sexuality to questions of gender, any absolute separation of sexuality and gender seems equally flawed (cf. Butler 1994; Spurlin 1998). After all, as Judith Butler has pointed out,

> Precisely because homophobia often operates through the attribution of a damaged, failed, or otherwise abject gender to homosexuals, that is, calling gay men 'feminine' or calling lesbians 'masculine', and because the homophobic terror over performing homosexual acts, where it exists, is often also a terror over losing proper gender ('no longer being a real or proper man' or 'no longer being a real and proper woman'), it seems crucial to retain a theoretical apparatus that will account for how sexuality is regulated through the policing and the shaming of gender (Butler 1993: 238).

I shall return in the final section of this essay to Butler's influential work, which brings together queer questions and feminist questions in an interesting fashion. I cite it here, though, to underscore my belief that feminist projects and queer projects, while not entirely reducible to one another, are likely to remain inextricably intertwined, due in no small part to the fact that both sets of projects have a stake in contesting the adequacy of hegemonic notions of proper gendered behavior—including those notions found in Hosea that I wish to interpret here.

It is important, however, to call into question from the beginning two assumptions that could in my view hinder an analysis of food, sex and manhood in Hosea: first, the assumption that men's relations with food and sex are, in radical distinction from those of many women, simple and uncomplicated; and, second, the assumption that Hosea's—indeed, patriarchy's—notions of manhood are necessarily more coherent or secure than the biblical notions about women which have been so convincingly critiqued by feminist scholarship. I will argue instead, through a somewhat circuitous route, that precisely by using food and sex to 'think' Hosea we can recognize the incoherence and insecurity of the views of both manhood and deity which the book presupposes; and that this recognition can make an important (if admittedly indirect) contribution to the contemporary 'queering' of the biblical texts.

II

In distinction from some biblical books, the book of Hosea refers to food most often in the context of references to agricultural production. These references have long generated questions about the role of agricultural concerns in the religious visions promoted and/or criticized by Hosea. At the same time, Hosea's references to food and drink frequently appear in or near passages in which Hosea's controversial sexual imagery is also utilized. As a consequence, attention to Hosea's references to food and drink can lead quite naturally to questions about Hosea's sexual rhetoric. The combination of language about food and language about sex occurs in ch. 2, for example, where Yhwh explains his motivation for punishing his symbolic wife, Israel, by stating:

> Because their mother was sexually promiscuous, she who conceived them brought about shame. For she said, 'I will go after my lovers; they give me my bread and my water, my wool and my flax, my oil and my drink' (2.7 [English 2.5]).[3]

One of the ways in which Hosea's imagery conjoins language about food and language about sex, then, is through representations such as this one in which, apparently, a sexually unfaithful wife seeks out lovers who give to her gifts of food, drink and agricultural products such as wool and flax.

Now the recognition that this passage and others in Hosea do contain references to both sex and agricultural products plays an important role in one influential theory about the situation in Israel to which Hosea is

---

3.   Except where otherwise noted, translations are my own.

supposed to have been responding. According to this theory, the Israelites of Hosea's day were falling away from a pure devotion to Yhwh into some sort of Canaanite 'fertility religion', either as a way of worshiping Yhwh or as a way of worshiping other gods instead of, or alongside, Yhwh. Within the framework of this reading of Hosea, the concern of the female speaker in 2.7 (English 2.5) for gifts or payments of food, drink and other agricultural products symbolizes the concern of the Israelites for a successful harvest, and the imagery of sexual infidelity used by Hosea was motivated by the cultic sex rites in which the Israelites participated as a way of insuring agricultural success. Indeed, in some versions of this hypothesis (e.g. Wolff 1974) Gomer, the wife of the prophet Hosea,[4] is herself supposed to have been a participant in such cultic sex rituals.

This interpretation of the book of Hosea (which I have admittedly oversimplified here) has recently fallen upon hard times, and with good reason. A growing number of scholars have pointed out that the detailed reconstructions of a Canaanite 'fertility religion' centered around sexual rites actually rest upon a rather flimsy set of arguments. There is, for example, remarkably little reliable evidence for such practices in Israel as 'cultic prostitution', practices that were long considered central to modern reconstructions of 'Canaanite fertility religion' (see Hooks 1985; Oden 1987; Westenholz 1989; Frymer-Kensky 1992: 199-202; Henshaw 1994; Bird 1997b; cf. Stone 1997b).

However, criticism of conventional accounts of 'Canaanite fertility religion', though absolutely necessary in my view, should not lead us to discount altogether the possibility that Hosea's rhetoric is motivated

---

4.   This is a convenient point at which to acknowledge (without solving) a problem of terminology caused by the fact that the name 'Hosea' is conventionally used to refer to several different entities: the prophet Hosea, a character in the book by the same name who is assumed by the language of the book to be the speaker or mediator of the book's oracles; a supposedly 'real' prophet Hosea who may have lived in ancient Israel and whose actual words and deeds, were they available to us, might stand at some greater or lesser distance from the words and deeds of the biblical character; the book that today carries the name of the prophet Hosea; and the actual author (or authors) and/or editors of the book. Although these variable uses of the term 'Hosea' can be confusing, I have not tried here to disentangle the complex issues involved in the confusion. Cf. Lemche 1992 for a provocative discussion of some of the problems. My own interest in this essay lies primarily in the literary text that we have before us and the cultural assumptions with which the text can be read as interacting.

in part by issues that have traditionally been associated with 'fertility'. Such a discounting seems to be partly at work, for example, in the very interesting thesis about Hosea put forward by Alice Keefe (1995). Keefe, who rightly critiques popular ideas about Canaanite fertility cults, argues that Hosea was not concerned principally with either the worship of other gods or the fertility of the land, as commentators have traditionally assumed, but rather with unjust practices of land appropriation associated with the commercialization of agriculture in eighth-century Israel. Prior to this time, according to Keefe, it was the patrilineal family, with its inalienable claim to land, which functioned as the foundational unit in Israelite social and political life. In the opinion of Keefe, the social chaos that accompanied the appropriation of land for commercial agriculture in the eighth century had as one of its features a breakdown in family structures, a breakdown signified by the chaos in Hosea's own family.

Like the older theories of an infiltration into Israel of a Canaanite sex cult, this interpretation of Hosea does account for Hosea's sexual rhetoric (by understanding it as an index of more widespread family disintegration in the eighth century) as well as the book's references to agriculture (and hence to food). It also takes a prophetic book that is somewhat difficult to fit into the popular portrait of the prophets as proponents of social justice and assimilates the book to that portrait by imagining the book to be a protest against unjust land policies—without, however, denying the book's patriarchal orientation. Moreover, the positing of a link in Hosea's time between familial breakdown and a wider social crisis will no doubt seem compelling to many in our contemporary political climate, especially in the United States (where such links are frequently asserted).

In spite of the fact, however, that Keefe calls our attention to possible sociopolitical dimensions of Hosea's rhetoric that are often missed, I am not convinced that one can go as far as Keefe does in disposing of Hosea's interest in either the worship of other gods or so-called 'fertility' concerns. With respect to the former, while some of the references to Israel's metaphorical 'lovers' probably do refer, as Keefe and others suggest, to political alliances rather than other gods, the traditional conclusion that Hosea is also, and perhaps even primarily, worried about the worship of other deities—and in particular the worship of Baal—seems to me inescapable. Keefe manages to downplay this possibility in part by choosing to exclude the third chapter of Hosea from consideration (Keefe 1995: 75-76 n. 2), for the first verse of that chapter tells us explicitly that the people of Israel 'turn to other gods' and it does so—significantly for my purposes here—by referring to both food and sex:

> Yhwh said to me again, 'Go, love a woman who is loved by another and is an adulteress, just as Yhwh loves the Israelites, though they turn to other gods and love raisin cakes' (3.1).

Hosea's concern about the worship of other deities is, in this passage, explicit, and such a concern needs to be integrated into an overall analysis of the book's rhetoric of food and sex more thoroughly than Keefe's thesis allows.

Moreover, while Keefe correctly criticizes the reading of Hosea that understands it to be a polemic against a sex-centered fertility cult, she paradoxically fails to question adequately a stubborn binary opposition which often sustained that reading, specifically, the opposition between the worship of Yhwh and the worship of Baal as two radically distinct types of religion. Yet as Yvonne Sherwood (1996: 207-35) points out in an important discussion, the language of the book of Hosea itself deconstructs the opposition between the worship of Yhwh and the worship of Baal that is so often proclaimed both elsewhere in the text and throughout the commentaries; and it does so in part by attributing to Yhwh characteristics frequently associated with the deities of so-called fertility religion, including Baal himself.

Thus, rather than rejecting fertility concerns altogether as concerns of Hosea, or explaining away apparent references to fertility concerns by arguing that they symbolize other social and political issues, it may be necessary instead to acknowledge that, for Hosea, the religion of Yhwh *is* a sort of 'fertility religion', but one in which fertility is credited to Yhwh rather than Baal. Such an acknowledgment raises difficulties of terminology, to which I return below; but for the moment I simply wish to recall that some of the pragmatic concerns which are generally in mind when the *phrase* 'fertility religion' is deployed— concerns about the production of food through agriculture, for example, as well as concerns about conception and childbirth—are more often associated with male than with female deities in the Northwest Semitic religions. As Jo Ann Hackett points out in her critique of popular rep-resentations of ancient Near Eastern 'fertility goddesses', it is actually male gods such as El and Baal who seem to be most often associated with childbirth and agricultural success among Israel's neighbors (Hackett 1989). Since, as is often acknowledged, biblical representations of the Israelite male deity Yhwh do incorporate features of both El and Baal (see, e.g., Smith 1990; Mettinger 1990), it is not surprising that some of these representations, including passages from Hosea, also attribute success in childbirth and agriculture to Yhwh.

So, for example, in Hos. 9 it is the male god Yhwh who, as part of Israel's punishment, demonstrates control over both reproduction and the successful nurturing of children:

> Ephraim, like a bird their honor will fly away—no birth, no pregnancy, no conception! Even if they bring up children, I will bereave them… Give them, Yhwh—what will you give? Give them a miscarrying womb and dry breasts… Ephraim is stricken, their root is dried up, they will not bear fruit. Even if they give birth, I will kill the precious products of their womb (9.11-12a, 14, 16).

According to these verses, Yhwh controls the bearing of fruit—which is to say, in this particular passage, the production of children. The attribution of such control to Yhwh coheres well with other biblical passages in which Yhwh 'opens' and 'closes' the womb (e.g. Gen. 20.18; 29.31; 30.22 ['God' rather than Yhwh]; 1 Sam. 1.6; Isa. 66.9).

But Yhwh also controls the more literal bearing of fruit; for Yhwh, who gives food to Israel, can punish Israel by preventing agricultural success and withholding food:

> She did not know that I gave her the grain, and the wine, and the oil, and multiplied silver for her, and gold which they made into Baal. Therefore I will turn back and take my grain in its time and my wine in its season, and I will take away my wool and my flax, that were supposed to cover her nakedness… And I will lay waste her vine and her fig tree, about which she said, 'These are my pay, which my lovers have given me'. I will make them a forest, and the beasts of the field will eat them (2.10-11, 14a [English 2.8-9, 12a]).

> For they sow in a wind, and they reap in a whirlwind. Grain without growth, it will not produce flour; if it does produce, foreigners will swallow it (8.7).

> Threshing floor and wine vat will not feed them, and new wine will fail them (9.2).

According to Hosea, then, both the fruit of the womb and the fruit of the earth are given to, or withheld from, Israel by Yhwh. It would appear from such passages that the issue in Hosea is not a conflict between an ethical worship of Yhwh and a fertility-centered Baal cult, as some of the older commentaries would have it; but neither is the issue primarily a critique of unjust land policies, as Keefe argues. The issue in Hosea is rather a contest between two male gods, Baal and Yhwh, both of whom are considered by adherents to be the source of agricultural and reproductive success. Hosea, standing clearly on one side of this conflict, wants to insist that Yhwh is the true provider for Israel, and had been known in this role already at the time of the wilderness wanderings:

> It was I who fed you in the wilderness, in the land of drought. When I fed them, they were satisfied; when they were satisfied, and their heart was proud, therefore they forgot me (13.5-6, NRSV).[5]

The reference to food here may not be a reference to agricultural produce, but its identification of Yhwh as the provider of food for Israel and the one whose food-providing abilities are more powerful than drought is obvious. From Hosea's point of view, those Israelites who worship Baal and thank him for the fruit of the land and the rain which nurtures such fruit sin thereby against the true provider, Yhwh. In this transgression they are encouraged by priests, who thus 'eat the sin of my people' (4.8). This latter verse has sometimes been taken as a reference to the greediness of priests who make haste to devour sin offerings (so Anderson and Freedman 1980: 358) or as a reference to priests who have exchanged the religion of true devotion to Yhwh for a religion of profit and prosperity (so Mays 1969: 70). In context, however, it is more likely in my view that these priests are described as eating 'sin' here precisely because they are eating offerings made to some other god (probably Baal) or gods rather than offerings made to Yhwh. Thus, several verses later eating is placed in parallel with the 'whoring' that clearly symbolizes, for Hosea, the worship of other gods:

---

5. The text here is widely acknowledged to be problematic. NRSV follows the Greek and Syriac in reading 'fed' rather than 'knew' in v. 5 and reconstructs the obscure Hebrew beginning of v. 6. Both moves receive support in the major commentaries (cf. Mays 1969: 173; Wolff 1974: 220; Anderson and Freedman 1980: 634-35). While the NRSV rendering clearly coheres well with my interpretation, I do not believe that the substance of my argument would be affected seriously by a more literal rendering of the Masoretic Text.

> They will eat, but not be satisfied;
> They will be sexually promiscuous, but not increase [i.e. by giving birth];
> Because they abandoned Yhwh to devote themselves to promiscuity
> (4.10-11a).

We see in this passage that eating and its desired result (satisfaction) are placed in parallel to sexual activity and its desired result (production of children). The illicit sexual activity, which I would argue is here as well as elsewhere a symbol for the worship of other gods, is unfruitful because Yhwh, the one who actually provides fruitfulness and fertility, has been forsaken. So also, the hunger of the Israelites will not be satisfied because Yhwh, the one who truly provides food for Israel, has been forsaken.

One of the issues underlying the rhetoric of Hosea, then, is a controversy over which god or gods can really provide, or has really provided, for Israel food that will satisfy. And, given on the one hand the book's use of the symbolism of female heterosexual promiscuity as a way of speaking about the worship of other gods, and on the other hand the book's references and allusions to Baal (e.g. 2.8, 16-17; 13.1), the controversy over provision of food seems to be primarily a conflict between the male gods Yhwh and Baal, characterized respectively as a husband and a male lover, between which Israel (characterized as a woman) must choose.

Now if the Israelites (or at least those whose views are represented in Hosea) associated agricultural success and the provision of food with male rather than female deities, this association may be due not only to the continuity between Israelite religion and some other Northwest Semitic religions but also to the fact that, among humans, too, agricultural success was sometimes more closely associated with men than with women. This association is quite clear in Gen. 3, for example, where it is the man rather than the woman who is condemned to spend his life extracting food from the earth through agricultural labor:

> Cursed is the ground because of you, in toil you will eat of it all the days of your life, and thorns and thistles it will put forth for you, and you will eat the plants of the field. By the sweat of your face you will eat bread until you return to the ground (Gen. 3.17b-19a).

What we have here, of course, is evidence for a *conventional notion* about the division of labor rather than empirical evidence about the *actual* division of labor in ancient Israel. Women in Israel may very well have played a more important role in subsistence activities (including the production of food) than the author of Gen. 3 acknowledges (cf. Meyers 1988: 47-63); and, by extension, there may also have been Israelites who associated food provision primarily with female rather than male deities (cf., e.g., Jer. 44.15-19). Nevertheless, based on the picture we get from Hosea and Genesis, we might conclude that Hosea, by attributing agricultural success ultimately to the male deity Yhwh, simply projects onto that male deity an association between manhood and agricultural labor that was already made, at least in some quarters, at the human level.

III

But how and why does this association between manhood and food provision come to be linked with the notorious sexual imagery that we find in the book of Hosea? With this question we confront more directly the issue of the relationship between food and sex. The question can perhaps be pursued most fruitfully when the book is read in an anthropological frame; for, as we noted earlier, various sorts of interrelations between food and sex have already been the focus of anthropological exploration. Since anthropological readings of Hosea, though rare, are not entirely novel, some of the groundwork for an anthropological framing of Hosea's rhetoric of food and sex has already been put in place.

So for example Gale Yee, in a brief but insightful discussion of Hosea (Yee 1992), suggests that Hosea's sexual rhetoric can plausibly be interpreted in relation to a network of conceptions about gender and prestige known to us from the anthropology of the Mediterranean basin and parts of the Middle East. Such conceptions, often associated (though somewhat simplistically; cf. Herzfeld 1980; Wikan 1984; Lindisfarne 1994) with the phrase 'honor and shame', emphasize among other things the cultural importance to men of the control of female sexuality (see, e.g., Gilmore 1987; Blok 1981; Pitt-Rivers 1977; Peristiany 1966; cf. Stone 1996: 37-49). As a way of insuring their own reputation and status, the paternity of their children, and above all their ability to be (in Michael Herzfeld's telling phrase) 'good at being a man' (Herzfeld 1985: 16), these men must demonstrate their ability to father children and to be absolutely vigilant with respect to both the sexual purity of the women of their household and the sexual intentions of other men. The failure to perform these tasks adequately puts one's manhood at risk, and leaves one open to a sort of symbolic castration in the eyes of others. Thus, as Yee points out, the scenario utilized by Hosea, in which one's wife and the mother of one's children is characterized as sexually promiscuous, represents a horrifying possibility that seems to haunt the men who share these cultural values. Such values are used by Hosea to characterize Yhwh, for Yhwh reacts to the religious infidelity of Israel in much the same way that (Hosea seems to think his audience will assume) an Israelite man would react to the sexual infidelity of his wife (see also Weems 1995).

But as productive as it is to read Hosea in the light of these notions about masculine honor and the control of female sexuality, it has perhaps been insufficiently noted by biblical scholars (including myself) that, in the anthropological literature generally cited in the explication of such notions, the domain of sexuality is only one of several domains in which a man must embody norms—and sometimes conflicting norms—of masculine behavior. Among the other components of a man's ability to demonstrate his skill 'at being a man' we also sometimes find references to the provision of food for one's dependents. Thus David Gilmore, one of the better-known anthropological interpreters of Mediterranean ideologies of manhood, agrees with John Davis that '[t]he ability of a husband to support his wife and children is as important a component of his honour as his control of his wife's sexuality' (Gilmore 1990: 43). Davis himself goes even further, suggesting that the display of economic success, including 'feeding a family', may actually be more important for a man's honor than the widely discussed displays of sexual vigilance (Davis 1977: 77-78). At the very least, a review of the relevant anthropological literature seems to indicate that these two components of male honor—sexual vigilance and the ability to provide—sometimes go together.

Let us suppose, then, that the ability to control sexual access to the women of one's household and the ability to provide food for one's dependents are often interrelated, as Gilmore, Davis and others suggest, in the 'honor and shame' cultures to which Yee directs our attention in her reading of Hosea. What might this tell us about the symbolic significance of attributing the results of one man's provisioning efforts to another man? Would not such misattribution be in some ways parallel to the claim that one's children are really those of another man, and that one has therefore been a cuckold? In both cases, within a certain cluster of cultural assumptions about masculine performance and male honor, a man's skill and success at manhood are at stake. Within the protocols of Mediterranean and Middle Eastern masculinity, both types of questioning demand a 'riposte', to borrow Pierre Bourdieu's term (Bourdieu 1979), which is to say, a response to the challenge that has been brought against one's socially acknowledged 'manliness', a demonstration of one's ability to embody the norms of masculine behavior successfully, and perhaps also a visible punishment of the individual or individuals whose conduct has opened the door for such questioning.

With these considerations in mind we can return to Hosea's rhetoric. As we have already seen, Hosea can be read as indicating that the Israelites (or some portion of them) were thanking Baal rather than Yhwh for their agricultural success. I would argue that Hosea, in response to this perceived misattribution of Yhwh's produce to Baal, ascribes to Yhwh emotions and reactions that were expected from any Israelite male whose produce, whose fruit in the literal sense, was credited to another man. Assuming that a human male would feel compelled, as a point of honor, to respond angrily and assertively to this sort of misattribution of provisioning ability, Hosea attributes just such a response to Yhwh, who (as Yee among others rightly notes) is characterized in Hosea through the projection onto the divine of certain norms and expectations about manhood. The misattribution of agricultural and economic success to other gods such as Baal triggers in Hosea's Yhwh the angry retort, 'She [Israel] did not know that I gave her the grain, the wine, and the oil' (2.10 [English 2.8a]). Such a retort serves a function not altogether dissimilar to the function of that retort made by Bourdieu's Algerian male informants who, playing upon the cultural link between facial hair and virility, insist 'I've got a moustache too' when they want to assert the equivalence of their manliness alongside that of other men (Bourdieu 1979: 100). Both Bourdieu's informants and Hosea's Yhwh are asserting their adequacy in the cultural protocols of manhood. Yhwh's male honor has been challenged by misattribution of his provisions to Baal, and the book of Hosea represents in part Yhwh's riposte.

Let us assume, then, that food provisioning *and* sexual vigilance *do* play a crucial role in the notions of manhood presupposed by Hosea. We can go on to ask whether Hosea's interpretation of Yhwh's anger and judgment as, at least in part, a response to Israelite misattribution of food and other provisions to the rival god Baal did not in fact generate the much more frequently discussed symbolization of Yhwh's relationship with Israel in terms of sexual infidelity and sexual vigilance. In order to see this it is important to recognize that the rhetorical strategies deployed by the book of Hosea rely to a very significant degree on the mobilization of male fears of emasculation, of being feminized. To borrow language used by Butler in a passage I cited earlier, Hosea capitalizes on male 'terror over…no longer being a real and proper man' (Butler 1993: 238). One relatively subtle way in which this mobilization of gender terror works is through the very comparison of God's relationship with the Israelites to the relationship between a man and his wife. As some commentators have noted (e.g. Eilberg-Schwartz 1994), this symbolic structure must itself have produced discomfort among Hosea's largely male audience since it represented that audience as a woman. Hosea further mobilizes male fears of emasculation, however, by utilizing the image of a sexually promiscuous woman, an image that is threatening in part because, within a certain framework of cultural assumptions, control of female sexuality is partially constitutive of manhood.

But in choosing this image, is Hosea simply making use of powerful and shocking rhetoric to communicate the message of covenant faithfulness? I believe the situation is somewhat more complicated than that and can be understood better precisely when we follow Pollock's recommendation to 'think' food and sex together. Yhwh's 'manhood' is first called into question when his Israelite 'wife' attributes agricultural fertility to Yhwh's rival, Baal. It is precisely in order to communicate, to a male audience, the scandal of this situation as well as the assumed need for a harsh divine response that Hosea compares such misattribution to the sexual infidelity of a wife. Hosea's vivid sexual language is largely a rhetorical tool for underscoring symbolically, and in a provocative fashion, the offense that Hosea assumes Yhwh must have felt when Yhwh's gifts of produce were attributed to Baal. Such a rhetorical tool was chosen by Hosea, I suggest, not because of any actual sexual misconduct on the part of the Israelites (male or female), but rather because of the parallel importance of both food provisioning and sexual vigilance to demonstrations that one is 'good at being a man'—or, in this case, good at being a male god.

IV

The possibility, however, that the manhood of Yhwh may be at stake in Hosea's language about food and sex brings us back to, among other complicated issues, the vexing question of 'fertility religion'; for the term 'fertility' tends not to be used primarily in connection with manhood but, rather, in connection with women, female deities and feminized entities such as the earth. Indeed, one compelling criticism made by Keefe against the notion of 'fertility religion' is the long and troubling history of association between that notion and the female body. It is difficult even to use the phrase 'fertility religion' today without calling to mind popular ideas about such phenomena as, for example, 'fertility goddesses'. Given the conceptions and misconceptions that have circulated, and continue to circulate, in connection with the phrase 'fertility religion' (cf. Hackett 1989), perhaps it is better to avoid such terminology altogether as a way of speaking about the worship of Yhwh.

But if we do abandon the phrase 'fertility religion', how are we to talk about the very real concern of biblical texts like Hosea with such issues as food production and childbirth, and link this concern with assumptions about gender and sexuality such as those that I have been utilizing in my analysis thus far? How are we to make clear that the major issue with which Hosea is concerned is not a contest between two different types of religion—one centered on agricultural fertility, and the other on ethics—but rather a contest between two Northwest Semitic male deities, both of whom, we increasingly recognize, were understood to play an active role in the generation of life and the products that sustain it? The problem here is not, in fact, a problem simply of terminology but also of the various conceptual frameworks within which relations are established among gender, sexual activity, reproduction, agricultural production and divinity.

One of the participants in the anthropological discussions of honor and shame, Carol Delaney, may offer us a way to begin to unravel this conceptual tangle when she suggests that 'honor and shame are functions of a specific construction of procreation', by which she means not simply sexual reproduction but a broader set of 'beliefs related to the question of how life comes into being...' (Delaney 1987: 36). As Delaney points out, folk models of procreation dominated by Judaism, Christianity and Islam tend actually to valorize, not so much the fertility of women and the earth (emphasized in so many modern accounts of 'fertility religion'), but rather what she calls 'the primary, creative, engendering role' of males, whether human or divine (Delaney 1991: 11). While the importance of women to the process of child*birth* is empirically obvious, the relative contributions of men and women to the process of *conception* are not. Thus, these contributions are said in some cultures (including some of the so-called 'honor and shame' cultures) to be analogous to the perceived relations between seed and soil. According to the terms of this analogy men plant the seed, in which one already finds the basic substance of life, in women, who as soil are more or less inert vessels in which the seed develops and from which it receives nutrition.

This analogy brings together agricultural production and sexual reproduction, but it does in a way that emphasizes male potency rather than (as reconstructions of 'fertility religion' sometimes imply) female fertility. The network of assumptions undergirding the analogy, already known to us from the ancient world (cf., e.g., DuBois 1988), is in fact referred to by Delaney with the term 'monogenesis'; for the analogy seems to presuppose that only one human parent, the father, is really responsible for the 'genesis' or 'generation' of new life (with the mother serving instead as something like an incubator).

Moreover, Delaney argues that the attribution to men of the primary role in contributing the substance of life is both justified by, and justifies in turn, the belief in a male creator god responsible for the generation and cultivation of life not only among humans but also in the wider cosmos. And, just as human males must water the soil (both literally and figuratively) for which they are responsible, so also the male creator god waters the soil with rain in order to produce the fruit of the field (Delaney 1991: 45). The symbolic associations at work in such language are of course complex, as one can see from the fact that Delaney's informants seem to speak about male contributions to intercourse as *both* seed *and* rain (in distinction from the female contribution of soil). Nevertheless, the effect of such imagery, in relation to both sexual reproduction and agriculture, is to conceptualize the contributions of both human males and divine males in terms of one another in such a fashion that, in Delaney's view, patriarchal beliefs and practices are reinforced.

Delaney goes on to argue for a close association between, on the one hand, the beliefs about gender and procreation that she explicates and, on the other hand, monotheism. Her analysis is itself developed in dialogue with monotheistic cultures, among which she includes ancient Israel; and in fact Delaney has argued more recently and more explicitly that a monogenetic view of procreation is presupposed in the Hebrew Bible (Delaney 1998). Indeed, biblical scholars have themselves sometimes noted the existence of a sort of 'monogenetic' view of procreation in the Hebrew Bible, though Delaney's terminology has not always been used and the view in question has not always been associated with the values of honor and shame as it is in Delaney's analysis (see, e.g., Rashkow 2000: 75-78).

Since, however, the application of the term 'monotheism' to ancient Israel and the Hebrew Bible may be more complex than Delaney's discussion sometimes seems to allow (cf., e.g., Halpern 1987; Smith 1990), it is important to note that there may not be a necessary relationship between monogenesis and monotheism. Marcia Inhorn, for example, has pointed out that versions of monogenesis can already be detected in writings from pharaonic Egypt, writings that clearly do not presuppose a monotheistic framework (Inhorn 1994: 53-55). The crucial dimension of monogenesis is not its (later) link with monotheism, then, but rather the fact that it attributes to male gods (and male humans) the principle role in the generation of life. As Inhorn points out (55), one of the most striking expressions of this attribution is found in those Egyptian myths that refer to masturbation on the part of male gods such as Atum in order to account for the generation of other gods and, finally, of human beings.

In any case, one could imagine from Delaney's own discussion of the ways in which these views play out on the human plane that such views might also be compatible with versions of henotheism or monolatry that involve, not a single male god, but rather an agonistic contest for precedence between two male gods. As Delaney points out, the symbolic understanding of human women as soil, waiting for the sowing of male seed, tends to be accompanied by language about an individual woman as a sort of field. This field, however, has to be protected by its male owner from other males. In order to be certain, as a point of male honor, that his wife bears children who are the product of his own seed, a husband has to put a fence around his field. This language about fencing a field, in Delaney's view, both symbolizes and justifies the segregation of the sexes, the 'vigilance' (Schneider 1971) with which sexual access to a woman is guarded, and the vehemence with which female sexual misconduct is punished. Such vigilance and vehemence result from anxiety about the possibility that children born to a man's wife are actually the result of another man's sowing. In order to insure that the fruit produced in one's field is one's own, one has to assert and guard one's rights as owner (and sower) of the field in question.

And is it not the case that such images circulate through the discourse of Hosea, as Hosea continually reflects upon the contest between Yhwh and Baal? Although the language of 'sowing' and 'reaping', which is used in more than one context in the book of Hosea, can take a human subject (see, e.g., 10.11-14), it also refers to activities carried out by Yhwh. Yhwh tells the prophet to name his firstborn son 'Jezreel', 'God sows', a name which (though not itself Yhwistic) contributes in context to Hosea's argument that Yhwh rather than Baal sows in Israel. Israel's god produces the food that Israel eats, a fact that is driven home at the end of the second chapter:

> And the earth will answer the grain, the wine, and the oil, and they will answer 'Jezreel' ['God sows'], and I will sow her myself in the land (2.24-25a [English 2.22-23a]).

The food staples listed here—grain, wine and oil—make up a conventional set (cf. Mays 1969: 41), appearing together in other texts both biblical and non-biblical, and even elsewhere in the book of Hosea itself, as we have already seen (2.10 [English 2.8]). Significantly for our purposes, this same series of foodstuffs seems to be attributed to Yhwh's rival, Baal, in the Ugaritic Keret text, for in that text it is precisely the scarcity of such staples that will be brought to an end by the arrival of the 'rain of Baal' (Gibson 1977: 98; cf. Wolff 1974: 39). In distinction from such texts, Hosea wants to insist that it is Yhwh who generates these food staples, that it is Yhwh who should be associated with the rain (cf. 6.3; 10.12), and, here in the second chapter, that it is Yhwh who 'sows'. Here as elsewhere, though, Hosea's rhetoric, insisting that Yhwh rather than Baal owns, sows, waters and generates life in the field of Israel, tends to slide from an agricultural to a sexual register. For while translations frequently substitute the personal pronoun 'him' in place of 'her' in 2.25 (English 2.23)—thus NRSV, 'I will sow him'— there is no textual warrant for this substitution. In fact Yhwh 'will sow her', that is, Israel, who thus serves as Yhwh's field in both senses of the term: Israel is Yhwh's land, and Israel is Yhwh's wife.

Jezreel is, of course, the only one of Gomer's three children who is explicitly said (in 1.3) to be born *to Hosea*. When we read about the next two children, by contrast, we are told that Gomer conceives and bears them, but not *to whom* they are born. Although some scholars have indeed understood these children to be born to Hosea (see, e.g., Anderson and Freedman's appeal [1980: 172] to 'the principle of successive abbreviation' in order to justify this interpretation), one could argue instead that the ambiguity of paternity for these last two children communicates what it means, from the point of view articulated in Hosea, for a man to take as wife a 'promiscuous woman' or 'woman of whoredom'. Such women are dreaded in part because their perceived trafficking with other men makes it impossible for any one man to know with certainty that particular children are the result of his sowing rather than another's. The symbolism of sexual promiscuity has of course been chosen by Hosea precisely in order to remind his male readers of this dread and of the appropriate male response—appropriate, that is, within a certain ideological framework—to women who provoke this dread through their behavior. The anxiety experienced by Hosea's readers, condemned by the ambiguity of the text to wonder about the paternity of Gomer's second and third children, therefore reproduces the anxiety of the man—or the god—whose field has no fence.

V

With this experience of anxiety, however, we confront one of the more paradoxical aspects of Hosea's use of cultural norms of manhood to characterize Yhwh. For anxiety is not a characteristic that readers of the Bible are generally inclined to attribute to God. Yet the notions about manhood that are utilized in Hosea's characterization of Yhwh are grounded in a profound sense of anxiety about masculinity. The anger with which a man responds to the implication that he has failed to embody adequately the 'poetics of manhood' (Herzfeld 1985) results from a certain fragility and instability of masculinity as a construct. As Gilmore points out, one has to 'prove' publicly one's manhood 'because it is undermined perpetually by incredulity and suspicion from within and without' (Gilmore 1987: 15). This reference to 'suspicion from within' points to a sort of insecurity about manhood that actually motivates the anxious demonstration of its protocols by male subjects who fear the symbolic castration that results from being exposed as something less than 'real' men. The fervor with which manliness is defended and publicly demonstrated has its roots in 'shared male anxieties about feminization' (Gilmore 1987: 11).

Thus, by characterizing Yhwh in terms of such recurring demonstrations of manhood as the vehement insistence that one is after all an adequate food provider, or the harsh punishment of women suspected of sexual infidelity, Hosea ironically leaves the Yhwh that he constructs open to the charge of revealing through anxious assertion a sort of divine insecurity about Yhwh's ability to be (playing here again on Herzfeld's phrase) 'good at being a male god'. That is, Hosea's rhetoric of food and sex exposes, on the part of Hosea's god, an anxiety about the possibility of symbolic divine castration.

Now Gilmore suggests at one point that extreme forms of such anxiety are especially characteristic of males raised in families from those areas of the Mediterranean basin and the Middle East that have so often served as objects of investigation and interpretation for the anthropologists of honor and shame. The predominant household structure within these areas is, according to Gilmore, often based on a sharp division of female and male spheres that young boys must negotiate in their riteless passage from boyhood to manhood. As Gilmore sees it, the uncertainties of this passage generate a lasting anxiety about its successful completion, which is to say, a lasting anxiety about the successful demonstration of one's manhood (Gilmore 1987: 8-16).

A reader familiar with accounts of sex and gender emerging at the intersection of feminism and queer theory, however, might well wish to place Gilmore's suggestion in a larger frame. If one finds compelling the argument of Judith Butler, for example, that gender is *always* a contingent effect of the 'stylized repetition of acts', and hence *always* subject to destabilization as a result of discontinuities from one repetition to another (Butler 1990: 139-41), then one might well imagine that the anxious assertions of manhood described ethnographically by anthropologists of honor and shame are simply context-specific cases of an insecurity that is inherent (at least as potential) within a great deal of what passes for 'manhood' elsewhere as well—including, perhaps, in the biblical texts.

After all, as Butler points out, gender norms may be demanded by culture but 'the compulsory character of these norms does not always make them efficacious'. Building upon a provocative combination of (among other things) feminism, poststructuralist readings of speech-act theory, and Foucault's theories of power, discourse and sexuality,

Butler argues that the coherence of the 'male/female' binary opposition which undergirds heterosexual relations (and which, I would add, is presupposed by Hosea's gender imagery) is maintained by the compulsory reiteration, citation and consequent materialization of social norms of sex and gender. Just as speech acts rely upon and reaffirm prior sets of sociolinguistic conventions and norms, so also the 'citation' of gender norms both presupposes and reaffirms the norms in question. Yet careful analysis reveals that the coherence of these norms of sex and gender is not total. Just as speech acts can 'misfire' (when, for example, the required context and conditions for a certain type of speech act—say, the 'performative' statement 'I now pronounce you man and wife'—are not met), so also the reiteration of gender norms frequently produces citations in which sex, gender and sexual practice are not, according to the dominant ideologies, aligned consistently. According to Butler, then, gender norms 'are continually haunted by their own inefficacy', and so they are accompanied by an 'anxiously repeated effort to install and augment their jurisdiction' (Butler 1993: 237). The repetition of gender norms seems, in Butler's view, to be closely related to the inherent instability of these norms; and this instability produces anxiety at the site of repetition.

It is therefore important to note that, while the book of Hosea can be seen as an instance (or perhaps a series of instances) of the representation of the stylized citation of gender norms (and I take this to be one way of recasting in Butler's terms the argument of Yee, Weems and others that Hosea makes ample use of audience expectations about appropriate gendered behavior in his characterizations of Israel and Yhwh), nevertheless the book itself is finally unable to sustain a coherent and consistent picture of the manhood that it presupposes and attempts to reproduce. This inability, which is exactly what Butler's view of gender might lead us to expect, manifests itself in several ways in Hosea's text, most of which have been pointed out by others: the hints of maternal imagery for a previously male Yhwh toward the end of the book (cf. Schüngel-Straumann 1995); the striking gender reversal accomplished by the representation of an intended Israelite audience that was composed largely of males as Yhwh's wife—and, hence, as female (cf. Leith 1989; Eilberg-Schwartz 1994); the implication that this wife finds her husband, despite his protestations to the contrary, to be inadequate as provider and/or lover, and so forth.

But among these slips in gender intelligibility, the one I would like to return to in conclusion is the one with which the book opens: the command by Yhwh that Hosea marry a 'woman of whoredom' or 'promiscuous woman' (1.2). Although this image, no doubt chosen in order to shock, is key to the symbolic communication of Hosea's overall message (that Yhwh has chosen a people, Israel, which has continually proven itself incapable of fidelity, as evidenced for example by Israel's tendency to expect Baal rather than Yhwh to supply food), the command to marry such a woman also tends to undermine the book's arguments. As Sherwood has shown, for example, the symbolism of a husband deliberately choosing to marry a whoring woman runs counter to the claim made elsewhere in the book that Israel's relationship with Yhwh, though now adulterated, was once pure (Sherwood 1996: 207-14). Moreover, the fact that Hosea, standing in for Yhwh, marries a woman whose character is already known undermines the force of Yhwh's/Hosea's recurring complaint about Israel's/Gomer's infidelity. As Carole Fontaine puts it, such a complaint ends up 'castigating the woman for the very behavior that caused her to be chosen in the first place' (Fontaine 1995: 63).

For my purposes, however, the intriguing fact about Hosea's/Yhwh's decision to marry a woman/nation whose infidelity is already known in advance is that such a decision may also undermine the divine manhood which, I have argued here, Hosea's rhetoric of food and sex elsewhere presupposes. For if, as Gilmore and others argue, a man is symbolically emasculated when his wife has sexual relations with other men (Gilmore 1987: 10-11; cf. Blok 1981: 431), then Hosea's culturally ascribed manhood—and, to the extent that Hosea symbolizes Yhwh here, Yhwh's culturally ascribed manhood as well—may paradoxically be *surrendered* from the start by virtue of Hosea's informed decision to marry a woman whose (supposed) 'promiscuous' or 'whoring' character is already known. With that decision Hosea/Yhwh actually transgresses in advance, or at least opens the door knowingly for a transgression of, the cultural protocols of masculinity according to which a man should insure the sexual purity before marriage (cf. Deut. 22.13-21) and the sexual fidelity within marriage of the women of his household.

I hasten to add that I would not want my language about the 'surrender' or 'transgression' of manhood to be misunderstood as an apologetic for Hosea's rhetoric of sex and gender. The devastating consequences of many of the gender notions that Hosea presupposes have been well documented by the feminist research on Hosea cited earlier, and I have no intention of minimizing the book's phallocentric norms. But, as we have already seen, Butler alerts us to the fact that the embodiment or materialization of gender norms (even, or especially, phallocentric gender norms) frequently fails to live up to the ideals on which it is based. It may be precisely this failure that offers opportunities for a certain sort of 'queering' of the biblical texts, a queering that works by destabilizing—or, better perhaps, by calling attention to the inevitable instability of—cultural imperatives surrounding gender and sexuality. The identification and proliferation of misalignments among sex, gender and sexual practice has become, in the wake of Butler's work, a goal for many queer theorists, for such misalignments in the 'sex/gender system' (Rubin 1975) represent both weak spots in the heterosexual matrix and openings for a reconfiguration of that matrix. As Butler argues, the 'institution of a compulsory and naturalized heterosexuality requires and regulates gender as a binary relation in which the masculine term is differentiated from a feminine term' (Butler 1990: 22-23). Thus, if such a 'compulsory and naturalized heterosexuality' is to find a secure grounding in the biblical texts (as many contemporary readers already assume it does), it should ideally be able to rely upon a clear and consistent demarcation of masculine characters, divine and human, from their feminine or ambiguously masculine counterparts (cf. Stone 2000b).

To the extent, however, that Hosea's characterization of Yhwh not only relies upon, but also transgresses, particular norms of manhood (such as those surrounding food and sex), the book does expose the inability of masculinities—including divine masculinities—ever to establish themselves over against the 'feminine term' in a consistent and nonproblematic fashion. And precisely this recognition, that even so relentlessly patriarchal a text as Hosea is in the end not entirely successful in constructing a consistent and secure representation of manhood, may allow us to imagine a space for alternative, even queer, scenarios that could involve the surrender, rather than the embrace, of the structures of agonistic masculinity.

THE GIFT OF VOICE, THE GIFT OF TEARS: A QUEER READING OF LAMENTATIONS IN THE CONTEXT OF AIDS

Mona West

In 1996 long-time AIDS activist Eric Rofes wrote a book that sought to speak of the devastation the AIDS epidemic has wrought on the gay community.[1] His opening chapters identify HIV as a mass catastrophe, a catastrophic death event similar to the Holocaust or Hiroshima. He claims,

> the literature that speaks to me these days is the literature of natural disasters and human atrocities... I finally had to ask myself what internal changes had brought on this new fascination? Slowly it became apparent that I had been seeking comfort and validation for the pain currently suffered by the gay community. The mythic scope of disasters spoke to the depth of tragedy in my own life.[2]

Rofes claims that AIDS is an event without a witness. As was the case with many survivors of the Holocaust, when one is in the middle of the tragedy it is impossible to step outside the event and bear witness to such a terrible atrocity. Yet the Holocaust has also taught us the historical imperative to bear witness to such events. It is only when survivors can bear witness, give testimony, and tell the truth about their tragedy that recovery can begin.[3]

In the remainder of his book, Rofes applies the work of trauma specialist Dr Judith Herman to Queer life and culture in epicenters where the impact of AIDS has been felt most. According to Herman, extreme trauma creates a second self—a traumatized self—and recovery involves reintegrating the traumatized self. There are three stages

1. Eric Rofes, *Reviving the Tribe: Regenerating Gay Men's Sexuality and Culture in the Ongoing Epidemic* (New York: Harrington Park Press, 1996).
2. Rofes, *Reviving the Tribe*, pp. 36-37.
3. Rofes, *Reviving the Tribe*, p. 23.

of recovery from trauma by individuals and communities: (1) the establishment of safety; (2) remembrance and mourning; and (3) reconnection with ordinary life.[4]

The book of Lamentations is trauma literature that describes the mass catastrophe of the destruction of Jerusalem—the epicenter of Jewish life and culture. It is a rare eyewitness account that seeks in its content, language and structure to bear witness—to give voice—not only to the destruction of the city, but to the loss and grief felt by those who were a part of the atrocity. The alphabetic acrostic structure of the book voices grief from A to Z. It is as if each poem seeks to bring literary order out of the chaos of destruction. Shifting voices from singular to plural, male to female, provide opportunities for many voices to be heard. The alternating speaking voices of the poet (1.1-11b; 2.1-10; 3.1-66; 4.1-16), daughter Zion (1.11c-22; 2.11-19) and the community (4.17-22; 5.1-22) produce a narrative movement among the individual poems that describe Jerusalem as a worthless woman, a worthless place, and a worthless community, because of her loss.[5]

In his Anchor Bible commentary on Lamentations, Delbert R. Hillers gives testimony to the importance of the book for any who struggle to express grief:

> Thus Lamentations served the survivors of the catastrophe in the first place as an expression of the almost inexpressible horror and grief they felt. Men (*sic*) live on best after calamity, not by utterly repressing their grief and shock, but by facing it, by measuring its dimensions, by finding some form of words to order and articulate their experience. Lamentations is so complete and honest and eloquent an expression of grief that even centuries after the events which inspired it, it is still able to provide those in mute despair with words to speak.[6]

The poetry of Lamentations provides those in the Queer community who are in 'mute despair' words to order and articulate their experience. These words are a gift of a voice that is an 'honest and eloquent' expression of grief. The poet's cry for comfort (vv. 1.2, 17, 21) and validation (1.9, 11-12, 20; 2.20; 3.48-51; 5.1) provides a voice for

---

4. Rofes, *Reviving the Tribe*, p. 61.

5. Mona West, 'Lamentations', in Watson Mills and Richard Wilson (eds.), *The Mercer Commentary on the Bible* (Macon, GA: Mercer University Press, 1995), pp. 667-72.

6. Delbert R. Hillers, *Lamentations* (AB, 7A; New York: Doubleday, 1972), p. xvi.

people like Rofes who search for literature that speaks to their pain and grief.

The book of Lamentations, like other biblical laments, also gives the Queer community a voice of resistance to suffering. Ken Stone claims that unlike early Christian martyr texts that tend to glorify suffering, the biblical laments resist it, claiming that suffering needs to be allevi-ated.[7] Stone goes on to say that the biblical laments construct a speak-ing subject that not only resists suffering, but resists neatly constructed theologies that do not speak to the reality of the suffering subject. This voice of resistance in the laments, and in the book of Lamentations, often confronts God directly as one who either causes the suffering, or is oblivious to it.[8]

Lamentations gives the Queer community the gift of a voice to speak the unspeakable about AIDS. It is a voice that allows us to describe the totality of the destruction that has been wrought on our physical bodies, our psyches and our communities. It is a voice of remembrance and mourning that allows us to move through the crucial second stage of truth telling in trauma recovery. It is also a voice that resists theologies that do not measure up to our experience, even if that means con-fronting God directly. It is a voice that leads us eventually to the healing gift of tears.

A Voice of Remembrance and Mourning

In 1998 Rofes wrote a follow-up volume on AIDS and the gay commu-nity, claiming that in light of many of the combination drug therapies, AIDS as an epicenter death event in the United States was over. According to Rofes, 'The collective gay community has left the emer-gency state'.[9]

While I agree with some of Rofes's observations about 'post-AIDS identities and cultures', I also believe that there is still much work to do with the Queer community's collective grief around AIDS. In an article on 'Sexual Orientation and Grief', Ron Wilder claims that in the Queer community there is grief at all levels concerning AIDS:

7.   Ken Stone, 'Safer Text: Reading Biblical Laments in the Age of AIDS', *TheolSex* 10 (1999), pp. 16-27 (21).
8.   Stone, 'Safer Text', pp. 24-25.
9.   Eric Rofes, *Dry Bones Breathe: Gay Men Creating Post-AIDS Identities and Cultures* (New York: Harrington Park Press, 1998), p. 15.

The symptoms of loss saturation, grief from multiple losses, in the community closely parallel the impact of grief on individuals. Most symptoms can be attributed to the emotionally and physically draining nature of grief, the lack of acknowledgment and support in the grieving process (disenfranchised grief), and feelings of helplessness, rage, and survivor guilt.[10]

The second stage of trauma recovery, remembrance and mourning, provides a way for the Queer community to deal with these multiple layers of grief by recounting, in detail, on an individual and communal level, losses due to AIDS.

Combination drug therapies, known as 'the cocktail', have gotten us to that first stage of trauma recovery known as the 'establishment of safety'. We can begin our work of remembrance and mourning, of bearing witness, now that we have the ability to stand outside the trauma. We have reached the 'post' stage of post-traumatic stress disorder.

Remembrance and mourning is a difficult stage of trauma recovery because a traumatized person's or community's natural response is to bury any memory of the experience. Yet the only way to healing from the trauma and reintegrating the traumatized self is to tell the truth about the terrible event.[11] Rofes claims that gay men resist detailing their experiences and instead speak in euphemisms or broad generalities, using 'off-the-cuff remarks and caustic asides over direct and serious testimony'.[12] He goes on to state that 'methods of healing from trauma are predicated upon self-examination and revelation. Casual references do not have the healing potential of full disclosure.'[13]

In the quotes that follow, Rofes recounts a visit to New York City which led him to realize the loss of physical structures of gay male life due to AIDS, the loss of pre-AIDS gay male sexual identity, and the geographic displacement of many because of the disease:

> Without consciousness or planning, I needed to stroll by what had been the Mineshaft, the quintessential gay male sex club of the 1970s. As I stood and stared at the door, tears flowed as I remembered both individual men and the spirit of optimism of the times.

10. Ron E. Wilder, 'Sexual Orientation and Grief', in Kenneth J. Doka and Joyce D. Davidson (eds.), *Living with Grief: Who We Are and How We Grieve* (Philadelphia: Hospice Foundation of America, 1998), pp. 199-206 (201).

11. Rofes, *Reviving the Tribe*, p. 74.

12. Rofes, *Reviving the Tribe*, p. 75.

13. Rofes, *Reviving the Tribe*, p. 75.

More than any other aspect of gay life, the A-bomb of AIDS exploded directly on gay men's sex culture. We have lost an entire series of gay male venues that held an extraordinary symbolic power in our pre-epidemic sexuality and communal culture. This is especially true in epicenter cultures which themselves held incredible meaning for gay men in the 1970s.

The impact of the epidemic on gay male geography, in addition to the elimination of key cultural landmarks, involves a mass confrontation with dislocation, displacement, exile, and repossession.

The geographic repercussions of the epidemic have ranged from lovers abandoning sick lovers, to AIDS widows being dispossessed of their homes because the deceased left no will, to men who felt it necessary after friends died to move to a new part of the country and 'start a new life'.[14]

Lamentations 1 gives voice to this remembrance by describing the loss of Jerusalem's status as an epicenter of communal culture:

How lonely sits the city that once was full of people!
How like a widow she has become, she that was great among the nations!
She that was a princess among the provinces has become a vassal.

She weeps bitterly in the night, with tears on her cheeks;
among all her lovers she has no one to comfort her;
all her friends have dealt treacherously with her, they have become her enemies.

Judah has gone into exile with suffering and hard servitude;
she lives among the nations, and finds no resting place;
her pursuers have all overtaken her in the midst of her distress.

The roads to Zion mourn, for no one comes to the festivals;
all her gates are desolate, her priests groan;
her young girls grieve, and her lot is bitter.

Her foes have become the masters, her enemies prosper,
because the Lord has made her suffer for the multitude of her transgressions;
her children have gone away, captives before the foe.

From daughter Zion has departed all her majesty.
Her princes have become like stags that find no pasture;
they fled without strength before the pursuer.

14. Rofes, *Reviving the Tribe*, p. 33.

> Jerusalem remembers, in the days of her affliction and wandering,
> all the precious things that were hers in the days of old (1.1-7a).

In these verses we hear the language of exile and dispossession. The metaphor of widowhood is invoked to describe not only the literal loss of loved ones,[15] but the identity loss of a fully functioning member of the culture.[16] There is also the loss of sexual freedom voiced in v. 6, 'Her princes have become like stags that find no pasture; they fled without strength before the pursuer'. Voice is also given to the loss of the precious things of culture such as physical places of 'festival making' (v. 4).

Chapter 1 of Lamentations allows gay men an explicit voice to describe the loss of the physical structures of gay community life and the 'reversal of fortunes' of many epicenters like New York City and San Francisco, that enjoyed favored status as burgeoning gay communities but became known for their death tolls. The opening verses of Lamentations also give voice to the individual loss of lovers, and the loss of pre-epidemic gay male sexual freedom.

This first chapter also speaks of the bodily shame associated with AIDS (vv. 8-10). In her article on Lamentations in the *Women's Bible Commentary*, Kathleen O'Connor observes that images of a woman's menstruating and naked body are used to describe the shame associated with daughter Zion's losses.[17] She notes that the Hebrew words for 'unclean' and 'mockery' denote the impure ritual status of a menstruating woman. In addition, references to daughter Zion's nakedness indicates 'profound disgrace'.[18] O'Connor concludes that in these images the 'degradation and bodily humiliation' of daughter Zion are clear.[19]

---

15. In speaking of the impact of loss and grief on gay and lesbian people, Wilder claims that while the loss of a life partner is devastating to anyone, for gays and lesbians it also entails the loss of a 'built identity as a gay or lesbian couple' (Wilder, 'Sexual Orientation', p. 201).

16. There were only two ways women were valued in Israelite society: unmarried virgin in the father's house, or child-producing wife in the husband's house. Childless widows had no status in Israelite society.

17. Kathleen O'Connor, 'Lamentations', in Carol A. Newsom and Sharon H. Ringe (eds.), *The Women's Bible Commentary* (Louisville, KY: Westminster/John Knox Press, 1992), pp. 178-82 (180).

18. O'Connor, 'Lamentations', p. 180.

19. O'Connor, 'Lamentations', p. 180.

When gay men who have watched lovers waste away and lose control over their bodily functions hear words like 'all who honored her despised her, for they have seen her nakedness; she herself groans and turns her face away', 'her downfall was appalling', they find a voice to name the shame and degradation they have experienced as the result of such a physically debilitating disease. These images also give voice to the fear and ignorance that surrounds disfiguring illnesses such as AIDS and cancer—fear and ignorance that keep victims of these diseases marginalized because of society's general discomfort and shame around the body.

A Voice of Resistance

Ken Stone has argued that a Queer reading of the biblical laments in the age of AIDS provides a shift from homosexuality as an *object* of biblical discourse (What does the Bible really say about homosexuality?) to homosexuality as a 'legitimate condition of knowledge about the Bible'.[20] This is done in the biblical laments by the construction of a speaking subject who resists suffering and confronts God.[21]

The laments found in the book of Lamentations construct such a speaking subject. In the middle of the poet's description of Jerusalem's losses in ch. 1, we find the direct speech of daughter Zion:

Look, O Lord, and see how worthless I have become.
Is it nothing to you, all who pass by?
Look and see if there is any sorrow like my sorrow, which was brought upon me,
which the Lord inflicted on the day of his fierce anger.

From on high he sent fire; it went deep into my bones;
he spread a net for my feet; he turned me back;
he has left me stunned, faint all day long (1.11c-13).

The language in this lament of daughter Zion confronts God on two levels. Zion demands that God take notice of her suffering, and she accuses God of being the source of her suffering. Images of 'fire deep in the bones' and feeling 'stunned' express the shock of an initial HIV diagnosis.

Daughter Zion resists and confronts again in ch. 2 of Lamentations:

20. Stone, 'Safer Text', p. 19.
21. Stone, 'Safer Text', pp. 21-25.

> Look, O Lord, and consider! To whom have you done this... The young and old are lying on the ground in the streets... You have killed them, slaughtering without mercy (2.20-21).

These verses provide a voice of resistance for the Queer community in the context of AIDS which speaks of the 'unacceptability of such suffering' and calls into question 'any theological discourse that is willing to construct a comforting God while refusing to confront the difficult question of evil'.[22]

This resistance consists of struggling with an honest assessment of one's own participation in the suffering. The reality of the Queer community's struggle with making sense of such mass destruction in the face of AIDS includes asking the hard questions of one's participation in the spread of the disease. Rofes indicates that when gay men engage in the kind of explicit testimony necessary for remembrance and mourning they are often faced with guilt, shame and responsibility around the tragedy of AIDS:

> How have we, individually and collectively, acted responsibly? How have we acted irresponsibly? What factors contributed to our becoming the primary initial vectors of HIV transmission in the United States and how did our community become the site of so much suffering? How has our belief in God been altered and our system of values changed?[23]

Verses such as 'the Lord has made her suffer' (1.5), 'Jerusalem has sinned grievously, so she has become a mockery' (1.8), 'Her uncleanness was in her skirts; she took no thought of her future' (1.9) give voice to these feelings.

However, as Stone cautions, there is quite a difference in reading the biblical laments from the perspective of the suffering subject giving voice to these kinds of questions, and these texts being used against the Queer community to perpetuate the notion that AIDS is God's punishment for homosexual behavior.[24] A major part of the Queer resistance to biblical laments being used in this way, and the resistance to suffering by the speaking subject within the laments themselves, is the challenge of neatly constructed theological systems that do not fit one's experience. Throughout the Bible, laments give voice to the resistance of what has been called the Deuteronomic theology of retributive justice which claims that suffering is always the result of wrong doing.

22. Stone, 'Safer Text', p. 25.
23. Rofes, *Reviving the Tribe*, p.78.
24. Rofes, *Reviving the Tribe*, p.78.

The biblical character Job comes to mind as one whose experience of suffering transcended such a neatly constructed theology. Israel's experience of the Exile, to which Lamentations bears witness, is another example of suffering that not only transcended this theological system, but constructed new theologies in spite of it.[25]

Part of this struggle to make sense of one's suffering by challenging bankrupt theological systems includes confronting God directly with the reality of one's suffering, and even accusing God of participating in the suffering. In language reminiscent of Job, the poet gives voice to this struggle in the third chapter of Lamentations:

> I am one who has seen affliction under the rod of God's wrath… He has made my flesh and my skin waste away… He has walled me about so that I cannot escape… He shot into my vitals the arrows of his quiver… My soul is bereft of peace; I have forgotten what happiness is (3.1, 4, 7, 13, 17).

In the middle of this intense experience of suffering and accusation of God, the poet is interrupted by another voice that almost sounds like one of Job's friends. It is the voice of the Deuteronomic theologian giving pat answers and advice:

> It is good that one should wait quietly for the salvation of the Lord… It is good for one to bear the yoke in youth, to sit alone in silence when the Lord has imposed it… The Lord will not reject forever. Although he causes grief, he will have compassion according to the abundance of his steadfast love; for he does not willingly afflict or grieve anyone… Let us lift up our hearts as well as our hands to God in heaven (3.26, 27, 28, 31, 32, 33, 41).

The suffering subject responds with the voice of resistance to such a neatly constructed theological world view:

> You have wrapped yourself with anger and pursued us, killing without pity; you have wrapped yourself with a cloud so that no prayer can pass through.

> You have made us filth and rubbish among the peoples.

> All our enemies have opened their mouths against us; panic and pitfall have come upon us, devastation and destruction.

---

25. See John Bright, *A History of Israel* (Philadelphia: Westminster Press, 3rd edn, 1981), pp. 343-60. For example, the development of the notion of the suffering servant, the resurrection of the righteous dead, Yahweh's relation to non-Israelite people as their God.

My eyes flow with rivers of tears because of the destruction of my people.

My eyes will flow without ceasing, without respite, until the Lord from heaven looks down and sees (3.43-50).

Lamentations as trauma literature bears witness to what survivors of such atrocities as the Exile, the Holocaust and AIDS have come to know through their experience: courageous confrontation with extreme historical events produces new values and theological systems. These theologies incorporate the experience of suffering rather than deny it, and for many trauma specialists, creation of such a world view is necessary to the victim's emotional survival:

> Rather than teaching trauma survivors ways to attain their pre-trauma levels of denial and numbness, how can we facilitate their integration of their painful new knowledge into a new ethic of compassion, feeling with, struggling with the web of life with which they relate?[26]

Remembrance, mourning and resistance are part of the truth telling about AIDS that is necessary in order to move the traumatized person into the third stage of recovery: reconnection with life. One begins this stage when one is able to see AIDS as an event in the past. The victim is able to see their life apart from the trauma and is able to reclaim their history and feel a sense of renewed hope and energy for engagement with life. This stage allows for a look again into the future.[27]

We see movement toward this stage in the third chapter of Lamentations, with some of the strongest language of hope in the book:

> The thought of my affliction and my homelessness is wormwood and gall! My soul continually thinks of it and is bowed down within me. But this I call to mind, and therefore I have hope: The steadfast love of the Lord never ceases, his mercies never come to an end; they are new every morning; great is your faithfulness. 'The Lord is my portion', says my soul, 'therefore I will hope in him' (3.19-24).

The Gift of Tears

Many of us in the Queer community know that giving voice to remembrance and mourning, as well as resistance, often brings tears of grief and anger. Throughout Lamentations the poet speaks of tears:

26. Rofes, *Reviving the Tribe*, p. 71.
27. Rofes, *Reviving the Tribe*, pp. 80-81.

> My eyes flow with rivers of tears because of the destruction of my people. My eyes will flow without ceasing, without respite, until the Lord from heaven looks down and sees. My eyes cause me grief at the fate of all the young women in my city (3.48-51; see also 1.2, 16; 2.11).

All of us who have grieved know that tears are a double-edged sword. They are necessary for release and healing, yet the thought of shedding them threatens to overwhelm us. Many of us hold back our tears because we believe that if we shed them, we are giving consent to the devastating power that HIV has had over our lives.[28]

The ancient church believed that tears were a gift of the Spirit in the same way that healing, miracles and faith were gifts given for the life of the community. These tears were evidence of a heart punctured by the reality of human sin and suffering and a desire for God. They had a purifying and renewing power that were thought to be an extension of baptism's renewing and creative waters.[29]

The poet of Lamentations tells us that shedding tears is an essential part of bearing witness to the atrocity of AIDS, and they are an essential part of our healing. The language of tears that we find in the book of Lamentations is a gift given for the life of the community. When we gather to view the AIDS quilt, or light candles during World AIDS Day ceremonies, we hear the poet's permission to cry 'rivers of tears because of the destruction of my people'. Our eyes 'flow without ceasing' for lovers, friends, colleagues and entire communities that we have lost to AIDS. The poet's testimony is that we will not be overwhelmed by our tears, but somehow renewed through their release.

Finally, not only is the Queer community recipient of the gift of tears in Lamentations, but our shed tears can become a gift we offer to a world grief-stricken over AIDS. While the Queer community may be at a 'safe place' with regard to the atrocity of AIDS, the phrase 'post-AIDS' does not exist in the global vocabulary of AIDS. There are 16,000 new infections per day and of the people living with HIV around the world, 6 in every 10 adult men, 8 in every 10 adult women, and over 9 of every 10 children infected are in the sub-Saharan region of Africa. In India, 4.5 million people have been hit by the virus and an estimated 1.6 million people are living with HIV/AIDS in Latin

---

28. Rofes, *Reviving the Tribe*, p. 79.
29. Wendy Wright, 'Tears of a Greening Heart', in *Weavings* XV.2 (Nashville: The Upper Room, 2000), pp. 6-14.

America and the Caribbean. In Mexico, AIDS is the third leading cause of death in men between 25 and 34 years of age.[30]

As a community that was one of the first to deal with the devastation of this disease, and as a community that has become acquainted with its grief, Queers in the United States have the unique opportunity to offer our gift of tears to the global community as wounded healers.[31]

30. 1999 statistics published by the AIDS Interfaith Network, Dallas, TX.

31. Henri Nouwen introduced the phrase 'wounded healer'. A wounded healer is one who is called to make his or her own wounds a source of healing for others. Henri Nouwen, *The Wounded Healer: The Ministry in Contemporary Society* (New York: Doubleday, 1979).

REMEMBERING PELOTIT:
A QUEER MIDRASH ON CALLING DOWN FIRE*

Michael Carden

Preamble

This essay is an exploration of the issues of homophobia and interpretation that cluster around the story of Sodom and Gomorrah found
in the book of Genesis. This story seeds and is embedded in a textual
and literary web that is diverse, expanding and politically potent, if not
toxic. As Paul Hallam says, 'There is no Sodom, there are only Sodom
texts' (Hallam 1993: 275). The Christian weavings of this web, in particular, have created an especially potent and toxic ideo-story on which
to base homophobic thought and practice.

What follows is an exercise in reweaving some of the threads of the
Sodom meta-text, both as an exercise in detoxifying its homophobic
application and as a way of confronting some of the other moral issues
implicit in the story. I have taken two texts as representative of the
Christian homophobic tradition. The first, an anonymous medieval
poem known as *Cleanness*, is identified by Elizabeth Keiser as a text
that, through 'its linkage of homophobic wrath and paradisal heterosexual pleasure', anticipates 'the dynamic interaction that modern
feminist theory and queer theory trace between compulsory heterosexuality and the continuation of oppressive features of male-dominant
culture' (Keiser 1997: 3). The second, an evangelical cartoon tract by
Jack Chick titled *Doom Town*, is illustrative of the snuff porn dimensions of contemporary homophobic Christian discourse.

* At the time of writing, a most wonderful (proudly bisexual) man has come
into my life. In an exercise of queer(y)ing biblical texts, I think it most appropriate
to celebrate the joys, the beauties of same-sex love. So I dedicate this essay to
Jason, to acknowledge his importance to me and to express my gratitude for our
lives being able to criss-cross-over and become so connected.

Throughout this essay, I weave around these two homophobic texts (so as to counter and invert them) a variety of additional textual strands, largely from Jewish tradition. This countering and inverting, I want to suggest, exposes different possibilities and patterns in our understanding of Sodom. Although one of the strands that appears here, Ps. 9, might not seem to have an obvious relevance for Sodom and Gomorrah, the sixteenth-century Kabbalist Isaac Luria observed that this psalm could well apply to the story of Sodom (Friedlander 1916: 183).

With some trepidation, I have called this exercise a queer midrash. Trepidation, because I am very conscious of the issues of appropriation involved in a Gentile, like myself, claiming to do midrash *and* using Jewish texts in such an exercise. However, I use the term in the sense captured by Alicia Ostriker when she describes the use of the imagination to yield from ancient tales new meanings to new generations, liberating meanings. As she reminds women:

> The texts plainly beg and implore women to read them as freshly, energetically, passionately—and even playfully—as they have been read by men. 'Turn it and turn it', the rabbis say of Torah, for everything is in it'. Besides, they tell us, God has intended 'all the meanings that He has made us capable of discovering' (Ostriker 1994: xiii).

As for women, so too for queer people; and so what follows below is a queer turning and turning of the many threads that make up the meta-tapestry that is Sodom.[1]

Prelude

…and so where to start; maybe at an ending but it is not a closure for this ending has released streams of malignant trajectories…

Standing upon a mountain top looking upon a broiling plain, erupting fire, belching columns of oily black smoke—constant rain of ashes. Ashes—desolation within, broken hearts, bereavements, shattered

---

1. I began this essay in the fires of bereavement and broken hearts in early 1998. It has incarnated in various drafts since then. In the writing of this draft, I must acknowledge and thank my supervisor, Professor Ed Conrad, and my colleague, Julie Kelso, who have read it and given criticisms, suggestions and affirmations. Thanks must also go to Jason Parker, with whom I bounced around a number of ideas and issues which are the subject of this essay, for his insights and observations.

dreams. My mouth tastes of ashes. Ashes and pain—sulphur screams echo on the mountainsides. Nearby stands Abraham wrestling to bind the beast within. A binding—who caused this?

Below cities smouldering, overturned—Sodom, Gomorrah, Admah and Zeboiim. Zoar remains untouched but abandoned, its people drowned in the boiling sea—fear and madness as the sky split apart possessed them like a herd of swine (*Cleanness* 990-91). Sodom, we all know Sodom, it's inscribed in the language—sodom/y/ite/ist/s—and the language has remembered Gomorrah, a terrible twin. But the other three, who remembers them?

Sodom—the story of the city has become a locus of what Eve Sedgwick describes as Christendom's 'desire that gay people not be' (1993: 164). (For Islam the story has come to represent that same desire, though the city there remains anonymous.) And Sodom's linguistic metonymy has fostered a (misleading) familiarity even though no one reads the story (who reads Bibles nowadays?). Sodom and Gomorrah, they were destroyed for homosexuality, weren't they? Sodom, definitely a poofters' city (and for the medievals Gomorrah was a hotbed of sapphistry [Johansson 1990: 1230]). And if lesbians have Sappho's Lesbos as their lost homeland, small wonder that gay boys want to reclaim Sodom for their nationality (Hallam 1993; O'Donovan 1996).

Looking Back on Sodom...

I am a self-styled sodom/olog/ist. How else for a (marginal Catholic) queer boy Bible scholar to start Bible scholaring? Sodom/olog/y—the study of Sodom's history—is not a study of a geographical or historical entity but rather of a story, its multiform mis/readings, its virulent and its forgotten trajectories. It is one of these forgotten or overlooked trajectories that I will explore in this essay; but, first, a quick tour of Sodom's story for those who have not journeyed there.

Sodom's story is found in the Hebrew Bible's first book, Genesis. The main protagonists are Abraham, Sarah, Abraham's nephew Lot, Lot's wife and daughters, two (or three) angels and, of course, the deity. Abraham and Lot are wanderers in Palestine but separate because of strife between their servants. Lot settles in Sodom, which is portrayed, along with the other cities in the Jordan plain around the Dead Sea, as abundantly rich and prosperous, the plain then being a richly fertile garden (Gen. 13.10). We readers are also told that these cities were wicked but the details of this wickedness are not given.

The main story opens in Gen. 18 with Abraham being visited by the angels and the deity, who promise that Sarah will conceive a son. Two angels then set off for Sodom and the deity tells Abraham that, as the outcry of Sodom's sin is very great, the situation is going to be investigated. If things are as bad as they seem the cities of the plain will be destroyed. Abraham challenges the deity's decision and the deity finally agrees that the cities will be spared if ten just men (women and children don't count) are found there.

Genesis 19 opens with the two angels arriving at Sodom in the evening. Lot is sitting at the city gate and offers these angels hospitality which they reluctantly accept. When they are at Lot's house, all the men of Sodom surround it demanding that the two visitors be brought out so that the mob can rape them. Lot offers his two virgin daughters in place of his guests but the mob rejects this offer. The angels intervene, striking the mob blind. They reveal to Lot who they are and that the cities are to be destroyed. The angels take Lot, his wife and the two virgin daughters out of the city at dawn (Lot also has sons-in-law who refuse to believe the warning and stay behind). As they flee the city, the deity rains down fire and brimstone upon the cities (save Zoar because Lot wants to shelter there). Lot's wife looks back on the destruction of Sodom and is turned into a pillar of salt. Lot and his daughters then flee into the mountains. The daughters believe that the whole world has been destroyed and so, to preserve the human race, they get their father drunk and rape him. Both daughters become pregnant with sons who are eponymous forefathers of the Moabites and Ammonites.

It is the attempted rape of the angels by the men of Sodom which has led Christians (and Muslims) to associate the fate of the cities with (male/male especially) homo-eros. Homophobic fundamentalists conflate consensual same-sex eros and the violence of rape. However, Judaism has sometimes read the story differently. Not homo-sex, but xenophobia, and abuse of outsiders and the poor have, for Judaism, been the sins of Sodom *par excellence*. And I have argued elsewhere, using Mediterranean/Middle Eastern anthropology, that male rape in the story should be read as an act of homophobic violence. Male rape of outsiders relieves the homosexual panic of the insiders, reinforcing their heterosexuality (honour) and inscribing the queer as outsider and the outsider as queer (Carden 1999). That article was an exercise to 'detox' the story of Sodom, as a locus of homophobia, from the perspective of the guest. But what about detoxing from the perspective of the daughter?

Rebellious Daughters…

'The outcry of Sodom and Gomorrah…her cry that has come to me' (Gen. 18.20-21). Jewish tradition presents some very interesting stories to explain more exactly what triggers the deity to investigate Sodom. *Genesis Rabbah*, for example, identifies this trigger as the execution of a young woman of Sodom who is burnt to death for giving food to another young woman who was poor (*Gen. R.* 49.6.3). Similarly, the Babylonian Talmud (*Sanh.* 109b) relates the incident of a young woman from Admah who is caught feeding a beggar (feeding or helping beggars or travellers being a crime in these cities). She is smeared with honey and hung from the city walls so that swarms of bees flock to her and sting her to death.

But it is the ninth-century rabbinic text the *Pirke de Rabbi Eliezer* that articulates a most graphic account of the execution of a rebellious daughter. She is not anonymous but is given a name, Paltit or Pelotit. Seeing a poor man begging in the street she is moved by his situation and smuggles food to him every day. The men of Sodom, wondering how the beggar can stay alive, investigate the situation. Pelotit's actions are uncovered and she is arrested, brought to trial and sentenced to death by fire. As she is led away to her death, she cries out, 'Sovereign of all the worlds! Maintain my right and my cause (at the hands of the men) of Sodom' (Friedlander 1916: 183).

> For you have maintained my just cause;
> you have sat on the throne giving righteous judgment…
> The LORD is a stronghold for the oppressed,
> a stronghold in times of trouble.
> And those who know your name put their trust in you,
> for you, O LORD, have not forsaken those who seek you…
> For he who avenges blood is mindful of them;
> he does not forget the cry of the afflicted (Ps. 9.4, 9-10, 12).

In Jewish tradition, the deity responds to the death cries of all these women, and this moment of decision is graphically portrayed in *Pirke de Rabbi Eliezer*. The deity decides to go down to Sodom to determine whether these things have been done to Pelotit. If so, the deity resolves to turn Sodom's 'foundations upwards, and the surface…shall be turned downwards…' (Friedlander 1916: 183).

I can't put these rebellious daughters out of my mind. Judith Antonelli refers to them as 'sister rebels' (Antonelli 1997: 43), a phrase which evokes the imagery of sisterhood and underground networks. I am reminded of those secret societies of women in southern China, who resisted marriage and formed strong bonds among themselves and who, in pre-Communist China, organized women's strikes in the silk mills (Rich 1993: 240). The images also call to mind Bernadette Brooten's study (1996) of female homoeroticism in the ancient Mediterranean world where it was seen as especially monstrous and unnatural. There were, however, counter-cultural trends in this world, especially in Helleno-Roman Egypt where evidence of female homoerotic love magic and woman/woman marriage has been found.

As I read Sodom and Gomorrah as hotbeds of patriarchy and homophobia I can't help but read these rabbinic tales of rebellious daughters and ask: Is it too much to imagine an underground sorority of tribades, frictrices, lesbians in the cities of the plain who are in ongoing conflict with the laws of their fathers? And, being a poofter myself, I think I'm justified in imagining a fraternity of fairies standing beside their dyke sisters.

Following Sodom's doom, Abraham will attempt to sacrifice his son, Isaac, 'withdrawn, haunted by the shadows in his mother's tent' (Zornberg 1996: 139; cf. Gen. 24.67). The bindings of Isaac ben Abraham and Seila bat Jephthah remind us that the Hebrew Bible is redolent of 'cinders...suggesting the sacrificial burning of children' (Linafelt and Beal 1995: 29). It is this image of child sacrifice that I want to pursue here because Pelotit, in Jewish tradition, is Lot's other daughter. Jewish tradition (unlike Christian) has consistently condemned Lot for offering his two virgin daughters to the mob. One of the more friendly commentators on Lot, Ramban, has this to say:

> From the praise of this man Lot we have come to his disgrace...he is ready to appease the men of the city by abandoning his daughters to prostitution. This bespeaks nothing but an evil heart for it shows that the matter of prostitution of women was not repugnant to him, and that in his opinion he would not be doing such great injustice to his daughters (Nahmanides 1971: 251).

Curiously, the *Cleanness* poet uses approvingly the same image of Lot as a pander or a pimp, eager to sacrifice his daughters to promote heteronormativity:

> I shall teach you a better device in accordance with nature. I have a treasure in my house, my two lovely daughters, who are virgins up to now, unspoiled by any men... They are fully grown, ripe and ready for men; it is a better pleasure to join naturally with them. I shall hand these

two lively attractive girls over to you, and you can play with them as you like... (865-72).

The *Cleanness* poet most graphically and pornographically illustrates how such a sacrifice of virgin daughters is essential to Christian homophobia.

Returning to Pelotit's burning to explore it as a father's sacrifice of his daughter, we find that Jewish tradition also says that Lot was appointed chief justice of Sodom (*Gen. R.* 50.3). This idea comes from the fact that the angels (and the reader) find Lot at the city gates. This rabbinic insight is echoed by Victor Matthews who points out that the 'one site specifically mentioned as a seat of judgement in biblical as well as in ancient Near Eastern texts is the city gate' (Matthews 1987: 25).

So now I offer the image of a father sitting in judgment on his daughter, sentencing her to be burned. As Gen. 19 has shown, Lot is not averse to offering his daughters on the altar of his own agendas. Likewise, long before a rampaging mob besieges his house, Lot offers his daughter, Pelotit, to be burned so as to appease Sodomite legality. In the majority opinion of Jewish tradition, as well, the only reason Lot is saved is on account of his uncle, Abraham, not for any virtue of his own. Furthermore, if the deity has overturned Sodom on account of the murder of Pelotit, is it surprising, then, that when the whole oppressive system is swept away, the rule of the father is reversed and Lot is raped by the two daughters he had himself offered for rape? Is that the real reason Lot is saved? (And let's name those daughters here—Antonelli tells us that the Jewish tradition names them Bechirah and Tsirah [Antonelli 1997: 44, see also Singer 1972]; paltry names, really, for they mean 'older' and 'younger' [cf. Gen. 19.31].)

To develop further this image of parent sacrifice of children I want to subvert a device of *Cleanness*. The *Cleanness* poet likens the generation of the Flood to the people of Sodom and Gomorrah to promote a homophobic agenda (Keiser 1997: 42). I will follow his example, but invert it by drawing on a horrific Jewish image of the Flood generation reported by Avivah Gottlieb Zornberg to illuminate my images of both Lot and the people of Sodom for my own anti-homophobic agenda. Citing Rashi, Zornberg recounts that the Flood generation used their many children as bungs to try to block the openings of the deeps thereby attempting to stop the influx of the waters (Zornberg 1996: 57). While the *Cleanness* poet links the two stories to pursue a homophobic objective, I, reading the Sodom story as indictment of homophobia, draw on Zornberg to put this image of the cruelty of the Flood generation beside Sedgwick's observations about the lethal dimensions of contemporary homophobic attitudes:

> I've heard of many people who claim they'd as soon their children were dead as gay. What it took me a long time to believe is that what these people are saying is no more than the truth. They even speak for others too delicate to use the cruel words... Seemingly, this society wants its children to know nothing; wants its queer children to conform or (and this is not a figure of speech) die; and wants not to know that it is getting what it wants (Sedgwick 1993: 2-3).

Therefore it is not a surprise to me that Lot and his fellow judges, men of Sodom, can condemn to death their daughters who, as rebels, must, of course, be queer. And while the *Cleanness* poet links the Deluge and Sodom by understanding them both to be due to homosexuality, Zornberg points out that where the Jewish tradition links the two stories to sexual sin it is not that of same-sex desire. Rather it is the evil of a rapacious sexuality hand in hand with robbery and exploitation and characterized by a lack of kindness, a lack of curiosity, 'that *attentiveness* to the self-made world of others' (Zornberg 1996: 53).

Pelotit's name is derived from the Hebrew root *plt* which can mean 'escape', 'bring to safety', and, in other forms, 'what has survived', 'fugitive/refugee' (Anonymous 1976: 54; Brown, Driver and Briggs 1977: 812). Marcel Proust, in 'Sodome et Gomorrhe', paints a delightful picture of the angels of the Eternal Throne standing by the gates of Sodom to prevent escape. Rather than being sternly efficient they are mercifully inefficient and let go anyone who appears suitably penitent and thus the race of Sodomites 'have established themselves throughout the entire world' (in Hallam 1993: 104). But I also like to imagine that the shade of Pelotit comes on the eve of Sodom's doom and spirits away everyone in those tribadic/fairy sororities/fraternities: something akin to the *Dragonlance* series (it's not necessary to like sci-fi/fantasy to be a Bible scholar but it helps) where the true clerics are spirited away by the gods they serve on the eve of Krynn's great cataclysm (Weis and Hickman 1986). So rather than a site of queer genocide, I can imagine a Sodom and Gomorrah that are doomed for homophobia and become a site of miraculous queer deliverance. And maybe, as in faerie lore of Europe, those dykes and fairies carried off the children of the cities of the plain.

Interlude

Pelotit stands astride the ashes of Sodom like Kali upon the corpse of Siva (Kripal 1998). She cries out in her pain and triumph:

> You have rebuked the nations,
> you have destroyed the wicked;
> you have blotted out their name forever and ever.
> The enemies have vanished in everlasting ruins;
> their cities you have rooted out;
> the very memory of them has perished...
> The nations have sunk in the pit that they made...
> The LORD has made himself known,
> he has executed judgment (Ps. 9.5-6, 15, 16).

Vindication is sweet and the Psalms reverberate with the tones of the vindicated oppressed. Pelotit's murder stands archetypally for all those homohate murders most internationally seared into our consciousness by the murder of Matthew Shepard. (But why, in this 'Great Southern Land', invoke a US experience? Down under, we have our own history of hate crime—drownings in Adelaide's Torrens River, the many homosexual panic murders now legitimated by the High Court [Marr 1999], a near-death bashing of a friend in Brisbane one night in 1993, AIDS Council offices bombed in Townsville in 1999.) Pelotit's triumph recalls Ulrike Bail's observation that, because the experience of violence is an experience of absolute powerlessness, 'from this perspective of powerlessness only the perpetrator's death can bring an end to the violence' (Bail 1998: 256). Friedlander tells us that there is another name for Pelotit in Jewish tradition, Kalah (Friedlander 1916: 183). The root, *klh*, brings with it a suite of meanings including the nouns 'completion', 'complete destruction', 'annihilation', and the verbs 'finished', 'accomplished', 'spent'; a related Assyrian word is *kalu*, 'put an end to' (Brown, Driver and Briggs: 477-78). Black with the fury of her pain, Kalah-Pelotit has called down fire to annihilate the homophobic cities of the plain.

But is it this simple to invert a site of homo-cide into a judgment of homophobia? On the one hand, Connell O'Donovan declares:

> I want that tiny hamlet of Sodom to be Queer Space. And really, it's ours whether we want it or not. Enough of our blood has been spilled in its name to warrant ownership of that land several million times over (O'Donovan 1996).

And John Linscheid throws down a further challenge:

> Do queer theologians, who note the rapacity or inhospitality of the city's inhabitants, unwittingly pitch camp with right-wing theologians who preach Sodom as the homosexual archetype? In both arguments we seek refuge by emphasizing our difference from those who were destroyed. Both theologies arise from our fear of destruction. We must reassure ourselves that the voice is wrong which whispers, 'you too deserve the fire' (Linscheid 1996).

Ezekiel, also, steps forward, saying, 'I will restore their fortunes, the fortunes of Sodom and her daughters… Sodom and her daughters shall return to their former state' (Ezek. 16.53, 55).

Shaking the dust away, Pelotit turns to me smiling and says, 'Embrace the fire? This is just like any other drag act. My fire, like Kali's sword, it's just a prop, a metaphor, so much glitter. Did I kill anyone? No one's got it yet—I rescued every Sodomite who was remotely queer. Just ask my mother.'

Remember Lot's Wife…

There is a site on the net, www.chick.com/tracts, at which Jack Chick has made available all his comic-book-format evangelical tracts. One of these tracts is called *Doom Town*, and in *Doom Town* Chick gives a thoroughly homophobic reading of the Sodom story (Chick 1998). In Chick's Sodom the only women in the city are Lot's wife and daughters, and all the men of Sodom are caricatures of the many looks you might see at, say, the Sydney Gay and Lesbian Mardi Gras Party. Chick, of course, doesn't miss an opportunity to indulge in homophobic demonization and especially utilizes the old libel of child sexual abuse. Page 9 of the tract includes a panel headed 'Even children were not safe from their gross perversions'. Below the heading is a picture of a small, cherubic child naked, pathetically clutching a sheet to itself. In the foreground is a rear view of the head and naked back of a hairy, brutish and overweight male saying to the child, 'It's that time again!' And below is the caption 'God heard the cries of these tortured little ones and took action'. Page 17 of the tract has two panels showing the destruction of Sodom, one of which shows figures burning in the conflagration, while the other shows Abraham looking down over the billowing clouds of smoke. The second panel is captioned 'Abraham watched from a distance as God cremated ALL who had rebelled against him'. As the tract only depicts Lot and his wife and daughters escaping from the city, I presume the 'ALL' who are 'cremated' include the 'tortured little ones' along with their torturers.

I am reminded of Eve Kosofky Sedgwick's insight about the relationship of genocide and omnicide and how this connection is most clearly revealed by homophobia—'the phobic narrative trajectory toward a time after the homosexual is finally inseparable from that toward imagining a time after the human' (Sedgwick 1994: 128). I am also reminded of the pattern for Christendom's other Demon Other, the Jew. Just as the existence of the synagogue challenges the claim of Ecclesia (I can't help but think of the Rowan Atkinson sketch where he plays Satan welcoming the damned to Hell, 'Christians, are you here? Yes, I'm afraid the Jews were right'), so the Jew must always be vilified, persecuted and murdered; and over the centuries 'Jewishness' becomes essentialized as an ontological pathobiology. But then, if there is a biological Jewishness, over the many centuries of forced (and willing) conversions (and didn't Christianity start as a Jewish sect?) who in Christendom is not tainted with biological Jewishness? But not only a biological demonology, Jewishness as pathogen releases a range of cultural toxins—Marxism, Psychology, (Christianity), non-heroic/non-realist art, Jazz (the Jew as Nigger), Rock 'n' Roll (ditto), Internationalism, 'bleeding heart'-ism, decadence and all the fun stuff that can be so disturbing. A spiritual Jewishness that can make one ask like Pilate, 'Am I a Jew?' (a terrifying question for a Nazi). Does it surprise, then, that the Nazi genocidal fantasy can end in a near Götterdämmerung of the Aryan master race? What an unstable category the Aryan really is. (A little voice whispers wondering if there isn't just a trace of lavender to that list of cultural toxins that so threatens to dissolve the Aryan.)

For Jack Chick, the 'tortured little ones' must die with their torturers. There will be no fairy/dyke pied pipers (probably recruitment, after all) or Proustian negligent angels. Like Aryanness in Nazi pathophantasma, heterosexuality is a highly unstable category in Christian fundamentalism. Even a taste of 'sodomy' is enough to destroy it for ever. And it occurs to me that in *Doom Town* the torture of these 'little ones' is equivalent to their 'recruitment' into homosexuality, the great fundamentalist homophobic blood libel. But I also wonder whence come these 'little ones'. Outside of Lot's family, there are no women in Sodom Doom Town and I also realize that the physiognomy of these Sodomites is quite distinct compared to Abraham and Lot. Are these

Sodomites (who are meant to represent us queer folks today) some sort of race apart? Does recruitment/torture involve some strange genetic component, something like the race pollution in Nazi anti-Semitic ideology? So while heterosexuality is unstable, it can remain fixed provided it is protected from the vampirish predations of latter-day sodomites (and why are the Sodomites of *Doom Town* orientalized in comparison to the almost Aryan Abraham and Lot?).

Doom Town illustrates well the universalizing/minoritizing dichotomy identified by Eve Kosofsky Sedgwick in Western homophobic ideology. It is this dichotomy which gives the omnicidal potential to genocidal homophobic fantasy:

> [O]ne of the few areas of agreement among modern Marxist, Nazi and liberal capitalist ideologies is that there is a peculiarly close, though never precisely defined, affinity between same-sex desire and some historical condition of moribundity, called 'decadence', to which not individuals or minorities but whole civilizations are subject. Bloodletting on a scale more massive by orders of magnitude than any gay minority presence in the culture is the 'cure', if cure there be, to the mortal illness of decadence (Sedgwick 1994: 128).

Chick's Sodom provides a means to imaginatively rehearse such massive bloodletting—it is, after all, a piece of snuff porn. Given that Sodom's story is told in Chick's tract as an admonitory tale to the character Sean, a latter-day sodomite, it is clear that this is a rehearsal with more than a degree of anticipatory glee. It is not only the spectacle of a past genocide that is presented but, through this presentation, the promise of a mass extermination to come, in New York City, in San Francisco, in Sydney, in Brisbane, in Ontario, California, in Enid, Oklahoma. Furthermore, the very explicit presentation of same-sex desire and a homosexual world enables a far more personal holocaust to occur. By entering Sodom Doom Town, the reader is invited to unleash the same-sex desire within, to participate vicariously in the revels of Sodom before personally exterminating that inner homosexual; and the reader can come back and do it again and again and again.

Interestingly, *Doom Town* leaves out the fate of both Lot and his wife, whose name in the Jewish tradition is variously Irith, Idith, Edis, Edith. I find the omission of Edith's fate especially telling in terms of Chick's homophobia. I have used Pelotit and her sisters to invert the Sodom holocaust into a judgment on homophobia. And I can use my imagination to envisage, like Proust, a host of refugees from Sodom through Pelotit's intervention. But that Pelotit herself calls down fire shows that the struggle for liberation is not itself without its geno-cidal/omnicidal implications (well illustrated by Stalin's Russia, Mao's China, Pol Pot's Kampuchea). Christians have always given Lot's wife, Edith, a bad press. She is portrayed as a backslider, someone who can-not give up the ways of Sodom (hence her looking back). Her turning to salt is understood by Christians as a punishment for that backsliding.

Irenaeus, however, remains an exception. For him Lot's wife is a salvific figure who

> remained in [the territory of] Sodom, no longer corruptible flesh, but a pillar of salt which endures for ever; and by those natural processes which appertain to the human race, indicating that the church also, which is the salt of the earth, has been left behind within the confines of the earth, and subject to human sufferings; and while entire members are often taken away from it, the pillar of salt endures, thus typifying the foundation of the faith which maketh strong, and sends forward, children to their Father God (*Adv. Haer.* 4.31.3).

Irenaeus links Edith's fate to the gospel saying from the Sermon on the Mount in Mt. 5.13 where Jesus calls his disciples 'salt of the earth'. Thus, rather than being a sign of disgrace, Lot's wife, the pillar of salt, represents the Church constantly enduring in the world. Lot's wife is not dead but is still alive, fertile, because, although a pillar of salt, she still menstruates (this image of saline Edith still alive and menstruating is found more explicitly in Pseudo-Tertullian's 'Strain of Sodom' [169-73]). She represents the Church in her fertility and fecundity and in her being left behind by her children. While for Irenaeus the Church is more important than Edith, because the Church still produces children that 'go on to the Father', it is the image of the fertile, salvific, Sali-nized Edith upon which I wish to focus and which I wish to link with Jewish understandings of her fate.

In Judaism, certainly, there are harsh negative images of Edith but there are also found somewhat different, more positive and sympa-thetic, understandings of her fate. Edith looks back out of compassion, she looks back for her other daughters (remember those sons-in-law) to see if they follow behind. Ellen Frankel has Edith look back 'on all that I left behind—my other daughter's grave, my friends and relatives, my home with its cherished mementos, my childhood—and I wept. And so hot...the brimstone...my flowing tears dried instantly, turning me into a pillar of salt' (Frankel 1996: 26). Rebecca Goldstein utilizes the imagery of the medieval rabbi David Kimhi (Radak), according to which the cities were destroyed by sulphur and salt, the place itself becoming sulphur while the people became pillars of salt. Goldstein portrays Edith turning back to look for her married daughters. Seeing that they do not follow her, she knows only one desire, to be one with her daughters. It was for this desire that she became a pillar of salt 'because God could not forgive her this desire…or because he could' (Goldstein 1995: 12). The medieval Levi ben Gershon, Ralbag, combines the image of Edith's compassion with the notion of her rebellion in a potentially subversive manner. Edith does not look back for her daughters alone but is moved with compassion for the 'hated of God' who lacked the faith to save themselves. Ralbag says that such compassion is sinful and caused her thoughts to cleave to the doomed Sodomites which meant that the punishment cleaved to her as well (Zlotowitz 1986: 707). Although I'm sure it is not Ralbag's intention, Edith's fate here becomes an act of martyrdom, in protest against the genocidal dimensions of the divine vengeance.

In *Doom Town*, however, Chick denies Edith by ignoring her fate. Combining Irenaeus's salvific image with Jewish notions of her rebellious compassion, it's possible to see why. Edith is one point upon which Chick's barque of homo-hatred founders. Perhaps that is also why Chick overlooks not only Edith's fate but also that of Lot himself. For, in opting to remain behind, Edith sets up the situation for Bechirah and Tsirah to rape their father and, by doing so, to initiate the line of the Messiah. The Messiah comes from Sodom and Edith's looking back is a messianic moment. This is the rub that Chick would deny. But, like Anna Akhmatova (and queer theologian John Linscheid), and in distinction from Chick, I will not deny Edith because I see her as a human protest against/judgment upon (warning against invoking?) the genocidal/omnicidal rage of God (the Father?).

Pelotit and Edith thus join hands and a new dimension of the queer vocation opens up.

Postscript

> I was worried, writing this. Too much autobiography? But the more I
> read the commentaries, the more they all seem like autobiographies,
> albeit disguised. Everyone so certain they've been there, seen Sodom
> (Hallam 1993: 84).

I live and grew up in the (curiously named) Australian state of Queensland, long known as the Deep North because of its conservatism, once
firmly entrenched in the 30-plus-year rule of a conservative state
government. Ten years ago, my sexuality made me a criminal in this
state. But ten years ago the conservative government was voted out and
replaced by a moderately reformist Labor party government. By the end
of 1990 homosexuality had been decriminalized. By mid 1992, anti-
discrimination laws had been introduced which outlawed discrimination on the grounds of, among other things, 'lawful sexual conduct'
(with an exception made for education and other areas dealing with
children). However, that Labor government also started spelling out in
law, wherever relevant, the definition of couples or spouses as being of
'opposite sex'.

In 1996, the Labor government lost office to the conservatives, who
made a number of attempts to turn back the clock, most notably in anti-
discrimination law by removing the clauses referring to lawful sexual
conduct. A number of us started a lobbying campaign which was
helped by the fact that the government wished to remove a number of
other areas covered by the Act. We were successful in stopping these
changes. Luckily, through its incompetence and arrogance, the conservative government alienated large sections of the Queensland population and was voted out of office in 1998. A minority Labor government was re-elected which in early 1999 gained a slender majority of
one following a by-election.

The new Labor government set out to introduce a variety of reforms
having to do with industrial relations, domestic violence and *de facto*
relationships. The Labor party had gone to the elections with a policy
of giving same-sex couples legal recognition equivalent to *de facto*
relationships in certain areas of property, custody and powers of
attorney. Needless to say, since they assumed office we have mounted a
continuous lobbying campaign to reverse the discriminatory definition
of partners and couples as being opposite-sex only. In June of 1999, in
a major reform of industrial relations law, the term 'spouse' was

broadened to include a partner of the same as well as the opposite sex, for the purposes of family and carer's leave. In November of 1999 a similar clause was introduced as part of the reform of the state's laws on domestic violence so that same-sex couples now have the same protection under the law as opposite-sex couples. In December 1999, the state government fulfilled its promises regarding the laws covering *de facto* couples. We are optimistic that in 2000 there will be further legal reform to ensure greater equality under the law for non-heterosexual people and same-sex couples and we will be continuing the lobbying efforts of the past.

It has been interesting for me, as someone involved to some extent in those lobbying efforts and as a sodom/olog/ist, to read the record of the Parliamentary debates around these reforms (*Queensland Hansard*, Legislative Assembly, 10/11 June 1999, 12 November 1999, 9 December 1999). Needless to say many Opposition members have proven almost rabid in the tone of their debate. Non-heterosexual people have been vilified as perverse, sick, filth, smut. The government has been accused of undermining the family, morality, Christianity, civilization. The Opposition parties have been particularly outraged because they see these law reforms as moving beyond mere tolerance of same-sex desire towards granting it a state of legitimacy.[2] Some Opposition MPs believe that such legitimacy is tantamount to making same-sex relationships compulsory for everybody! The government and the Labor party were accused of being 'sick' social engineers pandering to left-wing minorities.

The spectre of Sodom has also lurked in these debates. Government members were urged 'to listen to the oracles of God' and threatened with the prospect of Judgment Day. By bringing in such legislation the government was warned that it faced divine condemnation. Government members were threatened with the assertion that Jesus Christ would strike them dead if they passed the legislation. And if this threat were not enough the government was also warned that its actions would generate a community revulsion and outrage. I am pleased to say that, so far, no such outrage has eventuated, there has been no divine intervention, and no government member has been struck dead.[3] I am

2.   On the issue of tolerance, one conservative MP stated that 'those people' are tolerated 'because we have to; if we do not, we are told that we are small-minded'.

3.   In fact, with the final Bill concerning property rights of *de facto* couples, four Opposition members of the moderately conservative Liberal Party crossed the

also pleased to say that, while Sodom's spectre has lurked in the background, poor Sodom has not been named explicitly in these debates. And I hope that as we reclaim more and more our freedom and our dignity, poor Sodom will finally be allowed to rest; rest until awakened and renewed in the time of *Messiah*.

floor during the debate on 9 December to vote with the government to support the inclusion of same-sex couples as well as opposite-sex couples in the definition of a *de facto* relationship.

CRUISING AS METHODOLOGY:
HOMOEROTICISM AND THE SCRIPTURES

Timothy R. Koch

Preface

I am a gay man and therefore my own guiding sensibility is homoerotic; and I write from my experience. While I deeply treasure any
contributions I might make through my work here and elsewhere to
lesbians, bisexuals and transgendered persons—indeed to the human
community at large—the remarks that follow primarily regard the
experiences of gay men, simply because I cannot and do not presume to
speak for anyone else.

Introduction

Lesbians, gay men, bisexuals and transgendered persons (lgbt) continue to hunger for an effective strategy to deal with attacks (both
external and internalized) which are putatively based on a presentation
of anti-homosexual Scriptures. Thus, week in and week out, titles such
as Fr Daniel A. Helminiak's *What the Bible* Really *Says About Homosexuality* and Bishop John S. Spong's *Rescuing the Bible from Fundamentalism* continue to top the list of non-fiction bestsellers in lgbt
markets, demonstrating the need and the desire among us for what
scholarship calls a scriptural hermeneutic.

This paper critiques three of the most dominant hermeneutics
currently employed by gay men (and indeed the lgbt community) to
ward off anti-homosexual attacks, inasmuch as these approaches
actually—and, I believe, unfortunately—perpetuate a posture for us
that locates authority outside of our own, lived experiences. Audre
Lorde, in her incredible manifesto, *Uses of the Erotic: The Erotic as
Power*, warns, 'When we live outside ourselves, and by that I mean on
external directives only, rather than from internal knowledge and

needs, when we live away from those erotic guides from within our selves, then our lives are limited by external and alien forms, and we conform to the needs of a structure that is not based on human need, let alone an individual's' (Lorde 1978).

Following my critiques of the three hermeneutics that I label, respectively, 'The Pissing Contest'; 'Jesus Is My Trump Card'; and 'I Can Fit the Glass Slipper, Too!' I shall lay out some of my own principles of a homoerotic approach to Scripture, which I term *Cruising* (for those who are not familiar with that term, let me describe it obliquely as 'How we homosexuals meet one another in public, when we don't have anything but our wits about us!'), and then present some of the connections that I have scored in perusing the pages of Holy Writ, including that hairy leather-man, Elijah; his sidekick, Elisha, who would *not* be baited!; that boyishly flirtatious military ruler, Jehu; and Ehud the Erotic, whose sexy seduction of a Moabite king delivered Israel.

A homoerotic approach does not in any way require that others be convinced of our experiences, that others be able to 'score' the same connections that we do (which reflects real life, thank you very much!), that others be silenced as to their own experiences, or that others must choose between our approach and someone else's. This approach does not even expect that 'The Bible likes us, it really likes us!' Rather, it is an approach that seeks to integrate and align how we interact with the characters and stories of Scripture with how, as gay men, many of us interact with our world as we make our way toward joy.

The Critiques

Before taking on a critique of these particular hermeneutics employed to deflect hate-based attacks, let me state up-front that in no way do I hold the authors that I am here discussing—Fr Helminiak, Bishop Spong and the Revd Elder Nancy Wilson of the Universal Fellowship of Metropolitan Community Churches (UFMCC)—'responsible' for constructing a hermeneutic for gay men, particularly given that none of them identify as such. What I am critiquing is the adoption, adaptation and/or application of their particular approaches by gay men, or even worse, *on behalf of* gay men.

'The Pissing Contest'
For those whose sensibilities are offended by this particular colloquialism, I apologize. It refers, metaphorically, to one person laying down

an assertion that functions as a challenge, followed by the next person seeking to answer that challenge by a greater, more substantiated assertion, followed either by the first person coming forward again to outdo the second, or by a third person seeking to best the efforts of them both. Like an auction, the Contest continues until, well, no one has anything left to excrete.

The very title of Fr Helminiak's work, *What the Bible* Really *Says about Homosexuality* (with emphasis in the original), is a classic challenge in this Pissing Contest; he is responding to 'some people' (fellow contestants, as it were) who claim that '[t]he Bible condemns homosexuality. It says so in black and white', people who 'impressively back up their case with quotes from the Bible' (Helminiak 1994: 17). Fr Helminiak in turn proceeds to marshal an impressive array of scholarship on 'each of the Bible texts that supposedly talk about homosexuality' (Helminiak 1994: 20) and concludes the following:

> [T]he Bible takes no direct stand on the morality of homogenital acts as such nor on the morality of gay and lesbian relationships. Indeed, the Bible's longest treatment of the matter, in Romans, suggests that in themselves homogenital acts have *no ethical significance whatsoever* (Helminiak 1994: 108, emphasis added).

And of course, this conclusion now invites a response by which either Helminiak's arguments are, or he himself is, disassembled, repudiated, deconstructed and/or superseded by the opposition.

This Pissing Contest is played out again and again where issues of Scripture and homosexuality are concerned. You quote Leviticus; I cite cultural context. You say, 'Romans Chapter 1'; I reach for Fr Helminiak's book. You say, 'God's Word in black and white'; I say, 'But we eat shrimp and other shellfish, don't we?!' You say, 'The Church has *always* taught…'; and I say, 'Read John Boswell' and on and on, *ad infinitum, ad nauseam*.

What is obscured by this back-and-forth wrangling—this Pissing Contest between, on one hand, the open-minded, clear-thinking, humane scholars vs. the flat-earth, hate-mongering closed-minded bigots; or between, on the other hand, the God-fearing, Bible-believing, lovers of truth vs. the arrogant, self-absorbed, immoral sinners with their oh-so-fancy ways of obscuring plain truth in order to hide their degradation—what goes largely unchallenged here is the prize that goes to the ultimate winner: namely, the right to decide what behaviors I as a gay man may or may not 'rightfully' engage in!

Fr Helminiak shows that he is indeed after the same prize as his opponents when, in his concluding chapter, he writes,

> While the Bible makes no blanket condemnation of homogenital acts and even less of homosexuality, this doesn't mean that for lesbians and gay men anything goes. If they rely on the Bible for guidance and inspiration, lesbians and gay men will certainly feel bound by the core moral teachings of the Judeo-Christian tradition: be prayerful, reverence God, respect others, be loving and kind, be forgiving and merciful, be honest and be just. Work for harmony and peace. Stand up for truth. Give of yourself for all that is good, and avoid all that you know to be evil (Helminiak 1994: 108).

Yes, I suppose Helminiak allows a loophole of sorts for those gay men and lesbians who do *not* 'rely on the Bible for guidance and inspiration' but does he not make it sound like the alternative is to be counted among those who are *not* prayerful, reverent of the divine, respectful of others, loving, kind, merciful, peace-loving, truthful and just?!

No wonder these Pissing Contests evoke and consume so much passion on all sides: To the Victor belongs the Spoils of telling all others what codes of conduct they must bind themselves to!

'Jesus Is My Trump Card'

This approach is used widely by well-meaning *Christian* allies who themselves are averse to 'taking sides' in these Pissing Contests. Typically, their study of relevant texts frequently comes out (so to speak) where Bishop Spong does in his two works, *Living in Sin?* and *Rescuing the Bible from Fundamentalism*, with the hermeneutical 'conclusion' that:

> Even if one is a biblical literalist, the biblical references do not build an ironclad case for condemnation [of homosexuality]. If one is not a biblical literalist there is no case at all… (Spong 1988: 154).

This leads to the belief that squabbling about Scripture gets 'all of us' nowhere, and that what is truly important is the 'love of God that was seen in the life of Jesus…a terrifying, barrier-free love that…called for openness, for the death of prejudice… We cannot…escape the power of the fact that Jesus means love… Such love is the very essence of what we mean by God. God is love. Jesus is love. God was in Christ…' (Spong 1991: 238). And this belief flows from 'what we Christians believe to be an ultimate truth—namely, that somehow in and through the person of Jesus of Nazareth the reality of God has become an experience in human history that is universally available' (Spong 1991: 237).

What we have here as a scriptural hermeneutic regarding homosexuality is an 'all cats are gray at night' assessment, followed by the use of the 'Jesus is Love' Trump Card, which, when played, instructs one and all to return to their respective corners and come out loving instead of fighting.

The problems raised by this attempt to collapse debate are legion, and particularly difficult to get at because of the *very* beguiling call, 'Can't we all just get along?' which, however, is buttressed, yet again, with another notion about 'True Christianity' being The Universally Available, Ethically Superior Religion. The argument seems quite simple: Jesus is Love; Jesus said nothing whatsoever about homosexuality; therefore let us stop this arguing and love one another! Simple, yes, but this also means that I as a gay man am only able to enjoy the same 'Trumping' privileges if I am myself a True Christian. And, even should that be the case, beware! The bishop stands ready to explain in some detail the loving, honest, one-on-one committed relationships—grounded first in friendship, deep trust and responsibility—which are the *only circumstances* for Christians where 'sex outside of marriage can be holy and life giving' (Spong 1988: 215).

Funny how, when it's all said and done, it still turns out that the Hermeneutical Victor gets to tell me how to live my life—and have my sex!

'I Can Fit the Glass Slipper, Too!'
The last of the three hermeneutical approaches I am critiquing here is represented by the work of the Revd Elder Nancy Wilson in her passionate and compassionate work, *Our Tribe: Queer Folks, God, Jesus, and the Bible*, in which she seeks to 'out' a number of biblical characters in order to document our (queer) tribe's presence in the pages of Scripture.

The concern I have here is less with the methodology than with the agenda propelling this hermeneutic. Wilson, who cares deeply about the ways in which lesbians and gay men have been hurt by those quoting Scripture, is concerned with 'moving toward a positive lesbian and gay interpretation of the Bible...'; of 'reclaiming the Bible...for us'; of operating from the conviction that '[t]he Bible *must* be a holy text for gays and lesbians, because we are truly human, created by the

God who created heaven and earth' and of acting 'as if we *really have a right to be included*' (Wilson 1995: 84, 75, 111; emphasis original).

This argument, unfortunately, begins to sound a good deal like the argument that, if we search the pages of Scripture, there is a glass slipper that will fit *our* feet, too, and that we, *too*, will get to return to the Ball, for we, *too*, have the right to be there! The danger in this entire approach is actually that which befell Cinderella's stepsisters in *their* own, desperate attempts to fit that magical slipper themselves. If you recall the original story, one cut off her heel to squeeze into the slipper; the other cut off her big toe (both self-maiming and ultimately unsuccessful results). And with this already in mind, it was with a great deal of, shall we say, *discomfort* that I discovered that one main group of biblical characters that Wilson encourages me to squeeze myself into identity with are *eunuchs*! I for one certainly have no desire to cut myself to fit *that* particular slipper![1]

You see, each of these three approaches still grants to the Bible the power to authenticate or authorize human beings, and, with that power, the power to direct *my* behavior and the behavior of others, either in calling me to 'high moral standards' of love and decency (which so often sound strangely like reworked heterosexual norms) or even in calling those who would exclude me now to include me, to make room for me at *their* table.

No. No, indeed. I name the locus of my authority as intrinsic, and do not look to these or any texts to be normative for my life or my ethics. With Audre Lorde, I seek to allow my own deep knowing, my own homoerotic power, to be the light by which I do my reading, thinking, believing. For, as she so eloquently stated, 'when we begin to live from within outward, in touch with the power of the erotic within ourselves, and allowing that power to inform and illuminate our actions upon the world around us, then we begin to be responsible to ourselves in the deepest sense' (Lorde 1978).

---

1.   While Wilson does a compelling job of expanding the definition of eunuch to refer to a larger group of people than those who were physically castrated (Wilson 1995: 120), I nevertheless am quite alarmed by any invitation to see that I 'belong' by virtue of stories and reference to people whose lives were sexually and socially circumscribed.

Instead

Therefore, I propose a scriptural hermeneutic for gay men that moves 'from within outward, in touch with the power of the erotic within ourselves'. This hermeneutic I call Cruising the Scriptures, for cruising *is* the name gay men give to using our own ways of knowing, our own desire for connection, our own savvy and instinct, our own response to what attracts us and compels us. To cruise the Scriptures means to treat these women and men as we would any heterogeneous group, recognizing that there will be some friends, some enemies, a lot who don't care one way or the other (or else don't really 'do anything' for us!)— and a few really hot numbers! For, just as in our social lives, so also here choosing to cruise means taking our own authority and responsibility for following up on whatever comes our way, for it is this which speaks to our own desires. Cruising requires keeping our eyes and ears open, maintaining our awareness that attackers may lurk, recognizing that not all of our efforts will result in anything even remotely resembling success—yet all the while participating actively to create the possibilities of life-enhancing, thrilling contact with these texts!

Cruising the Scriptures, no less than cruising out in the world, involves being open to possibility, paying attention to what catches your own eye, pursuing your curiosity, following up on any promising signals, and simply 'taking it from there'. The goals really are not institutional validation, an external set of directives for life ethics, nor some 'proof' that we, too, can own a piece of the Rock. The *only* real motivations for even taking the time and energy to cruise then are because we want to, because we can, and because it is something we enjoy!

And so it is at this point that I wish to share just a little of the, shall we say, 'fruit' of my own labor, if you can call cruising laborious, and to detail where some of these connections have led me. By using my own sensibilities, my gay erotic knowledge, when coming to biblical texts, I have found that my life—my own scholarship, my own work, my own passion—has been expanded, stretched, and quite frankly and frequently blessed!

Four Scores[2]

1. *Elijah, the Hairy Leather-Man (2 Kgs 1.2-8, KJV)*

> And Ahaziah fell down through a lattice in his upper chamber that was in
> Samaria, and was sick: and he sent messengers, and said unto them, Go,
> enquire of Baal-zebub [lit., 'lord of the flies'] the god of Ekron whether I
> shall recover of this disease. But the angel of the LORD said to Elijah the
> Tishbite, Arise, go up to meet the messengers of the king of Samaria, and
> say unto them, Is it not because there is not a God in Israel, that ye go to
> enquire of Baal-zebub the god of Ekron? Now therefore thus saith the
> LORD, Thou shalt not come down from that bed on which thou art gone
> up, but shalt surely die. And Elijah departed.
>
> And when the messengers turned back unto the king, he said to them,
> Why are ye now turned back? And they said unto him [what Elijah had
> told unto them]. And the king said unto them, What manner of man was
> he which came up to meet you, and told you these words? And they
> answered him, He was an hairy man, and girt with a girdle of leather
> about his loins. And he said, It is Elijah the Tishbite.

Immediately, the following verse is the one that jumped out at me from
this text in the King James Version: 'He was an hairy man, and girt
with a girdle of leather about his loins'. Elijah as a leather man, as a
bear?! Sure it caught my eye, and it sent me to the original Hebrew.
Much to my surprise, where the English translation reads 'an hairy
man', the Hebrew states that the answer to the king's question is that
Elijah was *Ba'al Śēʿār*. Just as the earlier 'Baal-zebub' in the text
means 'Lord of the Flies' so, too, can these words mean 'Lord of the
Goats'—and the leather skins referred to, the ones that are girt around
his loins, are most certainly goatskins!

At this point in my cruising, I felt suddenly as if bells and whistles
were going off all over the place. Elijah as a goat god, wrapped in goat
skins?! Judy Grahn, in *Another Mother Tongue: Gay Words, Gay
Worlds*, devotes an *entire section* to detailing holy homosexuals who,
through history, dressed up in goat skins, channeling goat gods (gods

---

2.   In the section that follows, I have chosen to quote only from standard
biblical texts, readily available at most mall bookstores. This is to avoid any
distracting concerns that I have 'queered' the text through my own, 'special-
interest' translations! Nevertheless, it has been through cruising these standard
translations that I have found cause time and again to go back to the original
Hebrew or Greek, invariably leading me to deeper, more fruitful connections.

who were often thunder gods as well) (Grahn 1984: 95-99). Fascinating (to me, at any rate!)—and only the first of many possible connections I have begun to make with the entire cycle of stories associated with this hoary, hairy prophet!

2. Elisha, Who Would Not Be Baited (2 Kgs 2.23-25, NIV)

> From there, Elisha went up to Bethel. As he was walking along the road, some [male] youths came out of the town and jeered at him. 'Go on up, you baldhead!' they said, 'Go on up, you baldhead!' He turned around, looked at them and called down a curse on them in the name of the LORD. Then two bears came out of the woods and mauled forty-two of the youths. And he went on to Mount Carmel and from there returned to Samaria.

Having come across this passage, which occurs just after Elisha had lost Elijah, his companion and mentor, I immediately felt a chill go down my own back. The scenario felt to me, in my bones, just like a queer-baiting, one where young males go after a lone, supposed homosexual in order to harass and perhaps attack (and sometimes kill) him. It has all the elements: the lone, unmarried male; a deserted street outside of the city limits; young males jeering. And yet, what was this about baldness?!

Reaching for the Hebrew text to discover what this taunt was, I found that the youths were yelling at Elijah: '*ălēh qērēaḥ! 'ălēh qērēaḥ!* which, as it turns out, was essentially a way of telling him to 'Get the hell out of here, you person-who-made-yourself-bald-as-a-sign-of-mourning!' The reference to Elisha's hair-loss, far from being about male-pattern baldness, actually signifies the public sign of mourning that Elisha had made, presumably, on account of his recent loss of Elijah. And the boys were no doubt echoing sentiments they had picked up from their elders, namely: We don't want any of *your* kind around here!

As for the rest of this little tale, well, it certainly gives me the *very* clear sense that it is never acceptable for *any* of God's holy people to be baited!

3. Jehu the Zealous (2 Kgs 10.12-17, RSV)

> Then Jehu set out and went to Samaria. On the way, when he was at Beth-eked of the Shepherds, Jehu met the kinsmen of Ahaziah king of Judah, and he said, 'Who are you?' And they answered, 'We are the kinsmen of Ahaziah, and we came down to visit the royal princes and the

sons of the queen mother'. Jehu said, 'Take them alive'. And they took them alive, and slew them at the pit of Beth-eked, forty-two persons, and he spared none of them.

And when Jehu departed from there, he met Jehonadab the son of Rechab coming to meet him; and he greeted him, and said to him, 'Is your heart true to my heart as mine is to yours?' And Jehonadab answered, 'It is'. Jehu said, 'If it is, give me your hand'. So he gave him his hand. And Jehu took him up with him into the chariot. And he said, 'Come with me, and see my zeal for the LORD'. So he had him ride in his chariot. And when he came to Samaria, he slew all that remained to Ahab in Samaria, till he had wiped them out, according to the word of the LORD which he spoke to Elijah.

Now, in this story, the bloodthirsty, slaughtering he-man Jehu, fresh from the kill, encounters this Jehonadab on the roadside, a man who has purposely come out to meet him. *Seemingly* out of nowhere, Jehu pipes up and asks, 'Is your heart true to my heart, as mine is to yours?' This sounds a whole lot like asking, 'Are you thinking what I'm thinking?!' The answer is YES! and suddenly these men are holding hands and riding together in the chariot. Then, if there weren't enough, Jehu offers to show Jehonadab his 'zeal for the Lord' (what a line!) and commences another wholesale bloodbath. Talk about an ancient Lawrence of Arabia!

4. Ehud the Erotic (Judg. 3.12-26, NRSV)

The Israelites again did what was evil in the sight of the LORD; and the LORD strengthened King Eglon of Moab against Israel, because they had done what was evil in the sight of the LORD. In alliance with the Ammonites and the Amalekites, he went and defeated Israel; and they took possession of the city of palms. So the Israelites served King Eglon of Moab eighteen years.

But when the Israelites cried out to the LORD, the LORD raised up for them a deliverer, Ehud son of Gera, the Benjaminite, a left-handed man. The Israelites sent tribute by him to King Eglon of Moab. Ehud made for himself a sword with two edges, a cubit in length; and he fastened it on his right thigh under his clothes. Then he presented the tribute to King Eglon of Moab. Now Eglon was a very fat man.

When Ehud had finished presenting the tribute, he sent the people who carried the tribute on their way. But he himself turned back at the sculptured stones near Gilgal, and said, 'I have a secret message for you, O king'. So the king said, 'Silence!' and all his attendants went out from his presence.

Ehud came to him, while he was sitting alone in his cool roof chamber, and said, 'I have a message from God for you'. So he rose from his seat.

Then Ehud reached with his left hand, took the sword from his right thigh, and thrust it into Eglon's belly; the hilt also went in after the blade, and the fat closed over the blade, for he did not draw the sword out of his belly; and the dirt came out.

Then Ehud went out into the vestibule, and closed the doors of the roof chamber on him, and locked them. After he had gone, the servants came. When they saw that the doors of the roof chamber were locked, they thought, 'He must be relieving himself [lit., "covering his feet"] in the cool chamber'. So they waited until they were embarrassed. When he still did not open the doors of the roof chamber, they took the key and opened them. There was their lord lying dead on the floor. Ehud escaped while they delayed, and passed beyond the sculptured stones, and escaped to Seirah.

Perhaps the most fascinating story I've come across yet is this one found buried in the third chapter of the book of Judges, and it involves a young Israelite named Ehud. I invite you to read the above passage carefully, with an eye toward the following details:

- What is the significance of Ehud's being *left-handed*? In addition to whatever thoughts we may have today about the 'artistic' nature of left-handed men, it is perhaps important to consider how the left hand was and was not generally used in ancient Near Eastern culture, particularly as regards the handling of certain body parts and functions.
- A 'cubit' (roughly eighteen inches) would certainly be an impressive measurement for *anything* found snaking down (okay, okay, 'fastened' to) a young man's right thigh!
- Notice how Ehud has a sense of atmosphere and timing, turning back 'at the sculptured stones' once all the other Israelites had already departed, lingering so as to be able to suggest secrets that he has for the king's ears only. The king, not at all slow on the uptake, demands total privacy from his own attendants, and he and Ehud have the chamber all to themselves.
- What, may I ask, do you actually think that the king believes Ehud to be removing at that point from the folds of his garment, that cubit along his thigh?!

After considering this story, I for one believe that this belongs right alongside the seduction-then-murder-of-the-enemy-leader-for-the-sake-of-Israel tales, alongside those of Jael and Sisera and Judith and Holofernes!

In Conclusion

There are dozen of these gems scattered about and buried in the pages of the Bible.[3] And *of course* I may be convinced of something that leaves you saying, 'No way!' But, really, how many times have you been with a friend in public and had that very same interaction over some guy who walks by and you end up debating whether or not he's gay?! 'I'm sure he is!' 'No way!' 'Look at his walk!' 'Yeah, but look at that wedding ring!' and so forth. The point here is that an approach that we *each* base on our own erotic knowledge allows us *all* to pursue that which catches our eye, which calls to us, which holds out at least the hope of connection and transformation—whether our meeting takes place along a roadside, in a bar, in an Internet chatroom, or in the pages of Holy Scripture.

3.   Among the many passages which have caught my eye as a gay man, in addition to David and Jonathan and Ruth and Naomi, are the stories of a shrewd lesbian merchant (Acts 16.11-15); a very quickly advancing young man (1 Sam. 16.14-23); a raped lesbian sister (Gen. 34.1-7); and a huge number of slaughtered lispers (Judg. 12.4-6).

Part II

RESPONSES

(COR)RESPONDING: A LETTER TO THE EDITOR

Tat-siong Benny Liew

Dear Ken,

Congratulations on the completion of this volume on queer readings of the Hebrew Bible. I still remember our first conversation about the possibilities for such a volume three years ago. For me, the appearance of this volume registers a new chapter in biblical scholars' engagement in what Cornel West calls 'a new cultural politics of difference', as well as our endeavor to make biblical studies interdisciplinary. Queer theory is now part of the repertoire from which biblical scholars can learn and which biblical scholars can employ in our commitment to do the cultural work of biblical studies to help enact social, including sexual, justice.

I do find the word 'queer' an apt description for your volume (that is, 'queer' in the positive sense). First of all, at least a couple of your contributors (Michael Carden; Timothy Koch) 'come out' in writing about their sexual orientation. If the word 'queer' implies (as it often does in queer theory) the transgressing of norms, your volume has transgressed many. There are, for instance, the norm of biblical authority (clearly rejected by Roland Boer and Koch), the norm of tabooed subjects (pederasty as discussed by Ted Jennings; sadomasochism as discussed by Boer and Lori Rowlett), as well as the norm of form within academic writings (particularly Boer [again!] and, to a lesser extent, Carden). (By the way, I am writing you this 'personal' letter rather than a formal academic response essay to intensify this que[e]ry of form, for two reasons: first, when a friend of mine creatively proposed to write an '*Epistle* of the Closet' for one of my current projects, some senior biblical scholars expressed great hesitation about its form; second, matters of sex and sexuality are often evaded or neutralized by an apparent binary opposition between 'private' and 'public'.) If 'queer' is understood as overcoming binary opposites (originated from but not limited to the binary opposition between homosexuality and heterosexuality in lesbian and gay studies), the readings in your volume have bridged not only queer theory and biblical studies, but also (for lack of better terms) 'canonical' and 'non-canonical' resources. Carden, for example, uses various narratives from the Jewish tradition to comment on the Genesis story of Sodom, while Rowlett refers to oratorio and opera performances to talk about the biblical erotic between Samson and Delilah. In addition to covering some of the 'usual suspects' in the Hebrew Bible when it comes to homosexuality (David by Jennings; and Sodom by Carden), your contributors also bring in other (shall we say) 'non-queer' or 'less queer' texts like Lamentations (Mona West) and Ps. 9 (Carden). Finally, your volume brings together (to adapt Eve Kosofsky Sedgwick's terms [1997]) 'suspicious' and 'reparative' readings of the Hebrew Bible. In addition to the 'essays' that clearly challenge biblical authority (Boer; Koch), there are readings that seem ambivalent (Carden; Rowlett; and you) as well as positive (Jennings; M. West) about the material found in the Hebrew Bible.

With these numerous connections and deviations, your volume has (as far as I am concerned) the characteristic of a good collection. More importantly, these connections and deviations avert any essentialization of one, same queer identity, and thus strategically will help thwart any attempt at recuperation on the part of the dominant. Let me, however, talk 'straight' with you (forgive the pun) by offering some que(e)ries of my own. Because of my personal interests and investments, these que(e)ries will mainly focus on your volume's implications for inter-disciplinary biblical interpretation. I should also be clear that while I realize your volume is impressively international (two of your contributors are from Australia [Boer and Carden], and the collection is published in England), my comments and questions will in many ways be limited to the context and contest of US (multi)cultural dynamics. (Indeed, I would argue that the fact of globalization [which is also implied in M. West's essay] does not minimize, but rather maximizes the need for localized analyses.)

You and I have grumbled several times about the fact that current interdisciplinary work on the Bible fails to 'go both ways'. Biblical scholars read and 'borrow' from other disciplines, but our work is seldom read by, say, literary theorists or anthropologists. (I have not thought about this before, but the binary opposition between the concepts of 'influence' and 'intertextuality' that is popular in some literary circles may also be que[e]ried here: interdisciplinary work, as a specific kind of 'intertextuality', is itself not devoid of the anxiety of 'influence'.) I want to venture in this regard a psychoanalytic reading of Boer's psychoanalytically loaded 'essay' in your volume, and read it as a parable for interdisciplinary biblical studies. Of all the Freudian texts cited by Boer, one that is not cited but fundamentally structures Boer's piece is Freud's (1959) *Group Psychology and the Analysis of Ego*. Boer paints an almost 'return-to-Eden'-like vision where Yhwh sits together with a small number of men in a homosocial bonding process of mutual discourse. Their discourse on sadomasochism and the Bible becomes, in other words, Freud's 'leader' or the 'common object' that brings about the replacement of ego ideal, and thus the mutual identification of ego among group members. This fraternal connection or homoerotic 'paradise' (given Boer's erotic vocabulary) is, however, not without its own tensions and divisions. Yhwh, the initiator of this half-camp, half-conference discussion, becomes the investigated by the end; the other participants question both Yhwh's reality and identity (in terms of gender as well as sexuality). Moses also appears less than an active and equal participant in this discourse. From the very beginning, he needs special introductions to these other men (all 'theorists' of sadomasochism), and is somewhat 'nonplused' about meeting them (79). During the early part of the discussion, Moses is often puzzled. Since he has a difficult time keeping up with the conversation and identifying with the discourse, his mind—in a classic Freudian mixing of the identificatory and the erotic—often drifts to a kind of (homo)sexual desire for the other discursive partners (84, 89). Unable *to be* involved in the dialogue like the other men, he longs *to have* them ([homo]sexually). Despite occasional 'hint[s] of understanding' (95; see also 92, 97, 100-103) in the middle of the dialogue, Boer is clear that Moses ends up resigning and sighing in bewilderment (104).

How can one psychoanalyze this story of psychoanalysis and the Bible in light of the current scene within interdisciplinary biblical interpretation? Since Yhwh's 'reality' is in doubt according to Boer, I suggest that Moses is the lone biblical character who also represents biblical scholars (including, of course, Boer himself). Moses' confusion can then be understood as Boer's loathing of other biblical scholars' lack of knowledge (about psychoanalytic and queer theory), as well as Boer's self-loathing for his own lack of acknowledgment (by non-biblical cultural theorists). Note in this regard how Boer describes Moses in the beginning as someone who likes his tea 'unadulterated' and pure without sugar and milk (76), and who has a propensity for jealousy (78). In other words, Moses is partly Boer's alter ego (Boer has already shown us with the case of Yhwh that identity instability is something to look out for). In accordance with the Freudian paradox that affection and aggression coexist in identification as well as the Freudian response to unrequited love, Boer avenges this lack of acknowledgment by having Moses (along with Yhwh) whip these 'cliquish insiders' as the latter engage among themselves in (homosexual) intercourse as an interlude to a (homoerotic) discourse (86). Again, just as Freud suggests that the failure of intersubjective (homosocial) bonding would result in intrapsychic narcissism, we find Boer making several tacit referrals to his own work (91, 95, 104).

Boer's 'essay' demonstrates then not only sadomasochism in the Bible, but also the sadomasochism of an interdisciplinary biblical scholar. (Doesn't Rowlett insinuate that reading [the Deuteronomistic Historian] is itself a sadomasochistic play?) As those being whipped have suggested, Boer's sadistic whipping of them through Moses is inseparable from Boer's masochistic torment. Boer is angry with these men, but at the same time he has so thoroughly identified himself with these same men that he can literally become their ventriloquized voice. Boer's essay in particular, and your volume in general, confirm for me that if we ever hope to destabilize or change this 'top-and-bottom' arrangement in our so-called 'interdisciplinary' studies of the Bible, we must stop identifying with this discourse on 'theory' to the point of idealization or idolization. To be honest, this identification has resulted in the derivative tendency of much interdisciplinary biblical studies today, which, in turn, leads to this 'inequity' across disciplinary lines. We use queer theory to cultivate our sensibilities and then apply what is applicable to challenge 'conventional' readings of Scripture, yet we seldom challenge any conceptual emphasis that we find in a prevailing theory. What I am suggesting is that, as biblical scholars, we must not only read the Bible with the help of queer theory, but we must also use our reading of the Bible to interrogate, or even transform queer theory. We must no longer simply affirm what Sedgwick or David Halperin say, but must proceed to question, or at least point to a lacuna or an error that is revealed in our 'applications' of their insights to particular biblical texts. After all, what would entice a Judith Butler or a Michael Warner to read our work if we are just demonstrating over and over again the 'correctness' of their formulations? I trust that you have known me well enough by now to know that I am not advocating some kind of disciplinary warfare or a wielding of biblical authority to 'adjudicate' diverse thoughts. I am talking about what we (including myself first and foremost) must do as a next step to make biblical studies genuinely 'interdisciplinary'.

There is in my view one glaring example in your volume of such a missed opportunity to interrogate the prevailing emphasis of queer theory. Although you are right that 'Hosea's rhetoric...tends to slide from an agricultural to a sexual register' (134) and that questions of sexuality and gender are often intertwined, what you and other contributors to the volume continue to (dis)miss is how various texts elide nation and culture—and thus race and ethnicity—within sexuality and gender. You point out in your essay, after all, that Hosea frames its rhetoric about food and sex within a contest between the (male) fertility God of *Israelites* (Yhwh) and the (male) fertility God of *non-Israelites* (Baal). Likewise, Rowlett states that part of the power dynamics within the sadomasochistic play of Samson and Delilah has to do with the fact that Delilah is a foreign woman (110), but she does not go on to scrutinize the implications of this statement. In addition to what you and Rowlett have observed in the Hebrew Bible, Carden also finds in Jack Chick's 'comic', *Doom Town*, that Sodomites are 'orientalized in comparison to the almost Aryan Abraham and Lot' (163). Carden, however, raises this as a question that he does not bother to answer. Why are these issues of race and ethnicity mentioned in passing rather than que(e)ried in pursuit?

I think this is partly because of the way queer theory, despite its emphasis on queering more than just the norm of heterosexuality, tends to inherit from lesbian and gay studies the centrality of sex and sexuality. According to the editors of the popular *Lesbian and Gay Studies Reader*, for instance:

> [W]e can...describe lesbian/gay studies by saying that it intends to establish the analytical *centrality* of sex and sexuality within many different fields of inquiry, to express and advance the interests of lesbians, bisexuals, and gay men, and to contribute culturally and intellectually to the contemporary lesbian/gay movement (Abelove, Barale and Halperin 1993: xvi; my emphasis).

Similarly, Sedgwick declares:

> *Epistemology of the Closet* is a feminist book mainly in the sense that its
> analyses were produced by someone whose thought has been macro- and
> microscopically infused with feminism over a long period. At the many
> intersections where a distinctively feminist (i.e. gender-centered) and
> a distinctively antihomophobic (i.e. *sexuality-centered*) inquiry have
> seemed to diverge, however, this book has tried consistently to press on
> in the latter direction (1990: 15-16; my emphasis).

Wittingly or unwittingly, this (over)emphasis on center or centrality
has pushed other issues like race and ethnicity to the margins of queer
theory (despite the 'hope' that Teresa de Lauretis expresses in her
seminal essay on queer theory [1991: iii-iv]). As one can see from
Sedgwick's comment, even feminism and issues of gender, which from
my perspective have been (pardon the word) 'essential' to the
beginning of many different forms of que(e)ries, can now appear as
'divergent' within this rhetoric of 'centering'. This neglect of gender is
a problem in, for instance, Boer's piece. As evidenced by (1) the fact
that Boer cites only one woman writer (Annie Sprinkle); and (2) the
way Boer overlooks the women victims in the narratives and lives of
both Sacher-Masoch and Sade, Boer's dependence on Deleuze's concept of 'becoming woman' leads only to the disappearance of women.
(One can further relate this to Boer's depiction of Moses as a sort of
[homo]sexual predator. Leo Bersani has recently suggested that this
stereotypical view, and thus the homophobic fear of the gay man, result
from the projection of some straight men that the gay man will do to
them what straight men are supposed to do to all women of all orienta-
tions [Bersani 1995: 16-17]. Bersani's suggestion makes me wonder if
Moses' response to Yhwh's offer of sugar and milk for his tea, 'I like
mine *straight*, unadulterated' [76; my emphasis], is not a Freudian slip
on Boer's part. One may also wonder how this curious choice of word
['straight'] in a queering piece may relate to Moses' *subsequent*
[homo]sexual desires for the other men. Is Moses dis-oriented in more
than one sense? Is his sexual dis-orientation a result of, or a compensa-
tion for, his discursive dis-orientation? What do all these intimations
imply about Boer's own views on gender, [homo]sexuality, and the
[homo]social bond? There is [to follow your lead and use the language
of food] so much 'food for thought' here that I think my head is
suffering from a severe case of indigestion at the moment.)

The problem of this 'tunnel visioning' on sexuality is perhaps most visible in the essay by Jennings. What appears to link race and gender to sexuality in this highly stimulating essay actually pushes race and gender away into the background. His reference to homosexuality in Japanese culture features only a warrior emphasis that is similar to what he finds in ancient Israelite, ancient Greek and early feudal European culture. In other words, any cultural or racial difference that may be involved in this comparison is flattened out. Likewise, if his extolling of a 'virtue' of (gay) virility seems to undermine the stereotypical identification of 'femininity' with gay men, this disapproving of 'femininity' ends up demeaning women. Since (as you know) our colleague is too good a theologian to be ignorant of his own implied phallocentrism, Jennings attempts to diffuse and dispel 'gender trouble' with a note that he advocates feminist, class (which Gerald West described for me once as the 'most feared' category of the academy) and other readings to complement and challenge his queer reading (51). In contrast to Jennings's suggestion that multiple readings be made to supplement queer reading (which reminds me of a 'benign' form of multiculturalism that functions to assuage rather than address difference), I think queer theory should develop a multifocal reading that attends simultaneously to sexuality, gender, class as well as race and ethnicity. If Sedgwick starts her closet epistemology by arguing that any understanding of modern Western culture without consideration of sexuality is 'not merely incomplete, but damaged' (1990: 1), I would argue here that the same is true of any queer reading of the Hebrew Bible that is not multifocal. Shouldn't we have learned from Kimberle Crenshaw that numerous injuries that take place at *intersections* have gone unreported because of this 'one-thing-at-a-time' rhetoric? And isn't it ironic that for a theory that is supposed to be about the overcoming of 'either-this-or-that' binarisms, queer theory has developed its own rhetoric of mutually exclusive foci?

I am glad that within the volume, other essays (Carden's; Rowlett's; and yours) have made a greater effort to look at the intersection of gender and sexuality, although I am not sure if your non-agonistic masculinity will necessarily bring an end to patriarchy, as shown by Rowlett's brief comment (within her argument for gender flexibility) about the presence of 'all-male cast' and the absence of 'all-female cast' in musical performance. On the other hand, I am thoroughly disappointed that *no* essay makes a 'racy' attempt to look into the question of how sexuality can be racialized or ethnicity can be sexualized, even when the texts under examination (canonical or otherwise) beg for such an investigation. Instead of joining others who have used interdisciplinary studies to push queer theory in this direction in the last couple of years (for example, David L. Eng and Alice Y. Hom through Asian American studies), this que(e)ry of the Hebrew Bible has compromised the potential for reciprocal critique that interdisciplinary work provides.

This neglect of race and ethnicity has not only shortchanged some readings of some texts, it has badly skewed M. West's reading (as well as Eric Rofes's reading, upon which she relies) of AIDS in the US. If M. West would read AIDS as a composite problem of race, class, gender and sexuality, she would not have to appeal to the 'rest' of the world to emphasize the relevance of Lamentations. If M. West would heed the people of color within the US (particularly the Africans and Latinos/Latinas who have, to 'borrow' the nuanced word-play of Lavina Dhingra Shankar and Rajini Srikanth [1998], now become 'a part, yet apart' *within* this country), she would recognize that the 'safety' that she talks about belongs only to a queer community that is incredibly, and for some also invisibly, white.

Talking about invisibility, queer racial minorities are pretty much absent in your volume. They are not represented in either the literary or the political sense of the term. Not only do they not write as contributors, they are not even written about (except for Jennings's short reference to Japan). Although the rainbow flag has long been the symbol of queer pride and diversity, this collection of queer readings erases, in effect, the presence of colored queers. Is their absence in your volume because of a color line within the queer community, a color line within the community of biblical scholars, a divide over sexuality within communities of color, or all of the above? While queer theory has not been particularly keen to address issues of race, racial minorities within the US have been eager to join forces with mainstream media to expunge any appearance of queering in their communities. One only has to remember (to follow up on M. West's essay on AIDS) the incredible amount of resources that were spent to clarify the (homo)sexual 'innocence' of two high-profile minorities associated with HIV/AIDS: Arthur Ashe and Magic Johnson. Daniel Y. Kim has suggested that homophobia within US minority communities is related to a psychic anxiety over their marginal power status that is similar to Boer's and Rowlett's sadomasochism, and thus is an attempt to (over)compensate with an emphasis similar to Jennings's 'virile virtue'. This discussion does not only underscore (yet once more) the importance of multifocal queer readings, it also points to the need for queer readings to remain mindful of and sensitive to institutional(ized) power dynamics. To use the theatrical language made influential in queer (and gender) theory by Butler, performers of queer readings of the Bible must not forget the historical and materialistic specificities implicated in the process of production.

Since I have been talking about the absence of racial minorities in your volume, let me focus on one specific aspect of institutional(ized) power dynamics that is significant to interdisciplinary studies of the Bible: the authorization to write about the Bible. In my opinion, interdisciplinary biblical studies should involve conceptual as well as physical crossings. If we are to use queer theory to read the Bible, we should also 'allow' queer theorists to write about the Bible, particularly for an edited volume of collected essays like yours. Why is it that only people within biblical or theological studies are contributing and responding to this collection? Were people within queer theory but outside of biblical or theological studies invited to participate in this performance? If not, why not? If they were invited but declined to participate, what are some of the possible reasons behind their negative responses? If we do not wrestle seriously with these questions of institutional(ized) power dynamics, the only chance for biblical and non-biblical/non-theological scholars to sit at the same table may be (as Boer illustrates) a phantasmic gathering of our imagination. My concern here is not acknowledgment, but alliance, affinity, or what Antonio Gramsci (1971: 137, 168, 360, 366, 377, 418) calls a 'historical bloc' of 'organic intellectuals' that functions as a counter-hegemonic coalition (the same is true of my emphasis on multifocal queer readings).

If C. West's 'cultural politics of difference' makes interpretation and (socio-political) intervention inseparable, this question of authorization makes us reconsider the meanings of both intervention (now in terms of cross-disciplinary participation) and interpretation. The last issue I want to raise with you in light of your volume is 'interpretation', or what counts as 'good' interdisciplinary biblical interpretation. (Don't worry. I have gotten used to writing *short* emails by now rather than lengthy letters.) While you and M. West stay within a single book of the Hebrew Bible (Hosea and Lamentations respectively), Carden and Koch look at selected episodes of two books (Genesis and Psalms for

Carden; 2 Kings and Judges for Koch). As Rowlett starts with a relationship between two characters in Judges (Samson and Delilah) but eventually extends to the historical context of the Deuteronomistic Historian, Jennings begins with a relationship between two characters in the Deuteronomistic History (Yhwh and David) but ends up touching on almost every book in the Hebrew Bible. And there is of course Boer, who opens with a scene from Exodus, backtracks to Genesis, and fast-forwards to the Gospels and Paul in the Christian New Testament. What seems striking to me is that no 'essay' in your volume follows the traditional practice of looking at just a single pericope or passage of Scripture. Instead, what we find are readings that try to take an entire book into consideration, or readings that are organized around a topic (like sadomasochism). The issue of scope or quantity aside, Hebrew Scripture (in whatever length or range) is also read in diverse ways within your collection: it is closely and fully analyzed by Jennings, you, and M. West; 'cruised' through by Koch; and used as a pre-text provocatively by Boer, Carden and Rowlett. Unlike other contributors who more or less focus on reading the Scripture 'directly', Carden reads the Sodom story of Genesis through a 'history' of Jewish reception and interpretation. (Rowlett also presents a 'history' of musical performance on Samson and Delilah, but she does not look at how different composers or opera directors interpret the biblical narrative. Conversely, one can argue that a 'history' of interpreting sadomasochism [if only by European men] can be found in Boer.)

Given such diversities (as well as the previously mentioned diversity in form), I kept asking myself as I read through your collection of essays how one should evaluate the quality of interdisciplinary biblical studies. In fact, I found myself scratching my head at times wondering what makes interdisciplinary biblical interpretation 'biblical'. Since queer readings are reader-centered (as explicitly stated by Koch and Jennings, but implicitly assumed, I believe, by practically all the other contributors), they (along with other reader-centered interpretations, such as feminist and postcolonial readings) contest and force us to rethink the previously understood measure that biblical interpretation should result in the 'coming out' of a single, definitive original or intended meaning. And since queer readings are interdisciplinary and function as *one* site of sociopolitical resistance, they lead to an expanded and (as we see particularly from Boer, Carden and Rowlett) a somewhat eclectic notion of what constitutes biblical studies. I am glad and excited about all these things, but is there then not a need for us to articulate a different standard of measure (other than the two elements I have identified and argued for above: reciprocal critique and mutual engagement)? Or should we abandon this whole idea of measure as 'naïve objectivity', and thus obsolete and oppressive?

You have written an essay elsewhere about how gay male identity is formed *in* the practice of reading the Bible, or what you call (following Foucault) a 'technology of the self' (Stone 1997a). What you did not consider in that article is the 'other' identity that is also being formed in these interdisciplinary readings of the Bible: that of a biblical scholar. Is, for example, Sedgwick's implication that 'strong [queer] theory' should be coupled with New Critical skills of close readings (1997: 23) valid for us? I guess that this 'technology of the self' (Stone 1997a), like the other forms of technologies that we are more accustomed to talking about, is inevitably incalculable in effect and thus unpredictable in process. Does that mean, however, that *collectively*, we should not attempt some tentative but legible goals and directions as we fashion and refashion both our discipline and identity in our practice of interdisciplinary reading?

I think I should stop now. After all, you gave me a deadline that I have already missed! I look forward to talking more about this. Oh, before I forget, there is one more thing that I look forward to. I look forward to seeing other collections of queer readings that would take us into the New Testament as well as the often obscured and forgotten Apocrypha.

Benny

A GAY MALE ETHICIST'S RESPONSE TO
QUEER READINGS OF THE BIBLE

Daniel T. Spencer

'What are the goals and value of "queer readings" of the Bible?' When Ken Stone first posed this question to me and asked me to write a response to the essays in this volume from the perspective of a gay male Christian ethicist, my initial reactions were curiosity and delight: curiosity to see what new avenues of biblical interpretation queer readings are opening up; delight that such a project is even possible in academia today and has developed enough critical mass for an anthology.

As an openly gay scholar active in both academia and the church, I have long been interested in the broader issue of the Bible and homosexuality as it relates to society and the church. As one of an increasing number of openly queer seminarians seeking ordination in the early 1980s, I turned often to progressive scholarship on the Bible and homosexuality for survival and as a strategy to begin to open up queer spaces in the church and the theological guild. Yet virtually all of that scholarship was 'apologetic' in nature: it sought to offer alternative interpretations of a few dominant biblical texts used historically to justify homophobia and the exclusion and oppression of lesbian and gay Christians (bisexual and transgendered identities and liberation struggles were not yet on the table). In church conferences and in our classes we debated furiously the classic six 'Bible bullets': the Sodom and Gomorrah narrative in Gen. 19, the Levitical purity proscriptions against male homosexual acts in Lev. 18 and 20, the Pauline inclusion of 'catamites' and 'sodomites' in vice lists of people who would not see the kingdom of God in 1 Corinthians and 1 Timothy, and Paul's use of both male and female same-sex behavior in Rom. 1 to illustrate God's response to human idolatry. Queer readings of Scripture—nonapologetic, using the lens of lesbian, gay, bisexual and transgendered experience to shed light on biblical texts—were largely nonexistent or confined to seminary essays and journal entries.

By the end of the 1980s I had returned to Union Theological Seminary in New York to begin work on a doctorate in Christian ethics. A decade of trying to work in the church as an openly gay man had convinced me of the need to move beyond apologetic approaches to the Bible. I was determined to delve more deeply into biblical hermeneutics in order to examine the relationship of the biblical texts to ethics. For my doctoral exam in biblical ethics, I chose to survey the different hermeneutical approaches taken by biblical scholars toward the texts that address homosexual acts in order to outline what was needed for an alternative, liberationist, nonapologetic biblical hermeneutic. The opening paragraph of the essay, 'Bridging the Chasm, Reclaiming the Word: Toward Reconstructing a Liberating Biblical Hermeneutic', set the immediate context of that project:

> In the intense debates within the churches on issues related to homosexuality such as the blessing of gay and lesbian relationships and the ordination of gay men and lesbians to the Christian ministry, [the Bible] often is used as the definitive word to close debate on the issue and silence the voices of lesbians and gay men reclaiming our place in the Christian community. In our own lives [these] words cut like a knife as we experience daily the pain and humiliation of having our deepest forms of expressing love described as dishonorable, degrading, unnatural, shameful, full of lust, an abomination. Our delight at experiencing God's love in our lives turns to anger that smolders and erupts when confronted with a church that claims as Word of God these words that distort and lie about who we know ourselves to be.[1]

In reviewing my work on biblical hermeneutics a decade ago, what is most obvious is how much the field has changed with the infusion of several openly queer biblical scholars. Ten years ago most gay-affirming biblical studies were done by supportive straights (and a few closeted lesbians and gay men); today there is a growing body of queer biblical scholars working on a variety of texts.

As an ethicist whose work seeks to bridge feminist, queer, Latin American liberationist and ecological writings, I have been interested in biblical hermeneutics to the extent that it can aid in constructing a liberationist ecojustice ethic through liberationist readings of the

---

1. Daniel T. Spencer, 'Bridging the Chasm, Reclaiming the Word: Toward Reconstructing a Liberating Biblical Hermeneutic', unpublished doctoral examination in biblical ethics, Union Theological Seminary, New York, 4 March 1991.

Bible.[2] Reflecting the need to move beyond apologetic approaches, I have contended,

> [M]y conviction [is] that it is not enough to expose and name the ways the Bible has been used inappropriately to oppress gay men and lesbians and keep our voices silent. It is not enough simply to withdraw from churches whose practice is by and large oppressive rather than liberating for lesbian and gay people. We need to work at transforming this praxis. There will continue to be girls and boys who grow up within the church who will struggle with the contradictions between their own emerging lesbian or gay feelings and identity and the teachings and praxis of the church on homosexuality. Without challenging the church to transformation, gay men and lesbians in the wider society will continue to be denied opportunities, beaten and murdered, and have these acts justified by Christians quoting the Bible...it is imperative that lesbians and gay men in the churches understand what is at stake in the debates on the Bible, and that we understand the arguments in order to demystify their power. We need to turn from a hermeneutics informed by an apologetic stance that tries to justify our place in the church to engage in the reconstructive task of hermeneutics that enlists the Bible as a resource for our liberation and challenges those who seek to exclude and oppress us.[3]

In surveying and critiquing eight biblical scholars who dealt with the issue of homosexuality and the Bible, I drew on a fourfold typology for the use of the Bible in ethics that I had used in my work with feminist ethicist Beverly Harrison.[4] I include it here because it sheds light on the extent to which queer readings and queer hermeneutics have moved in new and promising directions.

> *Reactionary* approaches move directly from a literalistic interpretation of the text to ethical commandments or norms. They explicitly teach commitment to present alignments of sex and gender, and allegiance to a model of Divine–human relations that best protects this. Fundamentalism and the so-called Moral Majority are examples of this position. Homosexuality is explicitly condemned and vigorously opposed. Proponents of reactionary perspectives are willing to use power—to react—against positions opposing them.

---

2. See Daniel T. Spencer, *Gay and Gaia: Ethics, Ecology, and the Erotic* (Cleveland: Pilgrim Press, 1996), especially ch. 2, 'Crossing Bridges: Hermeneutics and Connections from the Margins'.
3. Spencer, 'Bridging the Chasm', p. 3.
4. Drawn from Beverly Harrison's ethics course on Sexuality and the Social Order at Union Theological Seminary, New York, October 1989.

Traditionalist approaches may use biblical criticism in exegesis, but still move directly from exegesis to ethical principles. They tend to utilize other contemporary resources such as sociopolitical analysis and the social sciences. They also seek to maintain the status quo in sex and gender relations, but do so by cleaving to certain theological and religious traditions rather than using power to try to return to an earlier arrangement of gender relations. Traditionalist theologies maintain powerful distinction between Divine–human and human–human relations which serves to curtail criticism of inherited patterns of power relations in society. They usually oppose homosexuality as sinful and morally wrong.

Liberal approaches use biblical criticism informed by insights from other contemporary resources before stating ethical norms or principles. They acknowledge the need for some change in both the church and in society which they see taking place through processes of reform. Liberal theologies try to discern what should be kept from tradition and what should be changed. Strategies focus on expanding access in society and the churches to include those who have traditionally been excluded, but without critical questioning of the church or society itself. Proponents of the liberal approach find themselves on both sides of the debate on homosexuality, with many arguing that while homosexuality is not normative, the church should be inclusive and accept gay men and lesbians. Homosexual relations should be judged by the same ethical standards used to judge heterosexual relationships.

Liberationist approaches begin from a stated commitment to justice and explicitly incorporate a critical consciousness of power relations in examining scripture and its historical context prior to stating ethical norms and principles. In contrast to the first three approaches which all accept the given reality in the church and society as something to be maintained or reformed, liberationist approaches see the dominant expressions of church and society as oppressive and therefore in need of radical transformation. Proponents of a liberationist approach with regard to sexuality critique the notion of a 'normative' heterosexual center to church and society. They focus on exposing and transforming heterosexist structures and homophobic attitudes in their call for justice for lesbians and gay men.

The queer readings in many of the essays in this collection lie closest to the liberationist approach described here. Since my own commitment is to developing a liberationist ecojustice ethic where just and sustainable relations with human and otherkind are fostered at each level of our lives, from our most intimate relations to our relations with the rest of the planet, in the remainder of my response I want to engage in a sampling of the queer readings in this collection from that perspective in order to 'flesh out' the distinctive contributions queer readings of the Bible might make to such a liberationist project.

Perhaps the essay with the most clear attention to issues of method and hermeneutics is Timothy Koch's 'Cruising as Methodology: Homoeroticism and the Scriptures'. Consistent with a liberationist approach's attention to social location in biblical interpretation, Koch begins by locating himself as a gay man whose 'guiding sensibility is homoerotic'; this gay male sensibility manifests itself cleverly and with a great deal of humor throughout his essay as he draws on many elements of gay male culture to illuminate otherwise hidden dimensions of biblical stories. While sympathetic to other members of the queer community, he makes no pretense to speak out of or to lesbian, bisexual, or transgendered experience.

Koch locates his article in the context of the ongoing 'hunger for an effective strategy' to ward off antiqueer attacks putatively grounded in anti-homosexual Scriptures. Three main strategies have dominated these efforts, which Koch provocatively labels (1) The Pissing Contest (we accept the traditional terms of the biblical debate, but marshal increasing amounts of evidence to show what the Bible *really* says, that it is really *not* anti-gay); (2) Jesus Is My Trump Card (collapse all detailed debate into 'God is love, so can't we just all get along?'); (3) I Can Fit the Glass Slipper, Too! (if we just look hard enough in the Bible, we'll find that we're included too). Koch's concern is that the essentially apologetic strategies employed in each of these efforts inadvertently 'perpetuates a posture for us that locates authority outside our own, lived experience'. Each implicitly accepts the external authority of Scripture, which—once correctly understood and interpreted— will include queer folks, but at the cost of telling us *how* we fit in. Or, as Koch puts it, 'Funny how, when it's all said and done, it still turns out that the Hermeneutical Victor gets to tell me how to live my life— and have my sex!'

Koch draws on Audre Lorde's work to argue that the locus of authority for queer folks must be intrinsic, where 'I seek to allow my own deep knowing, my own homoerotic power, to be the light by which I do my reading, thinking, believing'. To do this, he proposes a hermeneutic he titles 'Cruising the Scriptures', using this central and symbolic paradigm for gay men meeting each other to shape a queer reading of Scripture. Rather than 'cruising' the Bible to see how gay men either fit in or can defend ourselves, Koch outlines an approach 'that seeks to integrate and align how we interact with the characters and stories of Scripture with how, as gay men, many of us interact with our world as we make our way toward joy'. As in any act of cruising, some of the figures encountered will be friends, some enemies, and some may simply be indifferent—but there may also be that occasional 'hot number' that catches our eye and makes us move in for a closer look. So there is Koch cruising in on Elijah, the Hairy Leather-Man; on Elisha, Who Would Not Be Baited; on Jehu, the Zealous; on Ehud, the Erotic. In each case Koch uses his 'gaydar' to pick up clues in the text that merit a closer reading and an imaginative accounting, drawing on his gay sensibility. Koch has no illusions that what he finds attractive will be at all interesting to the next person, but that plurality of connections is one of the strengths of his approach: 'The point here is that an approach that we *each* base on our own erotic knowledge allows us *all* to pursue that which catches our eye, which calls to us, which holds out at least the hope of connection and transformation—whether our meeting takes place along a roadside, in a bar, in an Internet chatroom, or in the pages of Holy Scripture'.

Koch's 'cruising hermeneutic' reminds me of a gay nonapologetic approach I first encountered in Gary Comstock's 1993 book, *Gay Theology Without Apology,* where Comstock, too, rereads Scripture from a queer perspective: 'The "gay theology without apology" that I develop here examines the Bible and Christianity not with the purpose of fitting in or finding a place for them, but of fitting them into and changing them according to the particular experiences of lesbian/ bisexual/gay people. Christian Scripture and tradition are not authorities from which I seek approval; rather they are resources from which I seek guidance and learn lessons as well as institutions that I seek to interpret, shape, and change.'[5] Both Koch and Comstock, I think, offer a promising way to encounter the Bible nonapologetically, through the lens and from the ground of queer experience and insight. Elsewhere I have drawn on the metaphor of friendship to suggest the need for a relational hermeneutic in encountering Scripture.[6] Koch's cruising metaphor suggests that friendship is the wrong place to start, however, for in friendship both the friend and the relationship exercise already

5.   Gary D. Comstock, *Gay Theology Without Apology* (Cleveland: Pilgrim Press, 1993), p. 4.
6.   Spencer, *Gay and Gaia*, p. 39.

some authority on one. Koch suggests instead that we honor our own internal authority first by cruising the Scriptures—friendship with a text may or may not develop after the initial encounter.

I think Koch's approach to the Bible has much to offer a liberationist ethic, particularly in the way he draws on the work of Audre Lorde to construct a hermeneutic grounded firmly in one's own internal authority and experience. My ethicist's sensibilities leave me a little uneasy with Koch's somewhat individualistic and personalistic approach, however, which is largely devoid of political and historical context and meaning. In this regard Koch's approach ironically fits more closely with those liberal and libertarian perspectives that privilege individual experience without attention to social (or ecological) relations. Koch is up-front about this, arguing that 'the *only* real motivations for even taking the time and energy to cruise [Scripture] then are because we want to, because we can, and because it is something we enjoy'. I have argued elsewhere that pleasure and the erotic are foundational to our healthy sense of moral agency,[7] but these are always also connected to patterns of justice and injustice that must be discerned and either fostered or resisted. Without attention to relations of power and eco-social relations, our pleasure too often is derived at the expense of others, rather than being born out of mutuality and right relation. While Koch's four brief cruising excursions into Hebrew Scripture are likely intended to be more illustrative rather than substantive, I would like to see further development of how these encounters can contribute to our common as well as individual lives.

Attention to social power relations that infuse both the text and our contexts is one of the strengths of Ken Stone's 'Lovers and Raisin Cakes: Food, Sex and Divine Insecurity in Hosea'. In a fascinating essay, Stone draws on anthropological insights about connections between food and sex to examine ideologies of masculinity in Hosea, problematizing them through a queer filter with profeminist sensibilities to see what they reveal about notions of gender and sexuality. Stone is attuned not only to how his own social location as a queer scholar shapes his reading, but also to how contemporary assumptions about (the nonrelatedness of) food and sexuality influence the ethical bearing the Bible has on religious communities: 'Sex is a matter about which Christian denominations...argue and threaten to split. Practices

---

7. See Spencer, *Gay and Gaia*, ch. 5.

of food and eating, on the other hand...are often considered by Christians to be trivial matters that can safely be left to individual choice.'[8] Stone holds his own queer scholarship accountable to the findings of other critical liberationist scholars, especially feminists. Addressing the concern that a focus on food, sex and manhood in Hosea might simply reinforce the marginalization of women that has resulted from this problematic text, Stone responds that his 'own, rather queer, relation to norms of "manhood" leads me to agree with those feminist scholars who suggest that one important role for male biblical scholars working in the wake of feminism is to analyze critically the ideologies of masculinity constructed by biblical texts and their readers'. He links the work of queer and feminist projects in the efforts of both to contest 'the adequacy of hegemonic notions of proper gendered behavior'.

Following a detailed examination of Hosea through the anthropological lens of cultures of honor and shame, Stone argues convincingly that what is at stake in Hosea's language about food and sex is precisely Yhwh's 'manhood', his ability to provide for his Israelite 'wife' in the context of Yhwh's rivalry with Baal. Anxiety about his masculinity ends up paradoxically as one of the primary attributes of Yhwh in Hosea. Drawing on the work of Judith Butler about the inherent instability of all fixed notions of gender, Stone concludes that the book of Hosea finally is 'unable to sustain a coherent and consistent picture of the manhood which it presupposes and attempts to reproduce'. Stone therefore draws from this case study promising lessons for the potential for queering other biblical texts:

> It may be precisely this failure [of rigid gender norms] that offers opportunities for a certain sort of 'queering' of the biblical texts, a queering that works by destabilizing—or, better perhaps, by calling attention to the inevitable instability of—cultural imperatives surrounding gender and sexuality... To the extent, however, that Hosea's characterization of Yhwh not only relies upon, but also transgresses, particular norms of manhood...the book does expose the inability of masculinities—including divine masculinities—ever to establish themselves over against the 'feminine term' in a consistent and nonproblematic fashion. And precisely this recognition, that even so relentlessly patriarchal a text as Hosea is in the end not entirely successful in constructing a consistent and secure presentation of manhood, may allow us to imagine a space for

---

8.   Note also that Stone contextualizes this concern in the broader global context of inequalities in the distribution of resources.

alternative, even queer, scenarios that could involve the surrender, rather than the embrace, of the structures of agonistic masculinity.

Stone's nuanced placement of queer biblical hermeneutics in conversation with and accountable to other critical progressive approaches makes this approach ideal for a liberationist ethic. What we most need in our time is the ability to imagine new and more sustainable, life-giving possibilities for how we relate as sexual and gendered beings to others, human and otherkind, who share the planet. Stone's queer reading privileges queer experience and insights in its approach to the text, but not at the expense of critical insights from other communities. Like Koch, Stone seems to call into question any external authority dictating to gay men and other queer folk how we should live and love and have sex, but his attention to feminism holds those of us who are part of the queer community accountable to other historically marginalized communities—a critical component of a liberationist ethic.

One example of using a queer reading to make sense of queer experience is Mona West's 'The Gift of Voice, the Gift of Tears: A Queer Reading of Lamentations in the Context of AIDS'. Here West draws on Eric Rofes's observations about AIDS and gay men to read Lamentations as 'trauma literature' that gives the queer community a voice of resistance to suffering. West argues that 'Lamentations gives the Queer community the gift of a voice to speak the unspeakable about AIDS… It is also a voice that resists theologies that do not measure up to our experience, even if that means confronting God directly.' While in some ways West's text seems less a queer reading of Lamentations than a queer *appropriation* and *application* of the text to queer experience, she is attuned to the ways biblical texts such as Lamentations have been used against the queer community to justify AIDS as God's punishment for homosexuality. In distinction from such readings, West argues that a queer reading of Lamentations allows one 'to make sense of one's suffering by challenging bankrupt theological systems'. Hers is a perceptive appropriation of Lamentations for use in grieving and moving past AIDS, but I would like to see her develop further the queer dimensions of her reading of Lamentations.

In terms of queer readings that open up new possibilities for both the texts and how we live our lives, some of the most interesting (and certainly controversial) essays in the collection are those that read the text through the lens of the dynamics of S/M (sadomasochism). Lori Rowlett's 'Violent Femmes and S/M: Queering Samson and Delilah' employs a queer lens that sees in the Samson and Delilah story a 'pattern of domination by the exotic Other in a tale of bondage and degradation [which] emerges as a stock S/M scenario' where Delilah is the femme dominatrix and Samson the butch bottom. This reading allows Rowlett to examine not only the Samson and Delilah story, but also the character and relations of Yahweh throughout the book of Judges in terms of issues of gender, political identity and power to reveal deeper dynamics of 'divine control and relinquishment of control'. Like Stone, Rowlett draws on the work of Judith Butler to interrogate the illusion of the 'naturalness' or fixed nature of sexuality, arguing that 'hegemonic heterosexuality requires a constant and repeated effort to imitate its own idealizations'. Instead, male and female, as well as relations of dominance and submission in S/M, are inherently fluid and must constantly be renegotiated and reinscribed.

Rowlett uses her S/M reading of Delilah and Samson to explore the underlying power relations of the book of Judges as a constituent part of the Deuteronomistic History. Examining the cycle of hero stories in Judges, she argues that 'Yahweh, in the S/M pattern, alternates between being a top (deploying power) and being a bottom (relinquishing power), toying with the ancient Israelites, who (by definition) are not gods and therefore have considerably less power in the game. Yahweh emerges as a sadistic character in the Deuteronomistic Historian's schema in Judges because he/she has the power to do "good" on a grand scale, but chooses to dole it out in small doses and then pull back, letting people be overcome by "evil"'. Rowlett connects this theological strategy with the text's original social context, arguing that 'the violence of the cycle in Judges is therefore useful because it is exactly the same power strategy which the Deuteronomistic Historian wants to legitimate in his own context'. Monotheism emerged as a key component of the hierarchical authority of the centralization of power by the Jerusalem governing authorities, who identify religious diversity as the evil to be vanquished in recurring cycles. Rowlett concludes her article with this theological claim: 'Queering Samson and Delilah, viewing them as role players without fixed identities or essences, calls into question by analogy the stability of the divine/human dichotomy as well. If Yahweh has enormous divine powers, sufficient to establish his/her will globally many times over, then why does he/she allocate just enough of it to various heroes to keep the cycle of violence going? Perhaps he/she derives pleasure from the game, or perhaps the sadistic pleasure belongs to his/her (literary) creator, the Deuteronomistic Historian.'

Rowlett's essay thus serves as an excellent example of how queer reading strategies can simultaneously destabilize traditional, fixed interpretations of the text as well as expose and, at the same time, destabilize divine and social power relations that infuse the story. She is able to move beyond the text itself to relate this reading to the social-theological context that generated the book of Judges, exposing and critiquing the power strategy that the text serves to justify. In the process Rowlett opens up new spaces and possibilities for imagining both divine/human and human/social relations.

In many ways picking up where Rowlett leaves off, Roland Boer's 'Yahweh as Top: A Lost Targum' examines the character of Yahweh through a queer lens to explore the question of 'whether the Bible is a masochistic text or a sadistic one'. In an essay I found to be very challenging, yet equally fascinating, Boer imaginatively creates a conversation on Mount Sinai between Moses and Yahweh, who soon invite Leopold von Sacher-Masoch, Jacques Lacan, Sigmund Freud, Gilles Deleuze and the Marquis de Sade to join the debate. Queer form mirrors function here, as Yahweh emerges as something like a femme gay queen concerned with the finest interior decorating details of the tabernacle he wants Moses to build (reviewing Exod. 24–28), while Moses is more the hoary bear, sexually drawn to each of the characters as they make their way through the fine details of one another's works on sadomasochism and apply them to the biblical text. As the invited guests join the circle, Gilles Deleuze starts the conversation by posing the question, 'So, Yahweh, are you as much a top as a purveyor of high camp? The question for me, however, is whether you are a sadist or masochist.' Yahweh's important response is representative of both the clever style Boer employs throughout his essay and his sophisticated handling of the theory of each of the characters he addresses:

> Well, you know, sadomasochism—which is a single phenomenon with different parts, about which we'll have to ask Sigmund a little more in a few moments—is for many the end run of pornography, for it combines explicitly the dynamics of unequal power, pain and sex that are so assiduously sought for, it is commonly argued, in pornography itself. The power of such a critique lies in the moral coding assumed with these terms and its connections with gender: that is, power, pain and sex are understood to represent the relation between male and female, the heterosexual relation that belongs down the road somewhat in the

twentieth century. But what if the gender relation is not only historicized but also problematized in a queer fashion, if the willed dynamics of power are gay, lesbian, bisexual and transgender rather than merely heterosexual? And what if the moral coding of the key terms is negated or reversed? Power, sex and pain become either neutral or positive terms for one's sexual fantasy—mine, for instance. Is not all fucking some negotiation, an exploitation even, of the imbalance of power between the subjects of the act itself?

From there the conversation meanders through such topics as the creation of the top in sadomasochism, the role of the Law and the desire for its transgression, the connections between sadism and atheism, the 'covenant' between bottom and top, Yahweh's S/M relationship with the Israelites (here paralleling Rowlett's reading of Samson and Delilah), and Jesus as the vicarious bottom (with Christ as a masochist and Christianity a masochistic religion), to name just a few. Boer interweaves sophisticated theoretical analysis with a delightfully playful (and, perhaps, naughty) narrative that examines many different parts of the biblical story from a queer S/M perspective, while simultaneously engaging in vigorous debate between different schools and interpretations of sadomasochism. Moses interjects periodically, keeping the often heady dialogue somewhat grounded in the more earthy realities of sex, lust and desire.

The narrative ends with the appearance of a divine female figure (striking especially because of the noticeable absence of women in the story thus far) who asks, 'Why is there always such an easy fit between things such as masochism and the Bible? Is it possible that the Bible, in its very patterns, themes, relationships, the divine-human structure, preconditions any sexual relation (for masochism is sexual from beginning to end) that comes out of the West, or at least where the Bible has a deep and lasting cultural influence? So it turns out that the basic features of masochism appear first in the Bible: fetishes, fantasy, imagination, covenant, law, beating, whipping, binding, construction of the torturer, atmosphere, suspension, waiting, and even the oral mother.'

I suspect readers familiar with the literature of sadomasochism that Boer considers in detail will find this article particularly insightful; even without that familiarity, his playful narrative structure carries the reader along and rewards the reader's patience with several provocative insights about the biblical text, biblical religion and divine–human dynamics. While by no means explicitly 'political', Boer's reading succeeds brilliantly in opening up many new spaces and strategies for exploring the unstable configurations of power, gender and sexuality that infuse the biblical story and its cultural heritage.

In many ways the essay I find most fascinating and illustrative of the promise of multiple queer reading strategies is Theodore Jennings's 'YHWH as Erastes'. Like Koch, Jennings begins his essay by giving attention to issues of methodology. He distinguishes a queer reading strategy from both apologetic or 'homophobic-defensive' approaches (Koch's 'Pissing Contest') and 'gay affirmative' strategies (Koch's 'I Can Fit the Glass Slipper, Too!') that largely have dominated gay-affirming biblical interpretation in recent years. Jennings argues that a queer reading has some advantages over these other strategies, as it is not limited to texts that appear to cover same-sex relations, but rather can include a variety of sexualities. It also does not presuppose a definitive standpoint or perspective: 'It is here not a question of what everyone should see but of what may be seen from this standpoint as one among many possible standpoints'. As will be seen, this allows Jennings, like Stone, to listen to and learn from other reading strategies, such as feminist approaches, without compromising the legitimacy of his own reading. The strategy of this reading is thus also somewhat different than the previous approaches he cites: 'It is not then a question of contesting homophobia directly or of legitimating same-sex practice or relationships through the discovery of canonical precedents. Instead it simply presupposes that queerness exists, at least in readers, and that this provides a way of illuminating the texts.'

Jennings reads the story of David and YHWH with attention to 'how a certain homoeroticism operates in the development of this relationship'. To do so, Jennings draws on cross-cultural literature on what he terms 'warrior eroticism' to examine the development of the David–YHWH relationship within the larger context of David's (homoerotic) relations with Saul and Jonathan. In considering what kinds of cultural expectations or potentialities lie within these relationships as presented in these 'war sagas', Jennings notes the importance of social location in shaping hermeneutics: 'To which cultural sphere does the story of Saul, Jonathan and David correspond? To a certain extent the answer one gives will depend upon the experience of the reader. Those who have had sexual experience under such circumstances or who are familiar with persons or cultures that take such experience for granted will be inclined to read the story as inclusive of sexual potentiality while those who are inclined to regard this as unthinkable will not notice the

possibilities of such a reading or will even be outraged by its suggestion.' He concludes that there is nothing in the text that precludes erotic
or even sexual readings.

Jennings goes on to examine the rest of the David narrative in considerable detail, shedding much insight on the erotic and homoerotic
elements that infuse the story of David and YHWH's love relationship.
Particularly fascinating is his interpretation of the story of David
dancing before the ark as David dancing before the sheathed phallus of
his lover. A culmination of the story is YHWH 'promising lifetime
faithfulness, binding himself to David for life' in a parallel to a marriage vow.[9] Jennings's exposition is too rich and detailed for me to
review here, but what struck me repeatedly while reading it is how
much richer and more nuanced it is than most 'gay apologetic' readings
I have seen of the David and Jonathan story that attempt to see the
story as an example of a same-sex relationship validated by the Bible.[10]
As a result one sees not only the homoerotic elements in the story, but
also the complex transformation of both YHWH and David, lover and
beloved, as the narrative develops. It illustrates well the freedom from
some of the limitations of interpretation imposed by apologetic reading
strategies.

As an ethicist, I found Jennings's 'Concluding Reflections' on what
the David and YHWH narrative says about male same-sex relationships
to be particularly illuminating. He notes that in contrast to Greek divine
pederastic or asymmetrical homoerotic models, David is an actor, even
initiator in his relationship with YHWH, and their relationship takes
place fully within the realm of mortals. In contrast to the Greek gods,
YHWH lives out virtually his entire social, emotional and political life
among human beings. YHWH's and David's relationship is deeply
intertwined with the relation of both figures to the land and the people
of Israel. David as beloved is in many ways the paradigm for YHWH's

9.   Jennings notes here (as Ken Stone also does in his essay) the interesting
issue of the transgendering of Israel as YHWH's partner in this story, and the ways
in which Israel's unfaithfulness will call into question YHWH's own masculine
competence.

10.   An exception to this is Gary Comstock's reading of David and Jonathan in
his *Gay Theology Without Apology*. Comstock follows a warrior-lover model that is
in some ways similar to the model developed by Jennings, though Comstock draws
on Walt Whitman's homoerotic war poetry to provide a lens through which to read
the story of Jonathan and David.

relation to Israel. Jennings observes that 'this means that David as the male beloved of a male YHWH configures the relationship of Israel, Judah and Jerusalem to the same deity. Thus the homoerotic dimensions of the relationship between David and YHWH are, to a significant degree, transferred to the relationship between Israel and YHWH. Since, as I have suggested, David is, in contemporary parlance, set up as the "bottom" to YHWH's "top" this will have potentially crucial consequences for the distinctive features of Israelite and Jewish (and perhaps Christian) masculinity.' The warrior context of the relationship prevents the masculinity of the beloved from being questioned, as masculinity is associated more with boldness and loyalty than depending on one's relationships with women.

Yet Jennings is by no means blind to the other social dynamics, particularly of gender and class, that shape this story. In noting the positive potential for rethinking masculinity, he observes, 'In any case I do not believe it is helpful to read the homoeroticism of this relationship as existing on a scale of "more or less" masculine or, even worse, as entailing feminization. For this essentializes binary distinctions between male and female as well as casting feminization simply as a depletion of masculinity. Within the limits of the androcentric, phallocentric, militaristic, perhaps misogynistic and classist world of this narrative we may also find a helpful clue for exceeding the ill effects of a binary opposition of male and female and so a way to value the distinct masculinity of males in love (and thus the distinctive feminism of two women in love).'

Jennings concludes with the provocative observation that 'what seems to me to be remarkable is not the homoeroticism that may be read in the text but that the relation between the divine and the adherent may be read as erotic at all'. He concludes 'the erotic engagement of YHWH with Israel (and the believer) provokes an answering erotics of faith. It is this that may account for the rather troubled relation between faith and sexuality that has haunted Christianity perhaps far more than Judaism...at least in this narrative the erotic character of the relation between YHWH and David (and, by extension, Israel) does not serve to inhibit the erotic life of the human characters.' With my own interest in reclaiming the erotic as central to the moral life and to a biblically informed ethic, this is a very promising avenue for further exploration and reflection.

I am struck by the numerous ways in which Jennings's article, read in conjunction with the essays by Rowlett and Boer, illustrates the potential and promise of queer readings of the Bible. Where Rowlett and Boer choose an S/M hermeneutic, Jennings opts for a lens of warrior eroticism to tease out and illuminate homoerotic elements in the text, while also noticing additional insights available from other homoerotic and feminist approaches. It is a good example of how multiple readings from different stances need not compete but rather can mutually enrich interpretations. I also appreciate the way Jennings is alert to other progressive readings, particularly to issues of gender and class, without, however, having that prevent him from a critical reading and appropriation through a queer lens. He concludes his essay with further reflections on some of the implications of his queer reading for male same-sex relationships and broader configurations of gender, sexuality and class. The result is a richly nuanced essay attuned to the complex broader context of hermeneutical and political issues.

To conclude, what might we say about the question posed at the outset of this essay: what contributions, if any, might queer readings of the Bible make to ethics, to fostering just and sustainable relationships among human and otherkind? Perhaps here it is sufficient to quote Ken Stone's thoughtful essay on 'Gay Men and the Ethics of Reading': 'Biblical interpretation is a technology of the self inasmuch as it is one route by which new experiences of self and new ethical subjects are constituted. Gay male subjectivity does not simply produce, but also emerges from, practices of reading… When we evaluate such readings in relation to "the ethics of reading", it is necessary but not sufficient to ask whether they account for the experiences of marginalized peoples. We must ask whether they open up possibilities for new experiences and new forms of cultural existence; or, as Foucault might have put it a new "ethos".'[11] It is precisely in opening up possibilities for new experiences and new forms of cultural existence, possibilities for a new 'ethos', that we find the promise and potential of queer readings of the Bible. In resisting dominant, heterosexual normative readings, each of the essays here surveyed destabilizes dominant power relations and settings and opens up new possibilities for different configurations of gender, sexuality and other social dynamics that can be more conducive to just and earth-friendly relations. Key to this is the extent to which

11. Ken Stone, 'Biblical Interpretation as a Technology of the Self: Gay Men and the Ethics of Reading', in Danna Nolan Fewell and Gary A. Phillips (eds.), *Bible and Ethics of Reading* (Semeia, 77; Atlanta: Scholars Press, 1997), pp. 139-55.

these readings are sensitive and accountable to the experiences and perspectives of marginalized peoples—certainly to lesbian, gay, bisexual and transgendered persons, but also to other marginalized groups and commitments. The essays in this anthology are a promising addition to this project.

Yahwist Desires: Imagining Divinity Queerly

Laurel C. Schneider

This is a theological reflection on the twisted and twisting tales (tails?) of the character Yhwh and other gods of the Hebrew Bible. I am interested in the implications that queer readings of the Hebrew Bible have for divinity and its revelations: for its queerness and queerly divine desire. Thanks to the work of others, the Hebrew Bible is 'coming out', sometimes here, sometimes there, sometimes with embarrassing awkwardness, and sometimes with poignant depth. As a theologian (and not what could be called a biblical one at that) I am enchanted, fascinated, hopeful and really very troubled by the preliminary results. Many questions leap out of the wings like amateur tumblers and pile up in several uncertain heaps. The first pile contains variations on the matter of desire and fantasy; the second, variations on the matter of gender; and the third, variations on matters of authority, revelation and truth-production. Together these questions guide my thinking through some of the theological consequences and possibilities that may come of readings that queer the Bible.

To begin with, how can we now *not* see queer twists in the stories contained in the vast saga of the human–divine relationship that we call the Hebrew Bible? To presume a stable heteroeroticism and heteronormative social architecture throughout such a complex and multi-authored record of the events, myths and fantasies of a whole people is silly in terms of human history, sociology and what we know from contemporary histories of sexuality. It is also becoming an ill-advised presumption in light of biblical scholarship. Once opened, our eyes cannot be so easily shut, and the world that we imagine, superimposed on so many layers of retrieval, is changed.

Since Foucault (1980b), it is impossible to regard sexuality as a pre-cultural given, and since Butler (1990) it is impossible to regard gender or sexual difference that way either. Heteronormative interpretations are therefore no more given than are Eurocentric, patriarchal, feminist, Afrocentric or, for that matter, queer interpretations. So the question stands: how can we read the Scriptures now and not encounter their many and tantalizing traces of homoeroticism and queer possibility? And, encountering, how then do we think theologically about these possibilities, if Scriptures are to serve as any kind of source for thoughts about some presumed real divinity? What implications, in other words, do these particular readings have for all the rest of our biblical readings, and for the theology that we may generate from them?

These latter questions tend toward issues of biblical authority in constructive theology that are raised by any interpretation of the Bible, but they come into sharp relief particularly in response to those interpretations that overturn dominant customs or taken-for-granted social and moral norms. Before addressing these questions, however, I think that it is important to look more closely at what is queer about these readings in order to think more clearly about some of the theological implications that may result.

To begin with, a queer reading is, as I have argued elsewhere, one that 'takes on the outsider viewpoint, at least in terms of placements of power based on heteronormative presuppositions' (Schneider 2000: 206). Outsider interpretations, particularly sexual outsider interpretations of the Bible, encounter and disrupt a host of normative presuppositions that are hard-wired to the whole symbolic moral architecture of dominant Western culture. The commentaries in this volume postulate the plausibility of sexual diversity in the ancient stories and they consequently implicate the symbolic moral architecture on which heteronormativity is based. If evidence of sexual diversity in the ancient Hebrew world was the only substance in queer commentary, we could shrug our shoulders, brush off our hands and say, 'well, so there were also queer doings among important Israelites, Ammonites, Moabites, Babylonians, Canaanites and all the rest. Knew it, but nice to have it confirmed, if only to give pause to homophobes in the church.' But the moral universe founded on heteronormative and masculinist presumption is not fundamentally shaken by the presence alone of a few queers (or more specifically of some queer male sex) in the prophetic bloodlines, even if those bloodlines do lead to David and hence, reputedly, to Jesus. Christian theology can easily retain its traditional heteronormative presumption simply by discounting these tales as further evidence of the lineages of sin that Christ ultimately overcomes. This is not unlike other triumphalist, anti-Jewish tendencies in traditional Christian thought that often transformed would-be contradictions or other theological difficulties in the Hebrew Bible into apologetic strengths just by attributing their source to pre-Christian errors of the Jews. Something beyond the postulation of queer doings among the Israelites is at work here.

That something is the possibility of a more queer divinity. Using a new lens, these exegetes take on not only the character of some of the Bible's key cultural heroes, but suggest to theologians a radically queer dimension to the divine–world relationship itself. Queering this relationship may well threaten the whole symbolic architecture of heteronormativity in Western moral imagining, to the extent that that moral imagining rests on the mythic *hetero*paternity of the Bible's primary cultural heroes. More significantly, disruption of the heroic heteropaternity of the culture heroes (Moses, Saul, David and so on) reads sexual otherness (and not just homoerotic otherness) onto the divine–human/divine–world relationship and thus reads queer desire onto the divine. This, more than anything else, speaks to a theological challenge opened by these biblical scholars: a rethinking of the divinity that is supposed to reveal itself in the imagining of these tales. In other words, the opening in biblical scholarship that these queer readings represent makes the traditional presumption of biblical support for heteronormative sexual ethics shakier than ever.

Desire and Fantasy

Before we can imagine tantalizing new shapes of the god/s of Israel through queer readings of the Bible, we have to look at least briefly at the role of desire and fantasy both in reading the Bible and in constructing from it some meaningful notion of divinity. On one level, it is irritating to have to do this (since doing so further distances the theologian from any certainty about what the text might reveal, objectively, about God) but it is necessary because of the simple truth that both desire and fantasy help to shape whatever conclusions we may make about divinity. But why does the burden to account for the social construction of all readings seem always to fall on the outsider position? Certainly queer commentary on Scripture is no more laden with the interpreter's desires than any other kind of commentary. While that is true, the outsider position, by virtue of its vantage point and its status, cannot presume a voice or space in the scholarly conversation, and so must make one. Relativizing all voices by providing a lens into the social constructedness of all positions is one way to do this.

Apart from truth telling about social construction, however, queer theory in biblical interpretation also potentially offers the queer theologian an interesting avenue into the riches of biblical texts precisely through a greater attention to questions of desire and fantasy in the divine–human relation. Such readings may, oddly enough, be the very ticket we need to re-imagine the divine beyond heteronormative presumption. And who is to say that that is not revelatory of something other than our own desire? Still, the shock of reading homoeroticism into the characters of Yhwh and prophets, and sadomasochistic play into the lives of biblical heroes, raises the question of imagination and desire on the part of the interpreter more plainly precisely because such interpretations stretch imagination and taken-for-granted conclusions about the whole text and its history. We cannot deny the fact that, at least in part, the homoerotic potential of the Hebrew Bible stories is now exposed simply because of queer desire for visibility and recognition just as surely as it has been elided, consciously or unconsciously, on the basis of heteronormative desire for supremacy.

But I am suggesting here that desire and fantasy operate in theological reflection on biblical texts beyond just the issue of political goals or ends. When we look more closely at the issue of desire in developing theology out of biblical readings, other issues surface, such as the way that we construct (or fantasize our desires in) the divine in light of those readings and (much more hypothetically) how we might make room for thinking about divine desire and fantasy in turn.

Biblical scholars have long contended that the text does not stand alone and inert, receiving interpretation without interacting in some profound ways with the interpreters/readers/hearers who in turn construct and reconstruct the text itself. The same is true in theology. As Jürgen Moltmann and many other contemporary constructive theologians have pointed out, 'theology always includes the imagination, fantasy for God and his [*sic*] kingdom' (Moltmann 1985: 4). Imaginative retrievals and interpretations of the biblical text are accompanied, in theology, by imaginative constructions of God as second-order, intertextual reflections. And those imaginings return, insofar as people read theology, to the interpreter in the form of preconceived ideas about what the character of the divine–human relationship is and where it ought to be found. In other words, the texts of Bible, theology and interpretation become inter-texts that not only shape commentary, but also shape the possibilities for interpretation resident in the text.

By way of Mikhail Bakhtin's work on intertextuality, Julia Kristeva suggests that 'history and morality are written and read within the infrastructure of texts' (Kristeva 1980: 65). Outsider readings of those texts that form the foundation of Western imagining about morality, law and divinity highlight the infrastructure that positions queer commentary on the outside. By reading the outside in (reading homoerotic divine–human relationships into the Bible), queer readings dispose of the presumed infrastructure of heteronormative stability, thereby revealing the desire that established the presumption of that stability at its core. Desire funds the theological imagination, whether outside or inside the bounds of heteronormative presumption.

The fact that desire and fantasy play a role in the work of biblical scholars and theologians is not news, but the extent to which language and image—the stock in trade of both—are structured at their roots by the varieties of desire requires a critical, and sometimes difficult, distancing from most taken-for-granted views of reading, text and history. And sometimes the only way to glimpse the deep working of desire in imagination is through those stories, tellings and images that cavort with carnivalesque energy on the margins of intelligibility. Stretching past that which seems most familiar (in this case a heteronormative frame) helps us to gaze back on it and to see it as bounded—and so as not given—for perhaps the first time.

There is often more than a bit of carnival in queer life, and the testy wildness and performance of opposition characteristic of the carnival shows up in several of these commentaries, particularly when the repressed sexuality of the divine asserts itself, as in Jennings's and Boer's readings of Yhwh, or Koch's suggestion of queerness in the goat-clad prophet Elijah. Bakhtin's and Kristeva's interest in the carnival as that which exposes the law by opposing it and which reveals the dialogical and intertextual dimensions of all language applies to queer readings of biblical texts that distance the text (the stories and characters) from the laws and morality they supposedly inscribe/reinscribe. Kristeva argues that the carnivalesque is not parody (which strengthens the law) but

> *dramatic* (murderous, cynical, and revolutionary in the sense of *dialectical transformation*)... The laughter of the carnival is not simply parodic;

it is no more comic than tragic; it is both at once, one might say that it is *serious*. This is the only way that it can avoid becoming either the scene of the law or the scene of its parody, in order to become the scene of its *other* (Kristeva 1980: 80).

Certainly it would seem that, to the extent that queer readings of the Bible make plausible an enduring homoerotic tension in the mythic founding of Western culture, and explain this tension through a recasting of the characters as they play out erotic and sexual relationships that run counter to the 'law', a kind of carnivalesque mood develops that encompasses humans and divine alike. Queer commentaries on the biblical tales fit Kristeva's and Bakhtin's notion of the carnivalesque in that they do seem to depend on a kind of distance from the text-as-Scripture (in the sense of Scripture-as-revelation) even as they make themselves as reasonable as any other telling out there. The queered narratives *do* reveal their intertextual, dialogic character if only because they are so obviously 'composed of distances, relationships, analogies, and nonexclusive oppositions…[they are] a spectacle, but without a stage; a game, but also a daily undertaking; a signifier, but also a signified' (Kristeva 1980: 78). They transgress the abstraction of linear time by making the characters intelligible to a contemporary queer reader, almost present even, blurring the subject–object divide and wrenching a new distance between the characters and their historic sponsors in church, state and culture.

These readings are playful but deadly serious (murderous even?), and they demand a rethinking of the relationship between biblical interpretation and theology, particularly queer biblical interpretation and queer theology. If we can plausibly reread the story of Sodom along with Carden as Yhwh's rescue of the queers and a burning of the bashers, then we are reading a contemporary subject position funded by a very strong desire *into* the text perhaps more than we are reading some kind of mythic truth *out* of it. But the difference between these two positions may also be less relevant than the fruit such a reading can yield for our contemporary thoughts about a divine being whose founding tales *could* include such a deed. It is an apocalyptic reading of an apocalyptic text, to be sure. But queer readings of apocalyptic texts will, in the intertextual blurring of linear time, find a home in contemporary queer accommodations to, and desire for, a liberative faith tradition just as the accommodationist and liberative readings of every persecuted minority have done.

So there are queer imaginings and desires for 'God and his kingdom' at play here, some involving a deity who not only tolerates sexual difference but enjoys it from time to time himself, and who is willing to punish those who do not tolerate it (the refrain of the persecuted minority). There is also the queer imagining of divine desire here: the fantasy of God (our fantasy and, perhaps, God's?) as a fully eroticized deity who turns his gaze on the beauty of men and is rewarded for his power and authority by the adoration of the young and the well-sculpted. Yhwh emerges in these readings as a complex character who, when sexual, embodies the polymorphic sexual creativity and contractual subversions of power typical of much homoerotic sex when establishing 'his' covenant with Moses, and reveals a strong male homoerotic desire in establishing a kingdom in David. Or, more specifically, in the hands of queer readers, these tales lend themselves persuasively to the interpretive desire for a queer likeness of the deity and a queer construction in God's image. And they speak of a divine desire for us and for the world that is as sensual as it is passionate (dare we say embodied even?). In addition, it is promiscuous in its inclusivity (see Schneider 1999: 159-71).

But in what ways can theologians who seek to speak intelligibly of the divine beyond the biblical text take all of this seriously? What are we to do with a deity motivated by homoeroticism in 'his' selection of kings and in 'his' establishment of a people in history? Mustn't we exert all hermeneutical caution and remind ourselves that what we have here in queer commentaries are reader-responses that reflect the interpreter's/reader's desires alone? Queer commentary thus far looks like it primarily serves male fantasies of being made queer, in all the permutations of that term, in God's image. Who else but a latter-day queer would think to point out that keeping Moses locked in closed conference for forty days and nights on Mount Sinai just for the purpose of getting instructions for building and decorating the tabernacle indicates an interior-decorator god of the most anal-retentive, fruity, late-twentieth-century kind? And the amusing thing is, it does. In addition, placing Yhwh in the center (or on the top) of a young male beauty cult surely says as much about the longings of queer men for a god who desires them as it does about a god of a nation, or creator of a world. Or it says as much about older queer men who place on the deity their own desires to love young bucks who come at a high price (which usually is some form of kingdom). What is more, the intriguing similarity of the

Mosaic covenant to a sadomasochistic contract suggests in biblical terms what modernity has established since the beginning of the scientific revolution: that the imagined (and desired) God of omnipotence is really the creation—and trained hand—of the people he appears (by their direction) to control. Desire and fantasy shape imagination of the tale, and enflesh the divinity that rumbles throughout it.

Disrupting the Heteronormative but Not the
Ethnic Masculinist Presumption

Through the lens of queer imagining and desire, a distinct and pragmatic possibility of sexual fluidity and homoeroticism in Israelite understandings of the divine–human relationship comes into focus. But even as this possibility becomes gradually more concrete and shades into likelihood, spelling a welcome disaster for the Bible's presumed heteronormativity, a corollary regression seems also to occur. The preliminary readings in this commentary together suggest that, where the character of the divine is concerned at least, masculinity (however unstable, anxious and ethnically specific) is reinscribed on the divine in even more exclusive and troubling ways.

What does it mean for us today, in thinking about and configuring the divine–human relationship in light of and in some continuity with biblical imaginings, to find evidence of sexual diversity that further *masculinizes* divinity? The queer sexuality thus far unearthed is, as Ted Jennings so carefully points out, a fairly consistent hyper-masculine homoeroticism that leads, in the case of the founding of the kingdom of Israel at least, to a further marginalization of women. Yhwh, according to Jennings's, Boer's, and possibly even Stone's readings, relates so exclusively and erotically to men via male sexualities and Mediterranean/European constructions of masculinity that 'the chosen' really can come to suggest a misogynistic strain in the human–divine relationship. This leaves contemporary women exegetes of all kinds, and queer women in particular, in an awkward (and all too familiar) position.

On the other hand, as a white queer theorist in feminist theologies, I recognize a certain irony in my concern for 'female' vs 'male' queerings of the divine. The categories 'female' and 'male' are themselves problematic for queer imagining to the extent that the modern Western male-female binary is a large part of what feeds the heteronormative presumption in most cultures of the world today. But I am not so far gone into the mists of theoretical reversals to forget that the world in which we still *live* is structured by this binary notion, and that the extent to which the male symbolic stands in for the female is still the extent to which those who understand themselves to be female are made invisible in the discourse. Whether sexual difference is understood to produce gender through a kind of biologism that trumps questions of cultural production, ethnicity, race and so on, or whether gender is understood as produced through reiteration and repetition, the question of sexual difference is not resolved in queer theory and should remain alive and unresolved in our queer engagements with biblical tales (see Butler and Rubin 1997).

So what do we do with the apparent importance and reiteration of ethnically specific divine masculinities in the Hebrew Bible? Although this is hard for me to imagine, the extent to which Yhwh is persuasively imagined with a queer lens seems here to mean that 'his' masculinity becomes even more central than it did in traditionally patriarchal readings! I do not, at this preliminary stage, think that this is the result of oversight on the part of the interpreters so much as it is indeed the fruit that the Hebrew Bible most easily yields. Given this, I should not be surprised that these first queer readings of the Hebrew Bible are so focused on issues of particular (though not exclusive) importance to modern Euro-American gay male experience: masculinity, male homoeroticism, man-boy eroticism, sadomasochism, and AIDS. Certainly some female and other queer experiences are shaped by many of these issues as well. But a queer reading of, for example, Ruth's and Naomi's domestic conspiracy has to yield a far different set of concerns, as, I believe, more or less queer readings of Sarah and Hagar, Esther, Miriam, Judith, the unnamed daughter of Jepthah, and Michal might do. The problem is, how to do it? What is *queer* about these female-character texts in any homoerotic or sexual-outsider sense? Also, how can queer readings of female-character texts account more fully for the intertextual shaping of race, culture and ethnicity in the very formulation of 'female', 'male' and 'sex'?

The queerest stories of women in the Hebrew Bible may in fact be those about women who managed to have a voice at all, women who managed to survive and/or overcome with some kind of chutzpah their barrenness, widowhood, slavery, rape, virginity, abandonment, marriage, ugliness, or other signifiers of their male-derivative identity, economic dependency and status. These stories may be more queer tales, in a desexualized sense, than those stories (if such stories exist) that hint at female homoeroticism. It is clear in any case, as feminist biblical scholarship has demonstrated, that no treatment of potential female homoeroticism in the Hebrew Bible can avoid the issues of patriarchy, silence, ethnicity and the ways that femininity is constructed in male-derivative terms. Even then, there may simply be nothing in the biblical texts that also reveals a meaningful dimension of female homoeroticism in the divine–human relationship.

Indeed, the most provocative female possibilities for tales about the divine–human relationship speak clearly to the terrible violence of the male-imagined Yhwh against these possibilities. If, for example, scholars such as Gerda Lerner are correct in their hypotheses that the snake in the garden of Eden represents the powerful fertility goddess of Mesopotamia, then Her seduction of Eve and promises of freedom She whispers to Eve when they are alone are exhilaratingly provocative, while Her humiliation and apparent defeat by Yhwh speak both to His ethnic triumphalism and misogyny and to the rise of patriarchy (Lerner 1986: 193-98).

Similarly, a queer biblical scholar could take up the story of the two women who 'live in the same house' and who come before Solomon with a custody dispute (1 Kgs 3.16-28). What this story seems primarily to reveal is a brutal, sexist and classist precedent for heteronormative law. The child can have only one mother, and the claims of its second mother are denied, presumably regardless of the doubling of support that this would give to a poor child born to prostitutes in a patriarchal society.[1] In his decree that the child be severed in two to test the loyalty of the 'true' mother, Solomon mirrors Yhwh, who ordered Abraham to slaughter Isaac to test Abraham's loyalty. Funny, although the knife was poised above the bound body of his young son, *that* test did not result in a questioning of Abraham's paternity.

The overwhelmingly male aspect of what queerness there seems to be (yet) in the Hebrew Bible begs not only questions of gender and ethnicity but raises the issue of the implications of queer biblical scholarship for feminist, womanist and mujerista theologies. What is gained as a theological resource for contemporary gay, bisexual and female-to-male transsexual men may actually constitute a significant

---

1. I'm grateful to Bethany Schneider for this insight.

and more troubling loss for lesbian, bisexual and male-to-female women. Although the sexuality of the divine is always 'only' traceable through metaphor, and biblical sources for its imagining are always 'only' socially constructed productions, we all know that such psycho-cultural reductions do not account for the whole impact of the Bible on theological and cultural imagination. We have to face the very real possibility that the Bible is simply not a source for imagining female homoeroticism in the divine–human relationship except through extra-polation by example from the male tales read queerly here. There is little here to offer queer female sexualities or even straight female sexualities as they are actually experienced in the world, and no little danger in further eliding them altogether.

While there is some real usefulness to the challenge that we extrapolate something female from the male homoeroticism of Yhwh and his men, particularly when we understand 'queer' imagining to trouble gender categorizations, there are some more or less obvious problems with doing that. For example, Jennings has suggested else-where that it is not likely that the warrior culture and resulting homo-erotic relationship between Yhwh and Israelite men (via the nascent monarchy) is really helpful as a metaphorical template for female divine homoeroticism, and I would tend to agree. He has suggested, however, that the evolution of Yhwh's character from a tempestuous and fickle leather daddy type into a more considerate lover deserving of David's loyalty may provide a wider scope for imagining divine eroti-cism today.[2] The task of imagining a queer divine–human relation more recognizably female is still daunting, however, and the derivative aspect of it is as politically irksome and distasteful to many women as it may be unproductive.

What example there can be for a queerly conceived divine–human relationship in Boer's imagined gathering of minds on Mount Sinai is even more difficult to assess. The fact that he chooses a particularly misogynistic band of European men incapable of describing or address-ing women in non-reductionist, non-obsessive terms does not have to exclude the possibility of imagining a radically different gathering, with a different outcome (after all, anything can happen in 40 days!). The fact is that his creative exploration of Yhwh as effete top, turning

2.   I am grateful to Ted Jennings for his helpful suggestions in response to this question (Personal communication, 23 August 2000).

into a puppet front for some kind of tormenter Ur-goddess, would be more intriguing if it didn't reinscribe a Victorianesque cult-of-femininity muteness on her. She is as much the imagined creation of the pitiful gathering as Boer argues Yhwh to be. But that may be Boer's point. Either way, it is a discouraging start for queer readings that also seek to imagine the divine–human relation beyond maleness.

Perhaps the instability of Yhwh's ethnically produced and imagined masculinities in all of these texts is the queerest possibility that we have. But even in the case of Stone's persuasive argument that anxiety about Yhwh's masculinity in Hosea reveals gender instability both in the deity and in the (mostly male) intended audience, the resulting reinscriptions of gender in the text do little to alter the *imagined* weight of Yhwh's masculinity, however constructed and ethnically specific that masculinity may be (and the point is that we forget that it is both). The evidence that Stone gives us of the instability of divine masculinity is an opening particularly for queer women exegetes, but an opening into what? That is the question.

Why Read it at All?

Queer readings of the Hebrew Bible raise issues of biblical authority for theology more clearly and poignantly than any other readings I've encountered. Queer commentary on the Hebrew Bible overturns heteronormative presumption and stability. This is no small thing, given the mythic importance of Western cultural/religious imagining about moral origins in these texts. But as I have just suggested, queer readings also seem further to elide female sexualities, especially in their imagining of the divine–human relationship. How queer Hebrew Bible/s function in the life of faith or have authority in theological reflection is the issue here. If queer readings of the Hebrew Bible are ever to help undo some of the patriarchal, racist and kyriarchal biases of so many generations of commentary, teaching and theology, the further masculinization of the divine that emerges from these readings will have to be addressed.

There is no question that queer commentary is incompatible with fundamentalist/literalist approaches to biblical authority. But there is no reason to believe that queer readings are at all incompatible with a variety of faith-based approaches (unless faith is dependent upon heteronormative presumption).

The question of the Bible's authority as a source of information about divine reality is actually a large one for liberal people of some faith, even if theirs is a tentative faith, or even if they are people who are not sure what to believe. The extent to which key narratives from the Jewish and Christian Scriptures undergird and justify claims that people want to make about divinity, goodness, or right living (even if those same people do not consider themselves religious) speaks to the persistent importance of biblical interpretation for theological reflection, and of the mythic imagining in contemporary social and moral life that is rooted in these tales. It does not matter what questions the biblical scholar or theologian may wish to raise regarding the veracity or reliability of the biblical texts and their many authors as records and recorders of actual historical events. Even as a piece of literature or as a record of cultural imagination collected over the millennia into a socially effective product, the content of most of the Hebrew Bible is about the memory and *possibility* of human–divine relationship, and as such it brings that memory and possibility into our thinking with the accompanying demand that we take account of it.

This means that the uses to which the Bible is put—its valence in the larger social context of meaning and orientation—are as important to theology as specific interpretations of the text itself. The many and varied ways that the biblical texts serve to authorize and validate the social architecture of religious and social communities lies behind the question of what kind of authorizing (or de-authorizing) principles may emerge out of queer readings. Most clearly, the queering of key narratives in the founding texts of the Jewish and Christian traditions authorize a kind of return fire against those who commandeer the entire weight of Scripture against contemporary gay, lesbian, bisexual, transgendered and other 'queer' persons.

Whether queer readings are 'true' in some historical or objective sense is no more relevant, really, than whether homophobic readings are 'true'. What matters in this kind of situation is a sort of criminal trial logic. Can alternative scenarios be presented (in key biblical texts) persuasively enough to raise sufficient doubt about the veracity of biblical authority *against* gay, lesbian, bisexual and transgendered persons? If so, then the homophobic readings cannot rule the day. But the Hebrew Bible continues, reliably, to confound universalistic claims about the gods of any interpretation. For example, if Yhwh could plausibly have chosen David solely on the basis of his beauty and declared divine love and loyalty in a homoerotic pairing, how could that 'same'

Yhwh (albeit in a different context, imagined by a different generation) also have commanded the Israelites to put to death men who have sex together? If we are presuming some degree of theophanic consistency to the biblical text as a whole (a large presumption, to be sure, but an important one for questions of biblical authority), we may explain the divine homophobia in Leviticus and the divine homoeroticism elsewhere by going into the realm of the ridiculous and suggesting a homosexual panic defense for God, a kind of slimy Roy Cohn/gay persecutor complex for a profoundly unhappy and vindictive closeted gay deity. Or we could suggest a developmental movement out of the closet for Yhwh: he gave the laws to Moses long before Saul and David turned his eye. After all, there is something of a biblical tradition of persecutors who repent and cast their lot (come out?) with those they have persecuted.

If it is even possible (let alone probable or certain) to read queer intent and homoerotic action into the sacred accounts of the life of the god of Israel, surely the anti-queer Bible of the religious right is deflated. But what do such readings authorize beyond this? I am not suggesting that delegitimation of the righteous stranglehold that the religious right attempts to maintain on the Bible is a bad thing. I am asking if there are also some other authorizing dynamics made possible by a queered Bible. Certainly some will suggest that such scholarship simply authorizes a further trivialization of an already tenuous textual source. According to this logic, if so many divergent readings are plausible, none must be true. Irrespective of queer readings, the authority of the Bible as a source for information about some kind of 'real' divine–human relationship has long been challenged by the modern innovation of historical critical interpretation and the consequent recognition that the Bible is a historical product among other historical products. In addition, queer readings delegitimize biblical authority as a source of information about real divinity further because of their simultaneous outrageousness and plausibility.

For scholars and others on the queer margin, the Bible may suddenly become more interesting and, at the same time, less potent. It was used against us for so long, and to such effect, that the reversal wrought by queer commentary may merely neutralize the text rather than reveal any liberative or life-altering *scriptural* potential in it for ritual and/or cultic retrievals. On the other hand, a queered Bible might authorize a new religion and cultural formation altogether. Both are possible.

Queer interpretations of Moses, David, Elijah, Ruth, Naomi, Samson and Delilah, Jonathan, Elijah and a Bible-full of other possibilities that present such radical alternatives to patriarchal heteronormativity either provide a ground for inventing a new queer religious morality, or they can facilitate further the retreat of the Bible from social and religious reasoning about sexual morality altogether.

Either way, queer readings do not enter the contemporary social, political and religious stage without effect. Even to those horrified by homoerotic and sexually diverse possibilities in the Hebrew Bible, queer commentaries authorize interpretive social, religious, and theological response and action. Queer thinking is, as Ken Stone suggests in his introduction to this volume, greater than the sum of gay, lesbian, bisexual, transgendered or other sexual minority thoughts and experiences. Queer readings not only authorize a glimpse into the possibility that homoeroticism and other so-called sexually deviant practices were both present in the Bible and even favorably accounted for (given divine sanction, even); they also suggest a rethinking of the divine–human and divine–world relationship in terms that transgress the presumed stability of the identities of both.

What of Revelation?

What of the divine itself in all of this thinking about a queer Bible? What of divinity—that which is beyond thought but which still draws theologians, like flame draws moths? Does queer commentary further distance the Bible from relevance and access to divinity, or does it open new possibilities for both? I have begun to suggest here that I think that some new possibilities for queer biblical theology are opened up by queer biblical commentary.

The divine–human relationship long ago became desiccated by abstraction in both biblical interpretation and systematic theology, so reframing the divine in terms of a sexual-outsider position, indeed sexualizing divinity at all, does restore some wholism to the divine–human relationship. It also provides a context for thinking about divinity in the world according to more embodied frames of reference. And a more embodied frame of reference for the divine that takes the biblical text at all into account will necessarily undermine heteronormative presumption, as these readings already indicate.

Stone's argument that the rhetoric of food and sex in Hosea exposes an unstable and anxious ethnic masculinity in Yhwh, as well as 'slips in gender intelligibility' in Hosea's feminized male audience, becomes decidedly queerer when we think about incarnation and embodied notions of divinity. Indeed, if a less iconoclastic and more embodied thinking about the divine is a desired goal in biblical theology (and I believe that it is), then as Stone indicates here and Eilberg-Schwartz argues elsewhere, a homoerotically charged subtext in the relationship between God and the men (at least) of Israel cannot be avoided (Eilberg-Schwartz 1994).

There are some fascinating and provocative possibilities resident in any reading of the Hebrew Bible that ceases abstracting and over-spiritualizing the physical presence of the deity in the world. As Eilberg-Schwartz, Jennings and Boer have already made clear, the evident homoeroticism of a male-embodied deity in love with the male heroes of his story 'comes out'. And the Hebrew Bible contains only the (mostly masculinist) stories that have survived millennia of editing. But even with that, what a storehouse of theological riches the ancient tales become if we grant, just for an imaginative moment, the possibility of a divine freedom so bold that a single embodiment cannot hold it. What might come out differently as a result of such imagining? Everything, I suspect.

I have argued elsewhere that theological limitations on divine embodiment are unsupportable in concert with theological claims for divine freedom (Schneider 1999). That God cannot be embodied except, for example, in the ecclesiastically controlled, historical event of an individual man from Nazareth is hubris of the highest degree. If we take up a more humble theological position and allow for a multiplicity of divine embodiments based on our theological assertions of divine freedom and of divine love, how might we wrap our thinking around ancient texts that actually give us precisely that? The several clear divine embodiments in the Hebrew Bible, combined with the multitude of additional hints and subtexts in that direction, give ample material for queer biblical theology to take root. To play a bit fast and loose with verbs, if God 'bodies', then it stands to reason that God also 'sexes' in a polymorphic array. And if we can imagine divinity thus, we can also re-imagine the divine–world relationship in ways that finally may bring the richness and multiplicity of worldly and of divine experience together.

Despite these enchanting, imaginative possibilities, queer biblical theology (if we can even call it that yet) is in an odd place of formation. It stands uncertainly between the hermeneutics of cultural/literary theory that supports its own deconstructive stance toward heteronormativity and prelinguistic truth claims, on the one hand, and the real divinity that it presumably (as *theo*logy) has the task of imagining in conversation with the Bible on the other. But I have argued here that queer commentary may open the door for a theological rethinking of revelation and divine reality that may give us a language for thinking about imagination *and* divinity beyond the self-producing loop of social construction alone. However, those queer theologians who take up the question of God in the Bible may very well still conclude, along with other postmodern theological compatriots, that any so-called real divinity cannot be articulated as such precisely because there is no solid foundation for the 'real' outside of the social construction of the biblical text/identity/history/moral universe. If the divine is that which transcends our human constructions in *some* way (an assumption in and of itself) then it can only be the unspeakable other, and as such cannot enter discourse except as silence.

There is nothing wrong with this position vis-à-vis the divine in theology, except when the Bible is construed even marginally as a source for theological reflection and imagining of the divine–human relationship. Where is *divinity* resident in these ancient tales? How, in other words, can biblical readings fit into a process of tracing some real divinity, when we understand them simply as more or less colorful manipulations of the texts that have helped to form us and which we in turn formulate—a self-referencing loop of reading, social construction, rereading, reconstructing and so on? One possible answer, of course, is that they cannot. Queer biblical theology, in other words, cannot follow liberation theologies into the Scriptures in search of a plumb line to evidence for *divine* favor for and commitment to the poor and the marginalized. Nor can it follow more orthodox theologies into the Scriptures in search of historical evidence of *divine* relationship to the faithful so that queer folks today can extrapolate answers to contemporary questions about what *God* will do for or with them.

I think that a queer biblical theology need not concede claims to a real divinity resident in the text just because of its necessary commitments to intertextuality and the depths of fantasy to which desire will go. The Bible is a record of human imagining, memory and desire for the divine in relation to us. There is also the possibility, unfounded except through the lens of faith, that it is also a record of sorts of divine imagining, memory and desire *for us*. We are not at liberty, given the uses of the text in historical attempts to eliminate us, and our own weary awareness of the historical productions of all things symbolic, to read onto the Bible an uninterpreted revelatory content—a direct view into divine existence as it were. But neither are we at liberty to presume that divinity cannot breathe/aspirate/inspirit a heartbeat of recognition and revolution in these ancient tales, nor to deny the possibility of divine eros that casts a tissue of connection to us through a thing so thoroughly produced in all-too-human history.

While it is folly, of course, to try for revelation, theologians like myself are mostly a foolish lot. We are faced with the thrilling possibility that we need not always stand at the defensive when Bibles show up in the discussion, and I for one cannot resist thinking about the possibilities for re-imagining the divine through a queer biblical lens. After meeting Yhwh in all of his desire for David, and catching an all too brief glimpse of the goat-clad Elijah, and imagining for the first time a host of queer angels urging the beleaguered Sodomites out of the fire with gentle encouragements of 'that's it, honey, you're almost there' and 'thank god girls, we knew you wouldn't leave anyone behind', and even thinking that Delilah might have tired of Samson's self-destructive play for queer reasons all her own, I choose to think that there may be something revelatory in the Bible, in the old-fashioned theophanic sense of revelation, after all.

BIBLIOGRAPHY

Abelove, Henry, Michèle Aina Barale and David M. Halperin (eds.)
    1993   *The Lesbian and Gay Studies Reader* (New York: Routledge).
Ackroyd, Peter
    1971   *The First Book of Samuel* (Cambridge: Cambridge University Press).
Adam, A.K.M.
    1995   *What Is Postmodern Biblical Criticism?* (Minneapolis: Fortress Press).
Adam, A.K.M. (ed.)
    2000   *A Handbook of Postmodern Biblical Interpretation* (St Louis: Chalice Press).
Anderson, Francis I., and David Noel Freedman
    1980   *Hosea: A New Translation with Introduction and Commentary* (AB, 24; Garden City, NY: Doubleday).
Anderson, Bernhard W.
    1982   'The Problem and Promise of Commentary', *Int* 36.4: 341-55.
Anonymous
    1921   *Cleanness: An Alliterative Tripartite Poem on the Deluge, the Destruction of Sodom and the Death of Belshazzar* (ed. Israel Gollancz; trans. D.S. Brewer; Totowa, NJ, and Cambridge: D.S. Brewer and Rowman and Littlefield).
    1976   *Mimekor Yisrael: Classical Jewish Folk Tales*, I (collected by Micha Joseph Bin Gorion; ed. Emmanuel bin Gorion; trans. I.M. Lask; introduction by Dab Ben-Amos; Bloomington: Indiana University Press).
Antonelli, Judith S.
    1997   *In the Image of God: A Feminist Commentary on the Torah* (Northvale, NJ: Jason Aronson, Inc.).
Bach, Alice
    1993   'Reading Allowed: Feminist Biblical Criticism Approaching the Millennium', *Currents in Research: Biblical Studies* 1: 191-215.
Bail, Ulrike
    1998   ' "O God, hear my prayer": Psalm 55 and Violence against Women', in A. Brenner and C.R. Fontaine (eds.), *Wisdom and Psalms: A Feminist Companion to the Bible (Second Series)* (Sheffield: Sheffield Academic Press): 242-63.
Bailey, Derrick Sherwin
    1955   *Homosexuality in the Western Christian Tradition* (London: Longmans, Green & Co.).
Bailey, Randall
    1995   'They're Nothing but Incestuous Bastards: The Polemical Use of Sex and

Sexuality in Hebrew Canon Narratives', in Segovia and Tolbert 1995a: 121-38.

Barr, James
    2000   *History and Ideology in the Old Testament: Biblical Studies at the End of a Millennium* (Oxford: Oxford University Press).

Beal, Timothy K.
    1992   'Ideology and Intertextuality: Surplus of Meaning and Controlling the Means of Production', in Fewell 1992: 27-39.
    1997   *The Book of Hiding: Gender, Ethnicity, Annihilation, and Esther* (New York: Routledge).

Berlant, Lauren, and Michael Warner
    1995   'What Does Queer Theory Teach Us About *X*?', *Publications of the Modern Language Associations of America* 3: 343-49.

Bersani, Leo
    1995   *Homos* (Cambridge, MA: Harvard University Press).

Bible and Culture Collective, The
    1995   *The Postmodern Bible* (New Haven: Yale University Press).

Bird, Phyllis A.
    1997a   *Missing Persons and Mistaken Identities: Women and Gender in Ancient Israel* (Minneapolis: Fortress Press).
    1997b   'The End of the Male Cult Prostitute: A Literary-Historical and Socio-logical Analysis of Hebrew *QADES-QEDESIM*', in J. Emerton (ed.), *Congress Volume: Cambridge 1995* (VTSup, 66; Leiden: E.J. Brill): 37-80.
    2000   'The Bible in Christian Ethical Deliberation concerning Homosexuality: Old Testament Contributions', in David L. Balch (ed.), *Homosexuality, Science, and the 'Plain Sense' of Scripture* (Grand Rapids: Eerdmans): 142-76.

Blanchot, Maurice
    1963   *Lautreamont et Sade* (Paris: Minuit).

Blok, Anton
    1981   'Rams and Billy-Goats: A Key to the Mediterranean Code of Honour', *Man* 16: 427-40.

Boer, Roland
    1999   *Knockin' On Heaven's Door: The Bible and Popular Culture* (New York: Routledge).

Bordo, Susan
    1993   *Unbearable Weight: Feminism, Western Culture, and the Body* (Berke-ley: University of California Press).
    1999   *The Male Body: A New Look at Men in Public and in Private* (New York: Farrar, Straus and Giroux).

Bourdieu, Pierre
    1979   *Algeria 1960* (Cambridge: Cambridge University Press).

Boyarin, Daniel
    1995   'Are There Any Jews in "The History of Sexuality"?', *Journal of the History of Sexuality* 5.3: 333-55.
    1997   *Unheroic Conduct: The Rise of Heterosexuality and the Invention of the Jewish Man* (Berkeley: University of California Press).

Brenner, Athalya (ed.)
      1995   *A Feminist Companion to the Latter Prophets* (Sheffield: Sheffield Academic Press).
Bright, John
      1981   *A History of Israel* (Philadelphia: Westminster Press, 3rd edn): 343-60.
Brooten, Bernadette J.
      1996   *Love Between Women: Early Christian Responses to Female Homoeroticism* (Chicago: University of Chicago Press).
Brown, Francis, S.R. Driver and Charles A. Briggs
      1977   *A Hebrew and English Lexicon of the Old Testament* (Oxford: Clarendon Press [1907]).
Butler, Judith
      1990   *Gender Trouble: Feminism and the Subversion of Identity* (New York: Routledge).
      1993   *Bodies That Matter: On the Discursive Limits of 'Sex'* (New York: Routledge).
      1994   'Against Proper Objects', *differences* 6.2, 6.3: 1-26.
Butler, Judith, and Gayle Rubin
      1997   'Interview', in Elizabeth Weed and Naomi Schor (eds.), *Feminism Meets Queer Theory: Books from Differences* (Bloomington: Indiana University Press): 68-108.
Califia, Pat
      1994   *Public Sex: The Culture of Radical Sex* (Pittsburgh: Cleis Press).
Carden, Michael
      1999   'Homophobia and Rape in Sodom and Gibeah: A Response to Ken Stone', *JSOT* 82: 83-96.
Chauncey, George
      1994   *Gay New York: Gender, Urban Culture, and the Making of the Gay Male World, 1890–1940* (New York: Basic Books).
Chick, Jack
      1998   'Doom Town', 23 June 1998. http://www.chick.com/tracts/0273/0273.
Clines, David J.A.
      1995   *Interested Parties: The Ideology of Writers and Readers of the Hebrew Bible* (Sheffield: Sheffield Academic Press).
      1998   'From Salamanca to Cracow: What Has (And Has Not) Happened at SBL International Meetings', in *On the Way to the Postmodern: Old Testament Essays 1967–1998*. I (Sheffield: Sheffield Academic Press): 158-93.
Clines, David J.A., and J. Cheryl Exum
      1993   'The New Literary Criticism', in J. Cheryl Exum and David J.A. Clines (eds.), *The New Literary Criticism and the Hebrew Bible* (Sheffield: Sheffield Academic Press): 11-25.
Comstock, Gary D.
      1993   *Gay Theology Without Apology* (Cleveland: Pilgrim Press).
Counihan, Carole M.
      1999   *The Anthropology of Food and Body: Gender, Meaning, and Power* (New York: Routledge).

Coward, Rosalind
    1985   *Female Desires: How They Are Sought, Bought, and Packaged* (New York: Grove Weidenfeld).

Crenshaw, James L.
    1978   *Samson: A Secret Betrayed, A Vow Ignored* (Atlanta: John Knox Press).

Crenshaw, Kimberle
    1989   'Demarginalizing the Intersection of Race and Sex: A Black Feminist Critique of Antidiscrimination Doctrine, Feminist Theory and Antiracist Politics', *University of Chicago Legal Forum*: 139-67.

Crum, John
    1996   'Queer Music', *Performing Arts Journal* 53, no. 18.2: 118-26.

Davies, Philip R.
    1995   *Whose Bible Is It Anyway?* (Sheffield: Sheffield Academic Press).

Davis, John
    1977   *People of the Mediterranean: An Essay in Comparative Social Anthropology* (London and Boston: Routledge and Kegan Paul).

De Lauretis, Teresa
    1986   'Feminist Studies/Critical Studies: Issues, Terms, and Contexts', in Teresa de Lauretis (ed.), *Feminist Studies/Critical Studies* (Bloomington: Indiana University Press): 1-19.
    1990   'Eccentric Subjects: Feminist Theory and Historical Consciousness', *Feminist Studies* 16.1: 115-50.
    1991   'Queer Theory: Lesbian and Gay Sexualities: An Introduction', *differences: A Journal of Feminist Cultural Studies* 3.2: iii-xviii.
    1994   'Habit Changes', *differences* 6.2, 6.3: 296-313.

Delaney, Carol
    1987   'Seeds of Honor, Fields of Shame', in Gilmore 1987: 35-48.
    1991   *The Seed and the Soil: Gender and Cosmology in Turkish Village Society* (Berkeley: University of California Press).
    1998   *Abraham on Trial: The Social Legacy of Biblical Myth* (Princeton, NJ: Princeton University Press).

Deleuze, Gilles
    1991   'Coldness and Cruelty', in Gilles Deleuze and Leopold von Sacher-Masoch, *Masochism: Coldness and Cruelty and Venus in Furs* (trans. J. McNeill; New York: Zone Books): 9-138.

Deleuze, Gilles, and Felix Guattari
    1977   *Anti-Oedipus: Capitalism and Schizophrenia* (trans. R. Hurley, M. Seem and H.R. Lane; New York: Viking).

DeVault, Marjorie
    1991   *Feeding the Family: The Social Organization of Caring as Gendered Work* (Chicago: University of Chicago Press).

Douglas, Mary
    1975   *Implicit Meanings: Essays in Anthropology* (London and New York: Routledge and Kegan Paul).

Dover, K.J.
    1989   *Greek Homosexuality* (Cambridge, MA: Harvard University Press, 2nd edn [1978]).

Downing, Christine
1989   *Myths and Mysteries of Same-Sex Love* (New York: Continuum/Cross-road): 146-67.

DuBois, Page
1988   *Sowing the Body: Psychoanalysis and Ancient Representations of Women* (Chicago: University of Chicago Press).

Eco, Umberto
1981   'The Myth of Superman', in *The Role of the Reader* (London: Hutchinson): 107-24.

Eilberg-Schwartz, Howard
1990   *The Savage in Judaism: An Anthropology of Israelite Religion and Ancient Judaism* (Bloomington: Indiana University Press).
1994   *God's Phallus: And Other Problems for Men and Monotheism* (Boston: Beacon Press).

Eng, David L., and Alice Y. Hom (eds.)
1998   *Q & A: Queer in Asian America* (Philadelphia: Temple University Press).

Exum, J. Cheryl
1993   *Fragmented Women: Feminist (Sub)versions of Biblical Narratives* (Sheffield: Sheffield Academic Press; Philadelphia: Trinity Press International).
1996   *Plotted, Shot, and Painted: Cultural Representations of Biblical Women* (Sheffield: Sheffield Academic Press).

Fausto-Sterling, Anne
2000   *Sexing the Body: Gender Politics and the Construction of Sexuality* (New York: Basic Books).

Felder, Cain Hope (ed.)
1991   *Stony the Road We Trod: African American Biblical Interpretation* (Minneapolis: Fortress Press).

Fewell, Danna Nolan (ed.)
1992   *Reading Between Texts: Intertextuality and the Hebrew Bible* (Louisville, KY: Westminster/John Knox Press).

Fewell, Danna Nolan
1998   'Judges', in Carol A. Newsom and Sharon H. Ringe (eds.), *Women's Bible Commentary* (Louisville, KY: Westminster/John Knox Press, 2nd edn): 73-83.

Fewell, Danna Nolan, and David M. Gunn
1993   *Gender, Power, and Promise: The Subject of the Bible's First Story* (Nashville: Abingdon Press).

Fokkelman, J.P.
1990   *Narrative Art and Poetry in the Books of Samuel.* III. *Throne and City* (Assen: Van Gorcum).

Fontaine, Carole
1995   'A Response to "Hosea"', in Brenner 1995: 60-69.

Foucault, Michel
1978   *The History of Sexuality.* I. *An Introduction* (trans. Robert Hurley; New York: Vintage Books). Originally published as *Histoire de la sexualité 1: La volonté de savoir* (Paris: Gallimard, 1976).

1980	*Herculine Barbin: Being the Recently Discovered Memoirs of a Nine-teenth-Century French Hermaphrodite* (trans. Richard McDougall; New York: Random House).
1985	*The History of Sexuality*. II. *The Use of Pleasure* (trans. Robert Hurley; New York: Random House).

Fox, Everett
1999	*Give us a King* (New York: Schocken).

Frankel, Ellen
1996	*The Five Books of Miriam: A Woman's Commentary on the Torah* (New York: Putnam's Sons).

Fretheim, Terence
1982	'Old Testament Commentaries: Their Selection and Use', *Int* 36.4: 356-71.

Freud, Sigmund
1959	*Group Psychology and the Analysis of Ego* (ed. and trans. James Strachey; New York: Norton).
1977	'Three Essays on the Theory of Sexuality', in A. Richards (ed.), *The Pelican Freud Library*. VII. *On Sexuality* (Harmondsworth: Penguin): 31-169.
1979	'A Child is Being Beaten', in A. Richards (ed.), *The Pelican Freud Library*. X. *On Psychopathology* (Harmondsworth: Penguin): 159-93.
1984a	'Instincts and Their Vicissitudes', in A. Richards (ed.), *The Pelican Freud Library*. XI. *On Metapsychology: The Theory of Psychoanalysis* (Harmondsworth: Penguin): 105-39.
1984b	'Beyond the Pleasure Principle', in A. Richards (ed.), *The Pelican Freud Library*. XI. *On Metapsychology: The Theory of Psychoanalysis* (Harmondsworth: Penguin): 269-337.
1984c	'The Economic Problem of Masochism', in A. Richards (ed.), *The Pelican Freud Library*. XI. *On Metapsychology: The Theory of Psychoanalysis* (Harmondsworth: Penguin): 409-26.

Friedlander, Gerald (translator and annotator)
1916	*Pirke de Rabbi Eliezer (The Chapters of Rabbi Eliezer the Great): According to the Text of the Manuscript Belonging to Abraham Epstein of Vienna* (New York: Sepher-Hermon Press).

Frymer-Kensky, Tikva
1992	*In the Wake of the Goddesses: Women, Culture, and the Biblical Trans-formation of Pagan Myth* (New York: The Free Press).

Fuss, Diana
1989	*Essentially Speaking: Feminism, Nature and Difference* (New York: Routledge).
1991	'Inside/Out', in Diana Fuss (ed.), *Inside/Out: Lesbian Theories, Gay Theories* (New York: Routledge): 1-10.

Garber, Marjorie
1995	*Vice Versa: Bisexuality and the Eroticism of Everyday Life* (New York: Simon & Schuster).

Gibson, J.C.L.
1977	*Canaanite Myths and Legends* (Edinburgh: T. & T. Clark).

Gilmore, David (ed.)
  1987   *Honor and Shame and the Unity of the Mediterranean* (Washington, DC:
              American Anthropological Association).
Gilmore, David
  1990   *Manhood in the Making: Cultural Concepts of Masculinity* (New Haven:
              Yale University Press).
Goldstein, Rebecca
  1995   'Looking Back at Lot's Wife', in Christina Büchman and Celina Spiegel
              (eds.), *Out of the Garden: Women Writers on the Bible* (London: Harper-
              Collins): 3-12.
Goss, Robert E. and Mona West (eds.)
  2000   *Take Back the Word: A Queer Reading of the Bible* (Cleveland: Pilgrim
              Press).
Grahn, Judy
  1984   *Another Mother Tongue: Gay Words, Gay Worlds* (Boston: Beacon
              Press).
Gramsci, Antonio
  1971   *Selections from the Prison Notebooks* (trans. Quinton Hoare and Geof-
              frey Nowell Smith; New York: International, 2nd edn).
Greenberg, David
  1988   *The Construction of Homosexuality* (Chicago: University of Chicago
              Press).
Gregor, Thomas
  1985   *Anxious Pleasures: The Sexual Lives of an Amazonian People* (Chicago:
              University of Chicago Press).
Grimm, Veronika E.
  1996   *From Feasting to Fasting, the Evolution of a Sin: Attitudes to Food in
              Late Antiquity* (New York: Routledge).
Hackett, Jo Ann
  1989   'Can A Sexist Model Liberate Us? Ancient Near Eastern "Fertility"
              Goddesses', *JFSR* 5.1: 65-76.
Hallam, Paul
  1993   *The Book of Sodom* (London: Verso).
Halperin, David M.
  1990   *One Hundred Years of Homosexuality and Other Essays on Greek Love*
              (New York: Routledge).
  1995   *Saint Foucault: Toward a Gay Hagiography* (Oxford: Oxford University
              Press).
Halpern, Baruch
  1987   ' "Brisker Pipes Than Poetry": The Development of Israelite Mono-
              theism', in Jacob Neusner, Baruch A. Levine and Ernest S. Frerichs
              (eds.), *Judaic Perspectives on Ancient Israel* (Philadelphia: Fortress
              Press): 77-115.
Helminiak, D.A.
  1994   *What the Bible* Really *Says about Homosexuality* (San Francisco: Alamo
              Square Press).
Hennessy, Rosemary
  1994   'Queer Theory, Left Politics', *Rethinking Marxism* 7.3: 85-111.

Henshaw, Richard A.
　1994　　*Female and Male: The Cultic Personnel: The Bible and the Rest of the*
　　　　　Ancient Near East (Allison Park, PA: Pickwick Publications).
Herzfeld, Michael
　1980　　'Honor and Shame: Some Problems in the Comparative Analysis of
　　　　　Moral Systems', *Man* 15: 339-51.
　1985　　*The Poetics of Manhood: Contest and Identity in a Cretan Mountain*
　　　　　Village (Princeton, NJ: Princeton University Press).
Hillers, Delbert R.
　1972　　*Lamentations* (AB, 7A; New York: Doubleday).
Hooks, Stephen M.
　1985　　*Sacred Prostitution in Israel and the Ancient Near East* (unpublished
　　　　　PhD Dissertation, Hebrew Union College).
Horner, Tom
　1978　　*Jonathan Loved David* (Philadelphia: Westminster Press).
Inhorn, Marcia C.
　1994　　*Quest for Conception: Gender, Infertility, and Egyptian Medical Tradi-*
　　　　　tions (Philadelphia: University of Pennsylvania Press).
Irenaeus
　1883　　'Against Heresies', in A. Cleveland Coxe (ed.), *The Apostolic Fathers*
　　　　　with Justin Martyr and Irenaeus: The Ante-Nicene Fathers, I (Grand
　　　　　Rapids: Eerdmans): 309-567.
Jagose, Annamarie
　1996　　*Queer Theory: An Introduction* (Melbourne: Melbourne University Press;
　　　　　New York: New York University Press).
Jakobsen, Janet R., and Ann Pellegrini
　1999　　'Getting Religion', in Marjorie Garber and Rebecca L. Walkowitz (eds.),
　　　　　One Nation Under God? Religion and American Culture (New York:
　　　　　Routledge): 101-14.
Johansson, Warren
　1990　　'Sodom and Gomorrah', in Wayne Dynes (ed.), *Encyclopedia of Homo-*
　　　　　sexuality, II (New York: Garland Publishing): 1128-30.
Jordan, Mark D.
　1997　　*The Invention of Sodomy in Christian Theology* (Chicago: University of
　　　　　Chicago Press).
Katz, Jonathan Ned
　1995　　*The Invention of Heterosexuality* (New York: Penguin Books).
Keefe, Alice
　1995　　'The Female Body, the Body Politic and the Land: A Sociopolitical
　　　　　Reading of Hosea 1–2', in Brenner 1995: 70-100.
Keiser, Elizabeth B.
　1997　　*Courtly Desire and Medieval Homophobia: The Legitimation of Sexual*
　　　　　Pleasure in Cleanness and its Contexts (New Haven: Yale University
　　　　　Press).
Kim, Daniel Y.
　1998　　'The Strange Love of Frank Chin', in Eng and Hom 1998: 270-303.

Kripal, Jeffrey J.
    1998   *Kali's Child: The Mystical and the Erotic in the Life and Teachings of Ramakrishna* (Chicago: University of Chicago Press, 2nd edn).

Kristeva, Julia
    1980   *Desire in Language: A Semiotic Approach to Literature and Art* (ed. Leon S. Roudiez; trans. Thomas Gora, Alice Jardine and Leon S. Roudiez; New York: Columbia University Press).

Lacan, Jacques
    1990   'Kant with Sade', *October* 51: 53-104.
    1992   *The Ethics of Psychoanalysis 1959–1960. The Seminar of Jacques Lacan, Book VII* (trans. Dennis Porter; London: Tavistock/Routledge).

Lawrence, Marilyn (ed.)
    1987   *Fed Up and Hungry: Women, Oppression and Food* (New York: Peter Bedrick Books).

Leith, Mary Joan Winn
    1989   'Verse and Reverse: The Transformation of the Woman, Israel, in Hosea 1-3', in Peggy L. Day (ed.), *Gender and Difference in Ancient Israel* (Minneapolis: Fortress Press): 95-108.

Lemche, Niels Peter
    1991   *The Canaanites and Their Land: The Tradition of the Canaanites* (Sheffield: Sheffield Academic Press).
    1992   'The God of Hosea', in Eugene Ulrich *et al.* (eds.), *Priests, Prophets and Scribes: Essays on the Formation and Heritage of Second Temple Judaism in Honour of Joseph Blenkinsopp* (Sheffield: Sheffield Academic Press): 241-57.
    1998   *The Israelites in History and Tradition* (Louisville, KY: Westminster/John Knox Press; London: SPCK).

Lerner, Gerda
    1986   *The Creation of Patriarchy* (Oxford: Oxford University Press).

Leupp, Gary
    1995   *Male Colors: The Construction of Homosexuality in Tokugawa Japan* (Berkeley: University of California Press).

Lévi-Strauss, Claude
    1963   *Totemism* (trans. Rodney Needham; Boston: Beacon Press).

Linafelt, Tod
    2000   *Surviving Lamentations: Catastrophe, Lament, and Protest in the Afterlife of a Biblical Book* (Chicago: University of Chicago Press).

Linafelt, Tod, and Timothy K. Beal
    1995   'Sifting for Cinders: Leviticus 10:1-15', in George Aichele and Gary Phillips (eds.), *Intertextuality and the Bible* (Semeia, 69/70; Atlanta: Scholars Press): 19-32.

Lindisfarne, Nancy
    1994   'Variant Masculinities, Variant Virginities: Rethinking "Honour and Shame"', in A. Cornwall and N. Lindisfarne (eds.), *Dislocating Masculinity: Comparative Ethnographies* (London: Routledge): 82-96.

Linscheid, John
    1996   'Surviving Fire: A Queer Look at Sodom', http://www.seas.upenn.edu/~linsch/Sodomtxt.html.

Long, Burke O.
1997   *Planting and Reaping Albright: Politics, Ideology, and Interpreting the Bible* (University Park: Pennsylvania State University Press).

Lorde, A.
1978   *Uses of the Erotic: The Erotic as Power* (The Fourth Berkshire Conference on the History of Women, Mt Holyoke College; Freedom, CA: The Crossing Press).

Malson, Helen
1998   *The Thin Woman: Feminism, Post-Structuralism and the Social Psychology of Anorexia Nervosa* (New York: Routledge).

Marr, David
1999   'Hell Bent', *Sydney Morning Herald, Spectrum* 6 November 1999: 1, 6, 7.

Martin, Dale
1995   'Heterosexism and the Interpretation of Romans 1:18-32', *Bib Int* 3.3: 332-55.
1996   '*Arsenokoitês* and *Malakos*: meanings and Consequences', in Robert Brawley (ed.), *Biblical Ethics and Homosexuality: Listening to Scripture* (Louisville, KY: Westminster/John Knox Press): 117-36.

Matthews, Victor H.
1987   'Entrance Ways and Threshing Floors: Legally Significant Sites in the Ancient Near East', *Fides et Historia* 19: 25-40.

Mays, James Luther
1969   *Hosea: A Commentary* (OTL; Philadelphia: Westminster Press).

McKnight, David
1973   'Sexual Symbolism of Food Among the Wik-Mungkan', *Man* 8.2: 194-209.

Meigs, Anna S.
1984   *Food, Sex, and Pollution: A New Guinea Religion* (New Brunswick, NJ: Rutgers University Press).

Mettinger, Tryggve N.D.
1990   'The Elusive Essence: YHWH, El and Baal and the Distinctiveness of Israelites Faith', in Erhard Blum, Christian Macholz and Ekkehard W. Stegemann (eds.), *Die Hebräische Bibel und uhre zweifache Nachgeschichte: Festschrift für Rolf Rendtorff* (Neukirchen–Vluyn: Neukirchener Verlag): 393-417.

Meyers, Carol
1988   *Discovering Eve: Ancient Israelite Women in Context* (Oxford: Oxford University Press).

Milton, John
1963   *Samson Agonistes* (ed. John T. Shawcross; New York: New York University Press).

Moltmann, Jürgen
1985   *God In Creation* (San Francisco: Harper Collins).

Moore, Stephen D.
1998   'Que(e)rying Paul: Preliminary Questions', in David J.A. Clines and Stephen D. Moore (eds.), *Auguries: The Jubilee Volume of the Sheffield*

Department of Biblical Studies (Sheffield: Sheffield Academic Press): 250-74.

Nahmanides
1971   *Commentary on the Torah: Genesis* (trans. C.B. Chavel; New York: Shilo).

Nissinen, Martti
1998   *Homoeroticism in the Biblical World: A Historical Perspective* (trans. Kirsi Stjerna; Minneapolis: Fortress Press).

Nouwen, Henri
1979   *The Wounded Healer: The Ministry in Contemporary Society* (New York: Doubleday).

Nussbaum, Martha
1990   'Therapeutic Arguments and Structures of Desire', *differences* 2.1: 46-66.

Nygren, Anders
1963   *Agape and Eros* (trans. Philip S. Watson; New York: Harper & Row).

O'Connor, Kathleen
1992   'Lamentations', in Carol A. Newsom and Sharon H. Ringe (eds.), *The Women's Bible Commentary* (Louisville, KY: Westminster/John Knox Press): 178-82.

O'Donovan, Connell
1996   'Reclaiming Sodom', http://www.geocities.com/WestHollywood/1942/sodom. 5 May 1996.

Oden, Robert A. Jr
1987   *The Bible Without Theology: The Theological Tradition and Alternatives to It* (San Francisco: Harper & Row).

Olyan, Saul
1994   ' "And with a Male You Shall Not Lie the Lying Down of a Woman": On the Meaning and Significance of Leviticus 18:22 and 20:13', *Journal of the History of Sexuality* 5.2: 179-206.

Ostriker, Alicia Suskin
1994   *The Nakedness of the Fathers: Biblical Visions and Revisions* (New Brunswick, NJ: Rutgers University Press).

Pardes, Ilana
1992   *Countertraditions in the Bible: A Feminist Approach* (Cambridge, MA: Harvard University Press).

Parisi, Hope
1994   'Discourse and Danger: Women's Heroism in the Bible and Dalila's Self-Defense', in Charles W. Durham and Kristin Pruitt McColgan (eds.), *Spokesperson Milton: Voices in Contemporary Criticism* (London: Associated University Presses): 260-74.

Percy III, W.A.
1996   *Pederasty and Pedagogy in Archaic Greece* (Urbana, IL: University of Illinois Press): 53-58.

Peristiany, J.G. (ed.)
1966   *Honour and Shame: The Values of Mediterranean Society* (London: Weidenfeld & Nicolson).

Petersen, William
    1989   'On the Study of "Homosexuality" in Patristic Sources', *Studia Patristica* 20: 284.

Phelan, Shane
    1994   *Getting Specific: Postmodern Lesbian Politics* (Minneapolis: University of Minnesota Press).

Pitt-Rivers, Julian
    1977   *The Fate of Shechem or the Politics of Sex* (Cambridge: Cambridge University Press).

Pollock, Donald
    1985   'Food and Sexual Identity Among the Culina', *Food and Foodways* 1: 25-42.

Preston, John
    1996   'What You Learn After Thirty Years of S/M', in Michael Bronski (ed.), *Taking Liberties: Gay Men's Essays on Politics, Culture and Sex* (New York: Masquerade Books): 175-86.

Provan, Iain
    1998   'The Historical Books of the Old Testament', in John Barton (ed.), *The Cambridge Companion to Biblical Interpretation* (Cambridge: Cambridge University Press): 198-211.

Pseudo-Tertullian
    1870   'A Strain of Sodom', in *The Writings of Quintus Sept. Flor. Tertullian*. III (trans. S. Thelwall; Edinburgh: T. & T. Clark): 284-92.

Queensland Parliamentary Hansard
    1998   http://www.parliament.qld.gov.au/hansard/index.htm. 18 November 1998.

Rashkow, Ilona
    2000   *Taboo or Not Taboo: Sexuality and Family in the Hebrew Bible* (Minneapolis: Fortress Press).

Rich, Adrienne
    1993   'Compulsory Heterosexuality and Lesbian Existence', in Abelove, Barale and Halperin 1993: 227-54.

Rofes, Eric
    1996   *Reviving the Tribe: Regenerating Gay Men's Sexuality and Culture in the Ongoing Epidemic* (New York: Harrington Park Press).
    1998   *Dry Bones Breathe: Gay Men Creating Post-AIDS Identities and Cultures* (New York: Harrington Park Press).

Rosselli, John
    1992   *Singers of Italian Opera: The History of a Profession* (New York: Cambridge University Press).

Rowlett, Lori
    1996   *Joshua and the Rhetoric of Violence: A New Historicist Analysis* (Sheffield: Sheffield Academic Press).

Rubin, Gayle
    1975   'The Traffic in Women: Notes on the "Political Economy" of Sex', in Rayna Reiter (ed.), *Toward an Anthropology of Women* (New York: Monthly Review Press): 157-210.
    1984   'Thinking Sex: Notes for a Radical Theory of the Politics of Sexuality', in Vance 1984: 267-319.

Sacher-Masoch, Leopold von
 1991   'Venus in Furs', in Gilles Deleuze and Leopold von Sacher-Masoch,
         Masochism: Coldness and Cruelty and Venus in Furs (trans. J. McNeill;
         New York: Zone Books): 142-293.
Sade, Marquis de
 1991   *Justine, Philosophy in the Bedroom and other Writings* (London: Arrow).
Saikaku, Ihara
 1990   *The Great Mirror of Male Love* (trans. Paul G. Schalow; Stanford: Stan-
         ford University Press).
Saslow, James M.
 1986   *Ganymede in the Renaissance* (New Haven: Yale University Press).
Scherer, Barrymore Lawrence
 1998   'Song of the Orient: Saint-Saëns' *Samson et Delila*', *Opera News* 62.12
         (28 February 1998): 18-23.
Schneider, Jane
 1971   'Of Vigilance and Virgins: Honor, Shame and Access to Resources in
         Mediterranean Societies', *Ethnology* 10.1: 1-24.
Schneider, Laurel
 1999   *Re-Imagining the Divine: Confronting the Backlash Against Feminist
         Theology* (Cleveland: Pilgrim Press).
 2000   'Queer Theory', in Adam 2000: 206-12.
Schüngel-Straumann, Helen
 1995   'God as Mother in Hosea 11', in Brenner 1995: 194-218.
Schüssler Fiorenza, Elisabeth
 1999   *Rhetoric and Ethic: The Politics of Biblical Studies* (Minneapolis: Augs-
         burg Fortress).
Scroggs, Robin
 1983   *The New Testament and Homosexuality* (Minneapolis: Fortress).
Sedgwick, Eve Kosofsky
 1990   *Epistemology of the Closet* (Berkeley: University of California Press).
 1993   *Tendencies* (Durham, NC: Duke University Press).
 1994   *The Epistemology of the Closet* (London: Penguin Books).
 1997   'Paranoid Reading and Reparative Reading; or, You're So Paranoid, You
         Probably Think This Introduction Is about You', in Eve Kosofsky
         Sedgwick (ed.), *Novel Gazing: Queer Readings in Fiction* (Durham, NC:
         Duke University Press): 1-37.
Segovia, Fernando F., and Mary Ann Tolbert (eds.)
 1995a   *Reading From This Place*. I. *Social Location and Biblical Interpretation
         in the United States* (Minneapolis: Fortress Press).
 1995b   *Reading From This Place*. II. *Social Location and Biblical Interpretation
         in Global Perspective* (Minneapolis: Fortress Press).
Seidman, Steven
 1997   *Difference Troubles: Queering Social Theory and Sexual Politics* (Cam-
         bridge: Cambridge University Press).
Setel, T. Drorah
 1985   'Prophets and Pornography: Female Sexual Imagery in Hosea', in Letty
         M. Russell (ed.), *Feminist Interpretation of the Bible* (Philadelphia:
         Fortress Press): 86-95.

Shankar, Lavina Dhingra, and Rajini Srikanth (eds.)
   1998   *A Part, Yet Apart: South Asians in Asian America* (Philadelphia: Temple
              University Press).
Shaw, Teresa M.
   1998   *The Burden of the Flesh: Fasting and Sexuality in Early Christianity*
              (Minneapolis: Fortress Press).
Sherwood, Yvonne
   1996   *The Prostitute and the Prophet: Hosea's Marriage in Literary-Theoreti-
              cal Perspective* (Sheffield: Sheffield Academic Press).
Simpson, William Kelly (ed.)
   1973   *The Literature of Ancient Egypt: An Anthology of Stories, Instructions
              and Poetry* (New Haven: Yale University Press).
Singer, Isaac Bashevis
   1972   *The Wicked City* (trans. Isaac Bashevis Singer and Elizabeth Shub; New
              York: Farrar, Straus and Giroux).
Smith, Mark
   1990   *The Early History of God: Yahweh and the Other Deities in Ancient
              Israel* (San Francisco: Harper & Row).
Smithers, Howard E.
   1977   *A History of the Oratorio* (Chapel Hill: University of North Carolina
              Press).
Somerville, Siobhan B.
   2000   *Queering the Color Line: Race and the Invention of Homosexuality in
              American Culture* (Durham, NC: Duke University Press).
Spencer, Daniel T.
   1991   'Bridging the Chasm, Reclaiming the Word: Toward Reconstructing a
              Liberating Biblical Hermeneutic' (unpublished doctoral examination in
              biblical ethics, Union Theological Seminary, New York).
   1996   *Gay and Gaia: Ethics, Ecology, and the Erotic* (Cleveland: Pilgrim
              Press).
Spong, J.S.
   1988   *Living in Sin?: A Bishop Rethinks Human Sexuality* (San Francisco:
              Harper & Row).
   1991   *Rescuing the Bible from Fundamentalism: A Bishop Rethinks the Mean-
              ing of Scripture* (San Francisco: Harper San Francisco).
Sprinkle, Annie
   1998   *Post-Porn Modernist: My 25 Years as a Multimedia Whore* (San
              Francisco: Cleis).
Spurlin, William J.
   1998   'Sissies and Sisters: Gender, Sexuality and the Possibilities of Coalition',
              in Mandy Merck, Naomi Segal and Elizabeth Wright (eds.), *Coming Out
              of Feminism?* (Oxford: Blackwell Publishers): 74-101.
Stone, Ken
   1995   'Gender and Homosexuality in Judges 19: Subject-Honor, Object-
              Shame?' *JSOT* 67: 87-107.
   1996   *Sex, Honor and Power in the Deuteronomistic History* (Sheffield: Shef-
              field Academic Press).

1997a   'Biblical Interpretation as a Technology of the Self: Gay Men and the Ethics of Reading', in Danna Nolan Fewell and Gary A. Phillips (eds.), *Bible and Ethics of Reading* (Semeia, 77; Atlanta: Scholars Press): 139-55.

1997b   'The Hermeneutics of Abomination: On Gay Men, Canaanites, and Biblical Interpretation', *BTB* 27.2: 36-41.

1999   'Safer Text: Reading Biblical Laments in the Age of AIDS', *TheolSex* 10: 16-27.

2000a   'Sexuality', in Adam 2000: 233-38.

2000b   'The Garden of Eden and the Heterosexual Contract', in Gross and West 2000: 57-70.

Sugirtharajah, R.S. (ed.)

1991   *Voices from the Margin: Interpreting the Bible in the Third World* (Maryknoll, NY: Orbis Books).

1998   *The Postcolonial Bible* (Sheffield: Sheffield Academic Press).

Tarlin, Jan William

1997   'Utopia and Pornography in Ezekiel: Violence, Hope, and the Shattered Male Subject', in Timothy K. Beal and David M. Gunn (eds.), *Reading Bibles, Writing Bodies: Identity and the Book* (New York: Routledge): 175-83.

Thomas, Calvin (ed.)

2000   *Straight with a Twist: Queer Theory and the Subject of Heterosexuality* (Urbana, IL: University of Illinois Press).

Tolbert, Mary Ann

1990   'Protestant Feminists and the Bible: On the Horns of a Dilemma', in Alice Bach (ed.), *The Pleasure of Her Text: Feminist Readings of Biblical and Historical Texts* (Philadelphia: Trinity Press International): 5-23.

1995   'Reading for Liberation', in Segovia and Tolbert 1995a: 263-76.

Vance, Carole S. (ed.)

1984   *Pleasure and Danger: Exploring Female Sexuality* (New York and London: Routledge and Kegan Paul).

Warner, Michael

1993   'Introduction', in Michael Warner (ed.), *Fear of a Queer Planet: Queer Politics and Social Theory* (Minneapolis: University of Minnesota Press): vii-xxxi.

1999   *The Trouble With Normal: Sex, Politics, and the Ethics of Queer Life* (New York: The Free Press).

Weeks, Jeffrey

1985   *Sexuality and Its Discontents: Meanings, Myths and Modern Sexualities* (London and Boston: Routledge and Kegan Paul).

1989   *Sex, Politics and Society: The Regulation of Sexuality Since 1800* (New York: Longman, 2nd edn).

Weems, Renita J.

1989   'Gomer: Victim of Violence or Victim of Metaphor', *Semeia* 47: 87-104.

1995   *Battered Love: Marriage, Sex, and Violence in the Hebrew Prophets* (Minneapolis: Fortress Press).

Weis, Margaret, and Tracy Hickman
 1986 *Dragonlance Legends.* l. *Time of the Twins* (London: Penguin).

West, Cornel
 1990 'The New Cultural Politics of Difference', in Russell Ferguson, Marthat Gever, Trinh T. Minh-ha and Cornel West (eds.), *Out There: Marginalization and Contemporary Culture* (Cambridge, MA: MIT Press): 19-36.

West, Gerald
 1999 *The Academy of the Poor: Towards a Dialogical Reading of the Bible* (Sheffield: Sheffield Academic Press).

West, Mona
 1995 'Lamentations', in Watson Mills and Richard Wilson (eds.), *The Mercer Commentary on the Bible* (Macon, GA: Mercer University Press): 667-72.
 1999 'Reading the Bible as Queer Americans: Social Location and the Hebrew Scriptures', *TheolSex* 10: 28-42.

Westenholz, Joan Goodnick
 1989 'Tamar, *Qedesa, Qadistu,* and Sacred Prostitution in Mesopotamia', *HTR* 82.3: 245-65.

White, Edmund
 1999 *Marcel Proust* (New York: Penguin Books).

Wikan, Unni
 1984 'Shame and Honour: A Contestable Pair', *Man* 19: 635-52.

Wilder, Ron E.
 1988 'Sexual Orientation and Grief', in Kenneth J. Doka and Joyce D. Davidson (eds.), *Living with Grief: Who We are and How We Grieve* (Philadelphia: Hospice Foundation of America): 199-206.

Williams, Craig A.
 1999 *Roman Homosexuality: Ideologies of Masculinity in Classical Antiquity* (Oxford: Oxford University Press).

Wilson, N.
 1995 *Our Tribe: Queer Folks, God, Jesus, and the Bible* (San Francisco: Harper San Francisco).

Wolff, Hans Walter
 1974 *Hosea: A Commentary on the Book of the Prophet Hosea* (trans. Gary Stansell; ed. Paul D. Hanson; Philadelphia: Fortress Press).

Wright, Wendy
 2000 'Tears of a Greening Heart', in *Weavings* XV.2 (Nashville: The Upper Room): 6-14.

Yee, Gale
 1992 'Hosea', in Carol A. Newsom and Sharon Ringe (eds.), *Women's Bible Commentary* (Louisville, KY: Westminster/John Knox Press): 195-202.

Zizek, Slavoj
 1991 *For They Know Not What They Do: Enjoyment as a Political Factor* (London: Verso).

Zlotowitz, M.
1986   *Bereishis: Genesis: A New Translation with a Commentary Anthologized from Talmudic, Midrashic and Rabbinic Sources* (overviews N. Scherman; Brooklyn, NY: Mesorah Publications).
Zornberg, Avivah Gottlieb
1996   *The Beginning of Desire: Reflections on Genesis* (New York: Doubleday).

INDEX

INDEX OF REFERENCES

BIBLE

Old Testament

Genesis

3	126, 127
3.17-19	126
13.10	154
16.2	103
17.17	103
18	155
18.12	103
18.20-21	156
19	59, 155, 158, 193
19.4	59
19.31	158
20.18	124
21.1-7	103
21.7	103
22	102-104
22.1-3	103
22.4-5	103
22.2	102
22.7	103
22.8	103
22.10	103
22.11-12	103
22.20-24	103
24.67	157
29.31	124
30.22	124
34.1-7	180
38	39
39.6-7	43

Exodus

19.12	79
20	84
24–28	203
24.9	79
24.10	75
24.17	75
24.18	76
25.2-7	77
25.9	76
25.23	75
25.24	75
25.29	75
25.30	75
25.33	77
26.1	77
26.6	77
26.36	77
28.3-5	78
28.6-30	78
28.31-34	78
31.18	100
33.21-23	105
34.29	105

Leviticus

17	54
17.7	54
18	50, 193
20	50, 193

Deuteronomy

5	84
22.13-21	138

Judges

3.12-26	178
5	47
6	47
8	56
8.27	56
8.28	56
9	41
9.54	41
12.4-6	180
18	56
18.31	57
19	59

1 Samuel

1.6	124
5.2-5	58
5.9	59
6.6	59
6.19	66
8.5	43
8.7	43
9.1-2	43
9.2	39
9.3	40
9.5	40
9.7	40
9.8	40

1 Samuel (cont.)

9.22	40
9.27	40
10.14	40
11.11	40
14	40
14.1	40
14.3	57
14.6-7	40
14.12-14	40
14.18	58
14.23	40
16.7	44
16.12	44
16.14-23	180
16.21-22	41
20	41
20.7	65
20.8	65
21.5	39
23.6	58
23.9	58
30.7	58
31.3-6	41

2 Samuel

4.4	64
5.14	64
5.20	53
6	48
6.14-16	49
6.14	48
6.16	50
6.20-23	49
6.22	55
7	48, 54, 62, 69
7.14	64, 99
7.15	63
9	64
11.3	46
11.11	45
13.1-14	46
14.25	45
14.27	46
19.24-30	64
21	70

21.7	64
24	66, 70

1 Kings

1.1-4	46
1.6	45
3.16-28	219
11	62

2 Kings

1.2-8	176
2.23-25	177
10.12-17	177

1 Chronicles

9.4-5	41
15	49
15.13	49
15.27	49
15.29	50

Psalms

9	153, 183
9.4	156
9.5-6	160
9.9-10	156
9.12	156
9.15	160
9.16	160

Isaiah

13.1-22	54
13.21	54
34.14	54
53.2	44
66.9	124

Jeremiah

2–3	72
13.1-11	57
13.11	57
16.8	61
20.7	61
20.11	61
20.12	61
44.15-19	127

Lamentations

1	144-46
1.1-11	141
1.1-7	145
1.2	141, 150
1.4	145
1.5	147
1.6	145
1.8-10	145
1.8	147
1.9	141, 147
1.11-22	141
1.11-13	146
1.11-12	141
1.16	150
1.17	141
1.20	141
1.21	141
2	146
2.1-10	141
2.11-19	141
2.11	150
2.20-21	147
2.20	141
3.1-66	141
3.1	148
3.4	148
3.7	148
3.13	148
3.17	148
3.19-24	149
3.26	148
3.27	148
3.28	148
3.31	148
3.32	148
3.33	148
3.41	148
3.43-50	149
3.48-51	141, 150
4.1-16	141
4.17-22	141
5.1-22	141
5.1	141

Ezekiel

16	38

16.53	161	2.14	124	13.5-6	125
16.55	161	2.16-17	126	13.5	125
18	72	2.22-23 [Eng.]	134		
23	38, 72	2.23 [Eng.]	134	New Testament	
23.23	44	2.25	134	*Matthew*	
		3.1	123	5.13	164
Hosea		4.8	125		
1.2	138	4.10-11	126	*Luke*	
1.3	134	6.3	134	23.6-12	102
2	120	8.7	124		
2.5 [Eng.]	120, 121	9	124	*Acts*	
2.7	120, 121	9.2	124	16.11-15	180
2.8-9 [Eng.]	124	9.11-12	124		
2.8	126	9.14	124	*Romans*	
2.8 [Eng.]	129, 134	9.16	124	1	193
2.10-11	124	10.11-14	134	7	84
2.10	129, 134	10.12	134	13.6	125
2.12 [Eng.]	124	13.1	126		

OTHER ANCIENT REFERENCES

Apocrypha		Targum		Irenaeus	
Judith		*Gen. R.*		*Adv. Haer.*	
16.7	91	49.6.3	156	4.31.3	164
		50.3	158		
Talmud				Pseudo-Tertullian	
Sanh.		Early Christian Authors		*Strain of Sodom*	
109	156	Homer		169-73	164
		Iliad			
		20.233-35	67		

INDEX OF AUTHORS

Abelove, H. 186
Ackroyd, P. 59
Adam, A.K.M. 11
Andersen, F.I. 125, 135
Anderson, B.W. 12, 13
Antonelli, J.S. 156, 158

Bach, A. 119
Bail, U. 160
Bailey, D.S. 36
Bailey, R. 22
Barale, M.A. 186
Barr, J. 11
Beal, T.K. 25, 31, 157
Berlant, L. 12, 30, 33, 34
Bersani, L. 187
Bird, P.A. 18, 118, 121
Blanchot, M. 90
Blok, A. 127, 138
Boer, R. 12, 28-30, 32, 44, 182-85, 187,
    189-91, 203, 204, 208, 214, 217, 220,
    221, 225
Bordo, S. 118, 119
Bourdieu, P. 129
Boyarin, D. 18, 24, 70
Brenner, A. 118
Briggs, C.A. 159, 160
Bright, J. 148
Brooten, B.J. 18, 157
Brown, F. 159, 160
Butler, J. 25, 26, 32, 107-109, 119, 130,
    136, 137, 139, 186, 190, 200, 202,
    210, 218

Califia, P. 27
Carden, M. 18, 30-32, 155, 182, 183,
    186, 188, 190, 191, 215
Chauncey, G. 14, 15, 22

Chick, J. 152, 161-63, 165, 186
Clines, D.J.A. 12, 119
Comstock, G.D. 198, 206
Counihan, C.M. 116, 117
Coward, R. 118
Crenshaw, J.L. 110
Crenshaw, K. 188
Crum, J. 108

Davidson, J.D. 143
Davies, P.R. 29
Davis, J. 128
De Lauretis, T. 20, 21, 27, 187
De Vault, M. 118
Delaney, C. 131-33
Deleuze, G. 30, 89, 90, 92-95, 97-102,
    104, 187, 203
Doka, K.J. 143
Douglas, M. 117
Dover, K.J. 72
Downing, C. 67
Driver, S.R. 159, 160
DuBois, P. 132

Eco, U. 107, 112-14
Eng, D.L. 189
Exum, J.C. 12, 32, 51, 118

Fausto-Sterling, A. 25
Felder, C.H. 17
Fewell, D.N. 18, 31, 37, 51, 106, 110,
    111, 117, 208
Fokkelman, J.P. 48, 49, 51, 54, 62, 63, 65
Fontaine, C. 138
Foucault, M. 22, 25, 109, 117, 136, 192,
    210
Fox, E. 59
Frankel, E. 164

Freedman, D.N. 125, 135
Freidlander, G. 153, 156, 160
Fretheim, T. 13
Freud, S. 30, 78, 81-83, 86, 91, 184, 185, 203
Frymer-Kensky, T. 118, 121
Fuss, D. 20, 23

Garber, M. 24
Gibson, J.C.L. 134
Gilberg-Schwartz, H. 38, 39, 64, 73, 117, 130, 137, 225
Gilmore, D. 127, 128, 135, 136, 138
Goldstein, R. 165
Goss, R.E. 12
Grahn, J. 177
Gramsci, A. 190
Greenberg, D. 37, 47
Gregor, T. 116
Grimm, V.E. 117
Guattari, F. 83
Gunn, D.M. 18, 37, 51, 117

Hackett, J.A. 123, 124, 131
Hallam, P. 152, 154, 159, 166
Halperin, D.M. 22, 23, 28, 37, 39, 109, 185, 186
Halpern, B. 133
Harrison, B. 195
Helminiak, D.A. 169-72
Hennessy, R. 25
Henshaw, R.A. 121
Herzfeld, M. 127, 135, 136
Hickman, T. 159
Hillers, D.R. 141
Hom, A.Y. 189
Hooks, S.M. 121
Horner, T. 36

Inhorn, M.C. 133

Jagose, A. 14, 23
Jakobsen, J.R. 30
Jennings, T.W. 18, 19, 24, 30, 182, 183, 188-91, 205-208, 214, 217, 220, 225
Johansson, W. 154
Jordan, M.D. 60

Katz, J.N. 23
Keefe, A. 122, 123, 125, 131
Keiser, E.B. 152, 158
Kim, D.Y. 189
Koch, T. 182, 183, 190, 191, 197-99, 201, 205, 214
Kripal, J.J. 160
Kristeva, J. 214, 215

Lacan, J. 30, 75, 83-85, 88, 91, 203
Lawrence, M. 118
Leith, M.J.W. 137
Lemche, N.P. 22, 121
Lerner, G. 219
Leupp, G. 48
Lévi-Strauss, C. 116
Liew, T.-S.B. 22, 32
Linafelt, T. 17, 157
Lindisfarne, N. 127
Linscheid, J. 161, 165
Long, B.O. 13
Lorde, A. 169, 170, 174, 197, 199

Malson, H. 118
Marr, D. 160
Martin, D. 18
Matthews, V.H. 158
Mays, J.L. 125, 134
McKnight, D. 116
Meigs, A.S. 116
Mettinger, T.N.D. 124
Meyers, C. 127
Milton, J. 108, 109
Moltmann, J. 213
Moore, S.D. 12, 80

Newsom, C.A. 145
Nissinen, M. 18, 24
Nouwen, H. 151
Nussbaum, M. 117
Nygren, A. 71

O'Connor, K. 145
Oden, R.A. 29, 121
O'Donovan, C. 154, 160
Olyan, S. 18
Ostriker, A.S. 153

Pardes, I. 37
Parisi, H. 109
Pellegrini, A. 30
Percy, W.A. 67
Peristiany, J.G. 127
Petersen, W. 68
Phelan, S. 21
Phillips, G.A. 208
Pitt-Rivers, J. 127
Pollock, D. 116, 118, 130
Preston, J. 110, 111
Provan, I. 18

Rashkow, I. 117, 133
Rich, A. 157
Ringe, S.H. 145
Rofes, E. 140-44, 147, 149, 150, 189, 201
Rosselli, J. 107
Rowlett, L. 25, 29, 30, 32, 114, 182, 183,
    185, 186, 188, 189, 191, 201-204,
    208
Rubin, G. 117, 119, 139, 218

Sacher-Masoch, L. von 30, 80, 91, 93-97,
    99, 102, 105, 187, 203
Sade, M. de 30, 79, 85, 87, 88, 90, 93, 94,
    99, 187, 203
Saikaku, I. 48
Saslow, J.M. 67
Scherer, B.L. 107
Schnedier, J. 133
Schneider, L. 20, 27, 29, 211, 216, 225
Schüngel-Straumann, H. 137
Schüssler Fiorenza, E. 33
Scroggs, R. 36
Sedgwick, E.K. 23, 25, 119, 154, 159,
    162, 163, 183, 185, 187, 188, 192
Segovia, F.F. 17
Seidman, S. 21, 22
Setel, T.D. 118
Shankar, L.D. 189
Shaw, T.M. 117
Sherwood, Y. 12, 118, 119, 123, 138
Simpson, W.K. 60

Singer, I.B. 158
Smith, M. 124, 133
Smithers, H.E. 107
Somerville, S.B. 21
Spencer, D.T. 16, 30, 194, 195, 198, 199
Spong, J.S. 169, 170, 172, 173
Sprinkle, A. 92, 187
Spurlin, W.J. 25, 119
Srikanth, R. 189
Stone, K. 12, 18, 22, 32, 116, 118, 121,
    127, 139, 142, 146, 147, 192, 193,
    199-202, 205, 206, 208, 217, 221,
    224, 225
Sugirtharajah, R.S. 17

Tarlin, J.W. 28
Thomas, C. 28
Tolbert, M.A. 17, 20

Vance, C.S. 118

Warner, M. 11, 12, 28, 30, 33, 34, 186
Weeks, J. 22
Weems, R.J. 118, 128, 137
Weis, M. 159, 183, 189
West, C. 182, 190
West, G. 17, 188
West, M. 12, 17, 18, 24, 141, 183, 189-
    91, 201
Westenholz, J.G. 121
White, E. 31
Wikan, U. 127
Wilder, R.E. 142, 143, 145
Williams, C.A. 73
Wilson, N. 170, 173, 174
Wilson, R. 141
Wolff, H.W. 121, 125, 134
Wright, W. 150

Yee, G. 118, 127, 128, 137

Zizek, S. 84
Zlotowitz, M. 165
Zornberg, A.G. 157-59

JOURNAL FOR THE STUDY OF THE OLD TESTAMENT
SUPPLEMENT SERIES

178 Martin Ravndal Hauge, *Between Sheol and Temple: Motif Structure and Function in the I-Psalms*

179 J.G. McConville and J.G. Millar, *Time and Place in Deuteronomy*

180 Richard L. Schultz, *The Search for Quotation: Verbal Parallels in the Prophets*

181 Bernard M. Levinson (ed.), *Theory and Method in Biblical and Cuneiform Law: Revision, Interpolation and Development*

182 Steven L. McKenzie and M. Patrick Graham (eds.), *The History of Israel's Traditions: The Heritage of Martin Noth*

183 William Robertson Smith, *Lectures on the Religion of the Semites (Second and Third Series)*

184 John C. Reeves and John Kampen (eds.), *Pursuing the Text: Studies in Honor of Ben Zion Wacholder on the Occasion of his Seventieth Birthday*

185 Seth Daniel Kunin, *The Logic of Incest: A Structuralist Analysis of Hebrew Mythology*

186 Linda Day, *Three Faces of a Queen: Characterization in the Books of Esther*

187 Charles V. Dorothy, *The Books of Esther: Structure, Genre and Textual Integrity*

188 Robert H. O'Connell, *Concentricity and Continuity: The Literary Structure of Isaiah*

189 William Johnstone (ed.), *William Robertson Smith: Essays in Reassessment*

190 Steven W. Holloway and Lowell K. Handy (eds.), *The Pitcher is Broken: Memorial Essays for Gösta W. Ahlström*

191 Magne Sæbø, *On the Way to Canon: Creative Tradition History in the Old Testament*

192 Henning Graf Reventlow and William Farmer (eds.), *Biblical Studies and the Shifting of Paradigms, 1850–1914*

193 Brooks Schramm, *The Opponents of Third Isaiah: Reconstructing the Cultic History of the Restoration*

194 Else Kragelund Holt, *Prophesying the Past: The Use of Israel's History in the Book of Hosea*

195 Jon Davies, Graham Harvey and Wilfred G.E. Watson (eds.), *Words Remembered, Texts Renewed: Essays in Honour of John F.A. Sawyer*

196 Joel S. Kaminsky, *Corporate Responsibility in the Hebrew Bible*

197 William M. Schniedewind, *The Word of God in Transition: From Prophet to Exegete in the Second Temple Period*

198 T.J. Meadowcroft, *Aramaic Daniel and Greek Daniel: A Literary Comparison*

199 J.H. Eaton, *Psalms of the Way and the Kingdom: A Conference with the Commentators*

200 M. Daniel Carroll R., David J.A. Clines and Philip R. Davies (eds.), *The Bible in Human Society: Essays in Honour of John Rogerson*

201 John W. Rogerson, *The Bible and Criticism in Victorian Britain: Profiles of F.D. Maurice and William Robertson Smith*

202 Nanette Stahl, *Law and Liminality in the Bible*

203 Jill M. Munro, *Spikenard and Saffron: The Imagery of the Song of Songs*

204 Philip R. Davies, *Whose Bible Is It Anyway?*

205 David J.A. Clines, *Interested Parties: The Ideology of Writers and Readers of the Hebrew Bible*

206 Møgens Müller, *The First Bible of the Church: A Plea for the Septuagint*

207 John W. Rogerson, Margaret Davies and M. Daniel Carroll R. (eds.), *The Bible in Ethics: The Second Sheffield Colloquium*

208 Beverly J. Stratton, *Out of Eden: Reading, Rhetoric, and Ideology in Genesis 2–3*

209 Patricia Dutcher-Walls, *Narrative Art, Political Rhetoric: The Case of Athaliah and Joash*

210 Jacques Berlinerblau, *The Vow and the 'Popular Religious Groups' of Ancient Israel: A Philological and Sociological Inquiry*

211 Brian E. Kelly, *Retribution and Eschatology in Chronicles*

212 Yvonne Sherwood, *The Prostitute and the Prophet: Hosea's Marriage in Literary-Theoretical Perspective*

213 Yair Hoffman, *A Blemished Perfection: The Book of Job in Context*

214 Roy F. Melugin and Marvin A. Sweeney (eds.), *New Visions of Isaiah*

215 J. Cheryl Exum, *Plotted, Shot and Painted: Cultural Representations of Biblical Women*

216 Judith E. McKinlay, *Gendering Wisdom the Host: Biblical Invitations to Eat and Drink*

217 Jerome F.D. Creach, *Yahweh as Refuge and the Editing of the Hebrew Psalter*

218 Harry P. Nasuti, *Defining the Sacred Songs: Genre, Tradition, and the Post-Critical Interpretation of the Psalms*

219 Gerald Morris, *Prophecy, Poetry and Hosea*

220 Raymond F. Person, Jr, *In Conversation with Jonah: Conversation Analysis, Literary Criticism, and the Book of Jonah*

221 Gillian Keys, *The Wages of Sin: A Reappraisal of the 'Succession Narrative'*

222 R.N. Whybray, *Reading the Psalms as a Book*

223 Scott B. Noegel, *Janus Parallelism in the Book of Job*

224 Paul J. Kissling, *Reliable Characters in the Primary History: Profiles of Moses, Joshua, Elijah and Elisha*

225 Richard D. Weis and David M. Carr (eds.), *A Gift of God in Due Season: Essays on Scripture and Community in Honor of James A. Sanders*

226 Lori L. Rowlett, *Joshua and the Rhetoric of Violence: A New Historicist Analysis*

227 John F.A. Sawyer (ed.), *Reading Leviticus: Responses to Mary Douglas*

228 Volkmar Fritz and Philip R. Davies (eds.), *The Origins of the Ancient Israelite States*

229 Stephen Breck Reid (ed.), *Prophets and Paradigms: Essays in Honor of Gene M. Tucker*

230 Kevin J. Cathcart and Michael Maher (eds.), *Targumic and Cognate Studies: Essays in Honour of Martin McNamara*

231 Weston W. Fields, *Sodom and Gomorrah: History and Motif in Biblical Narrative*

232 Tilde Binger, *Asherah: Goddesses in Ugarit, Israel and the Old Testament*

233 Michael D. Goulder, *The Psalms of Asaph and the Pentateuch: Studies in the Psalter, III*

234 Ken Stone, *Sex, Honor, and Power in the Deuteronomistic History*

235 James W. Watts and Paul House (eds.), *Forming Prophetic Literature: Essays on Isaiah and the Twelve in Honor of John D.W. Watts*

236 Thomas M. Bolin, *Freedom beyond Forgiveness: The Book of Jonah Re-examined*

237 Neil Asher Silberman and David B. Small (eds.), *The Archaeology of Israel: Constructing the Past, Interpreting the Present*

238 M. Patrick Graham, Kenneth G. Hoglund and Steven L. McKenzie (eds.), *The Chronicler as Historian*

239 Mark S. Smith, *The Pilgrimage Pattern in Exodus*

240 Eugene E. Carpenter (ed.), *A Biblical Itinerary: In Search of Method, Form and Content. Essays in Honor of George W. Coats*

241 Robert Karl Gnuse, *No Other Gods: Emergent Monotheism in Israel*

242 K.L. Noll, *The Faces of David*

243 Henning Graf Reventlow (ed.), *Eschatology in the Bible and in Jewish and Christian Tradition*

244 Walter E. Aufrecht, Neil A. Mirau and Steven W. Gauley (eds.), *Urbanism in Antiquity: From Mesopotamia to Crete*

245 Lester L. Grabbe (ed.), *Can a 'History of Israel' Be Written?*

246 Gillian M. Bediako, *Primal Religion and the Bible: William Robertson Smith and his Heritage*

247 Nathan Klaus, *Pivot Patterns in the Former Prophets*

248 Etienne Nodet, *A Search for the Origins of Judaism: From Joshua to the Mishnah*

249 William Paul Griffin, *The God of the Prophets: An Analysis of Divine Action*

250 Josette Elayi and Jean Sapin, *Beyond the River: New Perspectives on Trans-euphratene*

251 Flemming A.J. Nielsen, *The Tragedy in History: Herodotus and the Deuteronomistic History*

252 David C. Mitchell, *The Message of the Psalter: An Eschatological Programme in the Book of Psalms*

253 William Johnstone, *1 and 2 Chronicles, Volume 1: 1 Chronicles 1–2 Chronicles 9: Israel's Place among the Nations*

254 William Johnstone, *1 and 2 Chronicles, Volume 2: 2 Chronicles 10–36: Guilt and Atonement*

255 Larry L. Lyke, *King David with the Wise Woman of Tekoa: The Resonance of Tradition in Parabolic Narrative*

256 Roland Meynet, *Rhetorical Analysis: An Introduction to Biblical Rhetoric*

257 Philip R. Davies and David J.A. Clines (eds.), *The World of Genesis: Persons, Places, Perspectives*

258 Michael D. Goulder, *The Psalms of the Return (Book V, Psalms 107–150): Studies in the Psalter, IV*

259 Allen Rosengren Petersen, *The Royal God: Enthronement Festivals in Ancient Israel and Ugarit?*

260 A.R. Pete Diamond, Kathleen M. O'Connor and Louis Stulman (eds.), *Troubling Jeremiah*

261 Othmar Keel, *Goddesses and Trees, New Moon and Yahweh: Ancient Near Eastern Art and the Hebrew Bible*

262 Victor H. Matthews, Bernard M. Levinson and Tikva Frymer-Kensky (eds.), *Gender and Law in the Hebrew Bible and the Ancient Near East*

263 M. Patrick Graham and Steven L. McKenzie, *The Chronicler as Author: Studies in Text and Texture*

264 Donald F. Murray, *Divine Prerogative and Royal Pretension: Pragmatics, Poetics, and Polemics in a Narrative Sequence about David (2 Samuel 5.17–7.29)*

265 John Day, *Yahweh and the Gods and Goddesses of Canaan*

266 J. Cheryl Exum and Stephen D. Moore (eds.), *Biblical Studies/Cultural Studies: The Third Sheffield Colloquium*

267 Patrick D. Miller, Jr, *Israelite Religion and Biblical Theology: Collected Essays*

268 Linda S. Schearing and Steven L. McKenzie (eds.), *Those Elusive Deuteronomists: 'Pandeuteronomism' and Scholarship in the Nineties*

269 David J.A. Clines and Stephen D. Moore (eds.), *Auguries: The Jubilee Volume of the Sheffield Department of Biblical Studies*

270 John Day (ed.), *King and Messiah in Israel and the Ancient Near East: Proceedings of the Oxford Old Testament Seminar*

271 Wonsuk Ma, *Until the Spirit Comes: The Spirit of God in the Book of Isaiah*

272 James Richard Linville, *Israel in the Book of Kings: The Past as a Project of Social Identity*

273 Meir Lubetski, Claire Gottlieb and Sharon Keller (eds.), *Boundaries of the Ancient Near Eastern World: A Tribute to Cyrus H. Gordon*

274 Martin J. Buss, *Biblical Form Criticism in its Context*

275 William Johnstone, *Chronicles and Exodus: An Analogy and its Application*

276 Raz Kletter, *Economic Keystones: The Weight System of the Kingdom of Judah*

277 Augustine Pagolu, *The Religion of the Patriarchs*

278 Lester L. Grabbe (ed.), *Leading Captivity Captive: 'The Exile' as History and Ideology*

279 Kari Latvus, *God, Anger and Ideology: The Anger of God in Joshua and Judges in Relation to Deuteronomy and the Priestly Writings*

280 Eric S. Christianson, *A Time to Tell: Narrative Strategies in Ecclesiastes*

281 Peter D. Miscall, *Isaiah 34–35: A Nightmare/A Dream*

282 Joan E. Cook, *Hannah's Desire, God's Design: Early Interpretations in the Story of Hannah*

283 Kelvin Friebel, *Jeremiah's and Ezekiel's Sign-Acts: Rhetorical Nonverbal Communication*

284 M. Patrick Graham, Rick R. Marrs and Steven L. McKenzie (eds.), *Worship and the Hebrew Bible: Essays in Honor of John T. Willis*

285 Paolo Sacchi, *History of the Second Temple*

286 Wesley J. Bergen, *Elisha and the End of Prophetism*

287 Anne Fitzpatrick-McKinley, *The Transformation of Torah from Scribal Advice to Law*

288 Diana Lipton, *Revisions of the Night: Politics and Promises in the Patriarchal Dreams of Genesis*

289 Jože Krašovec (ed.), *The Interpretation of the Bible: The International Symposium in Slovenia*

290 Frederick H. Cryer and Thomas L. Thompson (eds.), *Qumran between the Old and New Testaments*

291 Christine Schams, *Jewish Scribes in the Second-Temple Period*

292 David J.A. Clines, *On the Way to the Postmodern: Old Testament Essays, 1967–1998 Volume 1*

293 David J.A. Clines, *On the Way to the Postmodern: Old Testament Essays, 1967–1998 Volume 2*

294 Charles E. Carter, *The Emergence of Yehud in the Persian Period: A Social and Demographic Study*

295 Jean-Marc Heimerdinger, *Topic, Focus and Foreground in Ancient Hebrew Narratives*

296 Mark Cameron Love, *The Evasive Text: Zechariah 1–8 and the Frustrated Reader*

297 Paul S. Ash, *David, Solomon and Egypt: A Reassessment*

298 John D. Baildam, *Paradisal Love: Johann Gottfried Herder and the Song of Songs*

299 M. Daniel Carroll R., *Rethinking Contexts, Rereading Texts: Contributions from the Social Sciences to Biblical Interpretation*

300 Edward Ball (ed.), *In Search of True Wisdom: Essays in Old Testament Interpretation in Honour of Ronald E. Clements*

301 Carolyn S. Leeb, *Away from the Father's House: The Social Location of na'ar and na'arah in Ancient Israel*

302 Xuan Huong Thi Pham, *Mourning in the Ancient Near East and the Hebrew Bible*

303 Ingrid Hjelm, *The Samaritans and Early Judaism: A Literary Analysis*

304 Wolter H. Rose, *Zemah and Zerubbabel: Messianic Expectations in the Early Postexilic Period*

305 Jo Bailey Wells, *God's Holy People: A Theme in Biblical Theology*

306 Albert de Pury, Thomas Römer and Jean-Daniel Macchi (eds.), *Israel Constructs its History: Deuteronomistic Historiography in Recent Research*

307 Robert L. Cole, *The Shape and Message of Book III (Psalms 73–89)*

308 Yiu-Wing Fung, *Victim and Victimizer: Joseph's Interpretation of his Destiny*
309 George Aichele (ed.), *Culture, Entertainment and the Bible*
310 Esther Fuchs, *Sexual Politics in the Biblical Narrative: Reading the Hebrew Bible as a Woman*
311 Gregory Glazov, *The Bridling of the Tongue and the Opening of the Mouth in Biblical Prophecy*
312 Francis Landy, *Beauty and the Enigma: And Other Essays on the Hebrew Bible*
314 Bernard S. Jackson, *Studies in the Semiotics of Biblical Law*
315 Paul R. Williamson, *Abraham, Israel and the Nations: The Patriarchal Promise and its Covenantal Development in Genesis*
316 Dominic Rudman, *Determinism in the Book of Ecclesiastes*
317 Lester L. Grabbe (ed.), *Did Moses Speak Attic? Jewish Historiography and Scripture in the Hellenistic Period*
318 David A. Baer, *When We All Go Home: Translation and Theology in LXX 56–66*
320 Claudia V. Camp, *Wise, Strange and Holy: The Strange Woman and the Making of the Bible*
321 Varese Layzer, *Signs of Weakness: Juxtaposing Irish Tales and the Bible*
322 Mignon R. Jacobs, *The Conceptual Coherence of the Book of Micah*
323 Martin Ravndal Hauge, *The Descent from the Mountain: Narrative Patterns in Exodus 19–40*
324 P.M. Michèle Daviau, John W. Wevers and Michael Weigl (eds.), *The World of the Aramaeans: Studies in Honour of Paul-Eugène Dion*, Volume 1
325 P.M. Michèle Daviau, John W. Wevers and Michael Weigl (eds.), *The World of the Aramaeans: Studies in Honour of Paul-Eugène Dion*, Volume 2
326 P.M. Michèle Daviau, John W. Wevers and Michael Weigl (eds.), *The World of the Aramaeans: Studies in Honour of Paul-Eugène Dion*, Volume 3
327 Gary D. Salyer, *Vain Rhetoric: Private Insight and Public Debate in Ecclesiastes*
329 Wolfgang Bluedorn, *Yahweh Verus Baalism: A Theological Reading of the Gideon-Abimelech Narrative*
330 Lester L. Grabbe and Robert D. Haak (eds.), *'Every City shall be Forsaken': Urbanism and Prophecy in Ancient Israel and the Near East*
331 Amihai Mazar (ed.), with the assistance of Ginny Mathias, *Studies in the Archaeology of the Iron Age in Israel and Jordan*
332 Robert J.V. Hiebert, Claude E. Cox and Peter J. Gentry (eds.), *The Old Greek Psalter: Studies in Honour of Albert Pietersma*
333 Ada Rapoport-Albert and Gillian Greenberg (eds.), *Biblical Hebrew, Biblical Texts: Essays in Memory of Michael P. Weitzman*
334 Ken Stone (ed.), *Queer Commentary and the Hebrew Bible*
343 J. Andrew Dearman and M. Patrick Graham (eds.), *The Land that I Will Show You: Essays on the History and Archaeology of the Ancient Near East in Honor of J. Maxwell Miller*